PHILOSOPHY AND

Philosophy and Christian Belief

William Charlton

Sheed & Ward
London

ISBN 0-7220-6630-9

© William Charlton, 1988

Published in Great Britain in 1988 by
Sheed & Ward Limited,
2, Creechurch Lane
London, EC3A 5AQ

All rights reserved. No part of this book may be reproduced, stored in a retrieval system, or transmitted, in any form, or by any means, electronic, mechanical, photocopying, recording or any otherwise, without permission in writing from the publishers

Book production Bill Ireson

Photoset by Fakenham Photosetting Limited, Fakenham, Norfolk
Printed in Great Britain by A. Wheaton & Co Ltd, Exeter

Contents

Chapter		page
	PREFACE	vii
ONE	Christianity and Philosophy	1
TWO	The Existence of God	26
THREE	A Non-material Personal Creator	57
FOUR	The Divinity of Christ and Historical Truth	84
FIVE	Soul, Good and Evil	108
SIX	The Soul and God	127
SEVEN	Life After Death	141
EIGHT	The Incarnation	160
NINE	The Redemption	188
TEN	The Church	200
	NOTES	231
	INDEX	241

Preface

A professional philosopher who is also a believing Christian is bound to ask himself how far his religious beliefs are compatible with his philosophy. This book is the result of meditation on that question. I have tried to confine myself to beliefs which are shared by all Christian denominations, though the perceptive reader will probably see all too clearly from what part of the spectrum I view them.

For the convenience of readers who are just starting philosophical or religious studies I have suggested in the Notes some further reading which is fairly standard and accessible. For those who are in a position to push their enquiries further I have added some references to more technical literature and to primary sources like Migne's Greek and Latin Fathers (PG and PL).

Where not otherwise attributed translations are from the King James version of the Bible (checked, so far as is possible without Hebrew, against later versions) or by me.

I am grateful to Brian Davies O.P. and the Rt. Rev. Wm. Gordon Wheeler for reading drafts of this book and encouraging me to persist. Professor John Sawyer pointed me in the right direction on some issues of Old Testament scholarship; it is not his fault if I failed to reach the right conclusions.

PHILOSOPHY AND CHRISTIAN BELIEF

CHAPTER ONE
Christianity and Philosophy

I

Christianity is a philosophical religion. By that I mean two things. On the one hand it attaches value to being philosophically respectable. It does not ignore philosophical objections or dismiss them as irrelevant; on the contrary, Christians feel themselves obliged to reply to philosophical criticism and sometimes seem even to court it. The reverse side of this attentive and respectful attitude is a tendency to encroach on what philosophers may consider their private territory. Not content with defending themselves, Christians seize the initiative and launch their own attacks on philosophical doctrines they find distasteful. Tertullian in his treatise *On the Soul* (c. AD 203) speaks of philosophers as 'those patriarchs of heretics' (*PL* 2.651). There is, or Christians have believed there to be, a distinctively Christian ethics and metaphysics in a way in which no one has ever imagined there to be a distinctively Christian algebra or botany. Roman Catholics and other Christian bodies have their own universities, and in these philosophy is the subject over which the Church has traditionally exercised its most jealous control.

How did this come about? Jesus of Nazareth, as portrayed in the New Testament, is no sort of philosopher. He shows no interest in any philosophical issue, never supports any of his teaching by philosophical argument. In *The Acts of the Apostles*, which purports to relate the history of Christianity down to about AD 62, we read of only one encounter with philosophy: in *Ac.* 17.16–34 Paul addresses a philosophically minded audience in Athens, though his speech is religious instruction rather than a philosophical lecture.

It would be rash, however, to conclude that the philosophical dimension of Christianity is a late, post-apostolic development. For two centuries before the birth of Christ Judaism had been in contact with Greek culture, and Greek culture was steeped in philosophy. The book of Wisdom, which seems to have been known to New Testament writers, is now thought to have been written by a Jew of Greek education in the first century BC. The Alexandrian Jew Philo, a contemporary of Christ, offers a philosophical version of Judaism. For educated Greek-speaking Jews living outside Palestine Judaism was already in Christ's lifetime aspiring to philosophical respectability; and it was among these Jews that the apostles themselves, not just their successors, made most of their converts.

Those surviving Christian documents which seem to date from the end of the first century are still innocent of philosophy. But in the first half of the second century we find serious philosophical defences of Christian beliefs. The best examples are provided by Justin Martyr (died c. 150), who appears to have been trained in Greek philosophy, and who functioned as a freelance philosophical teacher first at Ephesus, at that time probably the most important Christian centre on the Aegean, and then at Rome.

In the second half of the second century, the part of the Mediterranean world which saw most active developments in doctrine was North Africa. At Alexandria in Egypt a formal catechetical school was set up.[1] Besides its famous Library, Alexandria possessed a residential institute, the Museum, which attracted the best minds in the Greco-Roman world. The only city of comparable academic prestige was Athens. The establishment of a Christian school at Alexandria, the purpose of which was to commend Christianity to the educated classes, gave a philosophical orientation to the whole of Christian thinking; and this effect was the more pronounced because either teaching at the school or associated with it were two men of outstanding intellectual capacity: Clement of Alexandria (c. 150–215) and Origen (c. 185–255). These men had a strong influence on the formulation of the doctrines of the Trinity and the Incarnation. Meanwhile further West, at Carthage, Tertullian (160–225) initiated the Latin theological tradition with philosophical as well as scriptural arguments concerning God and the soul. His short treatise *On the Soul* is directed especially against Plato.

By the beginning of the third century Antioch, capital of Syria and the leading see in the north-eastern quarter of the Christianised world, had Christian as well as non-Christian institutions of higher education. By the fourth century what might be called the philosophising of Christianity was complete. The Greek Fathers of this period who had most influence on Christianity's understanding of itself, John Chrysostom from Antioch and the three Cappodocians Basil, his brother Gregory of Nyssa and his friend Gregory of Nazianzum, were all trained in philosophy, and Gregory of Nyssa, at least, was a philosopher of the first rank. So, of course, was Augustine of Hippo (354–430). The influence of Augustine on Christian thinking in Western Europe has been so deep and prolonged that we are inclined to think of him as a Western European; in fact, however, apart from five years (383–388) in Rome and Milan his life was passed in or near Carthage, and his background, like Tertullian's, is that of Mediterranean Africa.

The effect of philosophy on Christian thought is crystallised in the decrees of the Council of Chalcedon (451). The famous Christological declaration of Chalcedon may be translated as follows:

> Following the holy Fathers, we all unanimously teach that our Lord Jesus Christ is one and the same Son, at once perfect in divinity and perfect in humanity, at once truly God and truly man, consisting of a rational soul and a body, the same in being [*homoousion*] with the Father in respect of divinity and the same in being with us in respect of humanity, similar to us in all things except sin. Before all times he was generated from the Father in respect of divinity, and in these last days, on account of us and

our salvation, he was generated from Mary the Virgin and Mother of God in respect of humanity.

We acknowledge one and the same Christ who is Son, Lord, sole-begotten and consisting in two natures without confusion, change, division or separation, the difference between the natures being in no way destroyed by the union; rather what is proper to each nature is preserved, and concurs to produce one person [*prosopon*] and one substance [*hypostasis*], not apportioned into two persons or divided, but one and the same Son, sole-begotten God, Word, Lord, Jesus Christ, as the prophets of old and he himself taught us, and the creed of the Fathers has handed down to us.

It is such statements as these which Maurice Wiles has in mind when he says that the philosophical atmosphere of the Eastern Mediterranean imposed on Christians of the first few centuries AD 'an approach to theology in which its affirmations are to be regarded as descriptive accounts (albeit very imperfect accounts) of ultimate realities existing in the spiritual world'.[2] Wiles and many other modern theologians consider this an unfortunate mistake: the affirmations of Christian doctrine should be regarded rather as poetry or myth than as statements of supernatural fact. I shall be suggesting that these modern theologians are themselves more influenced than they may realise by the philosophical atmosphere of Germany after Kant.

But would it have been possible for Christianity to evolve without taking on a philosophical character? I have already said that the Judaeo-Christian and the Greek traditions were mingling in Christ's lifetime. We must recognise too that the influence was not all one way. There were three strands in Greek philosophy, the Platonic, the Aristotelian and the Stoic. Christianity was drawn to Stoic ethics but to Platonic metaphysics. The ethical thinking which is standard in our civilisation today is very largely due to Christian acceptance of Stoic ethics together with the addition of an idea which is alien to Greek philosophy but prominent in the Bible, the idea of the will.[3] We owe the notion of natural law chiefly to the Stoics, but the belief that it is one thing to know what is right and another to do it, and that for the latter we need will-power, goes back to the Old Testament. At the same time Christianity helped to make Platonism, both in the Patristic age and later, the dominant system in metaphysics. The account of the soul which Plato puts forward in the *Phaedo* seems to fit in well with the Christian belief in personal immortality.

The obscure group of writers known as Gnostics and attacked by champions of Christian orthodoxy in the second century appear to have had both Christian and Platonic elements in their thinking. The greatest of the Neoplatonists, Plotinus (205–269/70), studied philosophy under the same master (Ammonius Saccas, apparently an ex-Christian) as Origen, and the resemblance of his system to Christianity is striking. He makes everything depend on three divine *hypostases*, the word later used by Christians for the Persons of the Trinity – the One, the Divine Mind and the Divine Soul. Not a little, then, that Christianity got out of philosophy it has already put into it.

In 451 Egypt and Syria were still firmly embedded in the Eastern Roman Empire, and therefore, one might say, in Christendom. Mohammed was born about 120 years later, and within ten years of his death in 632, Alexandria and Antioch with their schools and libraries had fallen to Islam. No doubt there was considerable destruction. Nonetheless some, at least, of the writings of the classical Greek philosophers were preserved and translated into Arabic. These writings contained material used by critics of the Moslem religion, and at least from the ninth century onwards Moslems tried to meet the critics with counter-arguments drawn from the same source. Moslem thinkers who engaged between 800 and 1200 in rational speculation about God and the soul divide roughly into Philosophers (the word 'philosophy' appears in Arabic, a little infelicitously, as 'falsafa') and Theologians ('mutakallimum'). Among other differences, the Philosophers adhered more closely to Greek philosophy and held that the universe has always existed, whereas the Theologians held it was created a finite time ago. The best known of the Philosophers are Ibn Sina or Avicenna (980–1023) in the East, and Ibn Rushd or

Averroes (1126-99) in Spain; of the Theologians, the greatest is Al-Ghazali (1058-1111).

Ghazali's *Incoherence of the Philosophers* (written against the party of Avicenna) would serve to this day as an introduction to the philosophy of religion. Ghazali begins by pointing out that the religious believer does not have to reject doctrines taught by the pagan philosophers which conflict with no religious principle, such as their theory of eclipses.

> The atheists would have the greatest satisfaction if the supporter of religion made a positive assertion that things of this kind are contrary to religion ... For these things have been established by astronomical and mathematical evidence which leaves no room for doubt. It you tell a man who has studied these things ... that they are contrary to religion, your assertion will shake his faith in religion, not in these things. (Introduction.)[4]

Ghazali then goes on to discuss questions on which there really is disagreement between the Greeks and orthodox Moslems: whether the universe has a beginning, whether God has knowledge of individuals, whether miracles are possible, whether there can be a bodily resurrection. His handling of these issues is not only philosophically sophisticated but entirely consistent with orthodox Christianity, and some of his points will be used below.

That Christianity became philosophical may seem a triumph for philosophy; but it was one philosophers might have done well to forego, since it brought them under the attention, and eventually the jurisdiction, of ecclesiastical authorities. In the fifth century there was freedom of thought in the great universities of Athens, Alexandria and Constantinople, and philosophy was taught, not exclusively but quite largely, by non-Christians. The Emperor Justinian (527-65) insisted on Christian teachers of philosophy at the University of Constantinople (which, being financed entirely by the government, was entirely under governmental control), and he closed the Platonic philosophy school at Athens. In provincial towns of the Byzantine Empire, although philosophy was taught it was

CHRISTIANITY AND PHILOSOPHY

not officially encouraged: teachers had to live off what fees they could obtain, whereas teachers of subjects thought more useful, like medicine and mathematics, were paid by the municipal authorities.

The Western Roman Empire had no universities, or at least no institutions which could compare with Athens, Alexandria or Constantinople. The monks of northern Europe, particularly those of Northumberland and Durham, are justly famous for their learning, but that learning was neither acquired nor imparted in universities. Perhaps the only figure in English history before the twelfth century who had a university education was Theodore, Archbishop of Canterbury 668–90, who had studied at Athens. Philosophy is a subject which cannot be well pursued independently of universities, and although it was not held in low repute in Western Europe, no progress was made in it. An unfortunate amount of authority was attached to the *Commentary on the Timaeus* by the (?) fourth-century cleric Calcidius. This was the main source in the West for the philosophical thought of Plato and Aristotle until their actual works began to be translated in the twelfth and thirteenth centuries, and it is unreliable. Until the very end of the dark, or University-less, Ages there seem to have been no attempts either to justify or to criticise Christian belief by philosophical reasoning.

A medical school existed at Salerno in the ninth century, but Western universities are generally considered to have started in the twelfth century with Bologna and Paris. Bologna began by teaching law, moved on to medicine and reached philosophy perhaps only in the thirteenth century. In Paris, however, thanks to William of Champeaux and his pupil Abelard, philosophy was being studied at Church schools even before the university was properly constituted, and the university specialised, and led the Western world, in theology.

This may have been partly due to St Anselm. He came to France from Northern Italy in the second half of the eleventh century, and entering the newly founded monastery of Bec, started teaching and writing philosophical theology. He does not suggest that philosophical argument can take the place of faith, but urges that we have a duty, 'once we are confirmed in faith, to try to understand the things we believe'. Anselm did not teach at Paris – in fact he became Archbishop of Canterbury in 1093 – but his work must have been influential. Perhaps even more important, historically if not philosophically, was Abelard's pupil Peter the Lombard. He became Archbishop of Paris in 1159, and bequeathed to the academic world his famous work the *Sentences*. This is a compilation of opinions (*sententiae*) on points of Christian belief, it became the main text-book for students of philosophical theology, and some of the best mediaeval philosophy which has come down to us is to be found in commentaries on it.

Perhaps nobody today would deny that the relationship between philosophy and theology in the mediaeval West was too close to be healthy. Philosophy was subjected to an ecclesiastical surveillance which was capricious and unpredictable and which did not stop short of violence; on the other hand philosophical methods let loose in the airy realm of theology where neither empirical observations nor natural intuitions can provide constraints, and where linguistic discipline is extremely difficult to maintain, produced a glut of facile and unwanted answers. The danger today is that we see only these bad consequences. But a society that wanted philosophy for its religion was not going to let the subject become dormant or ossified, and the universities of France and England were surely producing better philosophy in the thirteenth to fifteenth than in the sixteenth to eighteenth centuries. On the side of religion, the Anselmian hope of understanding what one believes and having faith and reason cooperate is neither ignoble nor limited to the scholastic mind; it may be said to reach its height in the age which followed that of scholasticism.

2

Modern philosophy is generally reckoned to begin with Descartes (1596–1650). A brilliant mathematician, Descartes formed the extraordinary belief that whatever is the case can be proved in the same way as the propositions of Euclid. In his own words:

> The long chains of simple and easy reasoning by means of which geometers are accustomed to reach the conclusions of their most difficult demonstrations had led me to imagine that *all things to the knowledge of which man is competent are mutually connected in the same way*, and that there is nothing so far removed from us as to be beyond our reach, or so hidden that we cannot discover it. (*Discourse on Method*, Pt. II. [Emphasis added.])

In particular Descartes thought he could prove the existence of God and the possibility of a life after death in this mathematical way. He entitled his main philosophical work *Meditations on First Philosophy in which the Existence of God and the Immortality of the Soul are Demonstrated*. To his disappointment, the demonstrations were not well received by contemporary theologians. It is doubtful, indeed, if any professional theologian, Catholic or Protestant, accepted any of them. Nevertheless the ambition of finding rigorous proofs of the fundamental doctrines of Christianity, like the ambition of discovering El Dorado, haunted the European mind for the next hundred years, a century distinguished from all others by its romantic confidence in human reason and rationality. The principal philosophers of the time, Spinoza, Locke, Leibniz and Malebranche, all offered arguments for the existence of God which they believed matched up to the standards for demonstration prevalent in mathematics.

Then, in the 1750s, came the reaction. David Hume (1711–76) composed his *Dialogues Concerning Natural Religion*, and they started circulating in manuscript. This work contains brilliant, and in the eyes of many readers devastating, criticisms of the traditional arguments for the existence of God; not only that, but Hume argues that the amount of evil and suffering in the world provides good rational grounds for holding there is *no* such God, all powerful, all wise, and at the same time benevolent, as Christians believe in. The attack on theism in the *Dialogues* is supplemented in other works. In his *Enquiry*

Concerning Human Understanding (s. 10) Hume argues that it is unreasonable to believe that any miracle has ever occurred. His short essay 'On the Immortality of the Soul' contains a classic version of the best argument against the possibility of life after death. To this day Hume is acknowledged by Christians and non-Christians alike as the foremost philosophical critic of Christian belief. Modern writers like Antony Flew and J. L. Mackie still use his arguments and would be willing to admit that they have little of substance to add to them.[5]

Immanuel Kant (1724–1804) is generally classed as the greatest of German philosophers, but it is perhaps significant that by descent he was a Scot like Hume. He saw Hume's *Dialogues* in 1780, the year before he published his *Critique of Pure Reason*, and whether or not he was influenced by Hume he was the means of transplanting Scottish scepticism to the naturally pious Teutonic soil. The second half of the *Critique* is a carefully planned attack on the whole project of natural or philosophical theology.

It has three parts: on the soul, the universe and God. In the first Kant argues that introspective self-knowledge does not (as Descartes thought it did) provide us with a notion of ourselves as conscious beings capable of existing without bodies. The significance of this is not just that it blocks arguments for a life after death. The theist has to suppose that God is a conscious being without a body, and Kant's argument, if successful, shows that the concept of such a being is not available to us. I would accept Kant's conclusion that no such concept is provided *by introspection*, though I do not find his arguments for it very cogent or clear.

The second part is an attempt to show that we cannot prove the universe had a beginning, and that it is never legitimate to explain an event, not by a prior cause, but simply by someone's wanting it to happen. In this way Kant hopes to cut the ground from under traditional theistic thinking, according to which the universe began a finite length of time ago because that was God's will.

In the third section Kant maintains that any argument for the existence of God must be of one of three kinds: it must be ontological, cosmological or physico-theological; and all three kinds of argument are fallacious. The terms 'ontological' and 'cosmological' have been retained by later critics of theistic belief, more, perhaps, because they are slightly absurd and make the arguments they are used to denote sound cumbersome and old-fashioned, than because they are appropriate. An ontological argument is an *a priori* argument which attempts to proceed from the concept or definition of God to his real existence. The following is an ontological argument:

God, by definition, has every desirable quality.
Existence is a desirable quality.
So God exists.

A cosmological argument is one which proceeds *a posteriori* from the physical universe as something which needs explaining to God as an explanation. The most plausible arguments for the existence of God are of this kind. Kant claims that any argument of this kind must include the crucial step of ontological arguments, the step from the concept of something to its real existence. If this were true the prospects of a sound rational argument for the existence of God would be poor. It is now, however, agreed by theists and atheists[6] alike that Kant's argument for this particular claim is fallacious.

In 1794 William Paley published his *Evidences of Christianity* in which he tries, among other things, to answer Hume's argument about miracles and the charge that the historical value of the Gospels is destroyed by their mutual contradictions. His book was welcomed by his fellow clergymen in the Church of England, but the intellectual tide in the last decade of the eighteenth century was running strongly against him. The deist Thomas Paine's *The Age of Reason* (written 1793–95) ends with the following verdict:

> Of all the systems of religion that ever were invented, there is none more derogatory to the Almighty, more unedifying to man, more repugnant to reason, and more contradictory in itself, than this thing called Christianity. Too absurd for belief, too impossible to convince, and too inconsistent for practice, it renders the heart torpid, or produces only atheists and fanatics. As an engine of

power, it serves the purpose of despotism; and as a means of wealth, the avarice of priests; but so far as respects the good of man in general, it leads to nothing here or hereafter. (Citadel Press, 1974, p. 186.)[7]

3

The first important response to the arguments of Hume and Kant was that of Friedrich Schleiermacher (1768–1834), a pastor and professor of theology at Berlin. In 1799 he published *On Religion: Speeches to its Cultured Despisers* – these being not the Parisian sceptics who had welcomed Hume but virtuous intellectuals in Germany. Schleiermacher does not try to convince them that Christian beliefs are, after all reasonable, but neither, to his credit, does he appeal to the consideration (developed by, among others, Louis XVI's minister Necker in 1788 in his *The Importance of Religious Opinions*) that they are needed to prop up morality. He tries to give religion a field of its own, separate both from that of thought and from that of practical activity: the field of feeling. Religious life consists in experiencing and renewing religious feelings. The most important part of his work is an attempt to explain exactly what these are.

Feeling in general is present in experience before consciousness. It is not identical with perception but it occurs with it:

> It is the first contact of the universal life with an individual. It fills no time and fashions nothing palpable. It is the holy wedlock of the Universe with the incarnated Reason for a creative, productive embrace. It is immediate, raised above all error and misunderstanding. You lie directly on the bosom of the infinite world. In that moment, you are its soul ... In this way every living, original movement of your life is first received. Among the rest, it is the source of every religious emotion. But it is not, as I said, even a moment. The incoming of existence to us by this immediate union at once stops as soon as it reaches consciousness. (Trans. Oman, J., Harper and Row 1958, pp. 43–4.)

We get religious feeling from being conscious of 'the divine unity and eternal immutability of the world' and from a sense of 'being at one with nature' (p. 71).

> Religion is to take up into our lives, and to submit to being swayed by them, each of these influences and their consequent emotions, not by themselves but as part of the Whole (pp. 48–9).

We are aware of action on us as 'an exhibition of the infinite in our life'. Religious contemplation is

> the immediate consciousness of the universal existence of all finite things in and through the Infinite, and of all temporal things in and through the Eternal (p. 36).

What, in the light of this, can we say of the traditional religious beliefs? We do not jettison God, since we count a feeling as religious only insofar as 'it affects us as a revelation of God' (p. 93). But since religion is not a matter of ideas, we should not insist too strongly that God is a person. The religious man may well be conscious of 'the limitation of personal existence, and particularly of personality joined to consciousness' (p. 97). Like Spinoza, he may give a higher place to supra-personal necessity. 'The usual conception of God as one single being outside of the world and behind the world' is always 'inadequate', and may be formed 'from the need for such a being to console and help' (p. 101).

Similarly with life after death. The goal of religious life is not

> the immortality that is outside of time, behind it or rather after it, and which still is in time. It is the immortality which we can have in this temporal life (p. 101).

> If our feeling nowhere attaches itself to the individual, but if its content is our relation to God wherein all that is individual and fleeting disappears, there can be nothing fleeting in it, but all must be eternal. In the religious life... we are actually enjoying immortality (p. 100).

But immortality as usually conceived is 'opposed to the spirit of piety' because it is too personal; besides, 'Who can endure the effort to conceive an endless temporal existence?' (p. 100).

In response to doubts about miracles (raised by Reimarus and Lessing in Germany as well as by Hume) Schleiermacher says that everything is miraculous because everthing is wonderful and significant; but in a footnote (p. 114) he concedes that 'absolute miracle' is to be rejected, and that nothing ever happens for which a naturalistic explanation is not possible.

Schleiermacher's ideas about God and immortality constitute a kind of high-tide mark which *avant-garde* theology since his day has reached more than once (particularly in recent years) but hardly yet transcended. He also influenced philosophy to an extent unusual for a theologian. What he says about religious experience could more naturally be offered as an account of aesthetic experience, and is in fact echoed in the aesthetic writings of Benedetto Croce and Clive Bell. Bell's *Art* is one of the canonical writings of the far from Christian Bloomsbury Group, but we read in it that we feel authentic aesthetic emotion for a thing when and only when:

> Instead of recognising its accidental and conditioned importance, we become aware of its essential reality, of the God in everything, of the universal in the particular, of the all-pervading rhythm.[8]

More important for our present study, Schleiermacher's interpretation of the New Testament can be viewed as the inauguration of the modern discipline of Hermeneutics. Developed philosophically by Heidegger and Gadamer, hermeneutics has returned in this century to influence theology by licensing and indeed demanding the sort of non-propositional understanding of Christianity of which I shall speak in a moment.

The influence of Schleiermacher was canalised, at least initially, through G. W. F. Hegel (1770–1831). Hegel would be important even if the Russian Revolution had not caused a materialistic version of his system to become the Bible of half the world. After his death the universities of Germany and the

German-speaking intelligentsia of Europe were dominated by his pupils. He is the principal source of state socialism in Germany and Britain, and it was his pupils also who led the way not only in theology but in history and the new critical study of the Bible which was to reinforce so powerfully the conclusions of eighteenth-century philosophy. Hegel applied to his distinctive method of philosophising the German word *Wissenschaft* which is rendered in English by 'science' although its original meaning is rather more broad. It is thanks to him that the term 'scientific' became, in the nineteenth century, a general term of praise, and his influence may be suspected wherever there is enthusiastic talk of 'scientific socialism', 'scientific history', 'theological science'[9] or a 'scientific' approach generally.

Hegel wrote and lectured extensively on the philosophy of religion. At first he seems to be opposing Schleiermacher's view that religion is simply a matter of feeling. He does not suggest, however, that there can be any return to the situation as it was before Hume. He is extremely difficult to interpret, and readers have disagreed about whether he believed in a personal God distinct from the universe; but however that may be, it seems to me that his aim is less to deny that religious life consists of religious feeling, than to establish that religious feeling and experience still fall under the authority of philosophy. Religion for him is an aspect or partial expression of a process which as a whole is the subject-matter of philosophy: the emergence of the Absolute. Whether or not this interpretation of Hegel's own intentions is correct, it is plain that his followers, far from repudiating Scheiermacher, go beyond him.

Of these followers the foremost on the philosophical side is Ludwig Feuerbach (1804–72). His *Essence of Christianity* (1841; translated into English by George Eliot in 1854) takes Schleiermacher's conclusions as its premises and says little that is not at least foreshadowed in *On Religion*. Schleiermacher had made religion consist in consciousness of the infinite; Feuerbach argues (not very cogently) that this can only be consciousness of ourselves. In a similar manner he reasons that if feeling is 'the organ of religion' it is itself God. From this he infers that religion is 'the earliest and most indirect form of self-knowledge' (1.2). The object of religious feeling is not something superhuman; it is man's highest feeling of himself, the feeling of himself as free (Appendices 1–3). But man does not recognise this, and projects the idea of himself as the idea of a divine being distinct from himself. In this way man alienates himself from himself, and religion is the result of this alienation.

Feuerbach claimed (Appendix 22) to be siding with Protestantism against Catholicism; but his speculations led directly (witness Marx's *Theses on Feuerbach* of 1845) to atheism on philosophical grounds. At the same time Christian belief had to face an attack on historical grounds. A number of writers had already expressed doubts about the historical value of much of the Old Testament; 1835 saw the publication of Strauss' *Life of Jesus* (translated into English ten years later by George Eliot) in which it was argued at the length of some 1500 pages that the narratives of the New Testament too are largely false.

D. F. Strauss (1808–74) was teaching philosophy at Tubingen when he started work on this book, and while strongly influenced by Schleiermacher he seems to have found his chief inspiration in Hegel. In the Introduction he declares that there are two criteria by which we can tell that an account is not historical: 'First, when the narration is irreconcilable with the known and universal laws which govern the course of events ...'[10] and secondly, inconsistency. The first of these criteria makes the containing of a miracle itself sufficient to condemn a narrative as unhistorical. We may feel that Strauss here begs the question. In a later work, however, with a similar title, *A New Life of Christ for the German People* (1864) he defends himself by appealing to Hume:

> On the side of the sceptical and critical philosophers, Hume's Essay on Miracles in particular carries with it such general conviction that the question may be regarded as having been by it virtually settled. (English translation 1865, Vol. I, p. 199.)

Strauss takes it that Hume's argument (which will be discussed below) shows incontrovertibly that the miracle-narratives of the New Testament cannot rationally be believed, and this being so, the Gospels cannot be taken seriously as historical evidence for the events they appear to relate.

In his 1835 Preface Strauss is careful to say that his book is not intended to be subversive of Christianity:

> The author is aware that the essence of the Christian faith is perfectly independent of his criticism. The supernatural birth of Christ, his miracles, his resurrection and ascension, remain eternal truths whatever doubts may be cast on their reality as historical facts.[11]

How can they be eternal truths if they are not historical facts? Strauss did not explain that in 1835, but in the Preface to the 1854 *New Life* he says that 'a principal, if not the sole consideration' of this later work is

> that in the person and acts of Jesus no supernaturalism shall be suffered to remain; nothing which shall press upon the souls of men with the leaden weight of arbitrary, inscrutable authority. (E.T. Vol. I, p. xii.)

> So long as Christianity is considered as something given from without, its Author as literally heaven-descended, the Church as a machinery for procuring the expiation of human offences through his blood, Christianity, though claiming to be the religion of the Spirit, must remain unspiritual, and in fact Jewish. Only when it is seen that in Christianity man did but become more deeply conscious of his own true nature, that Jesus was the individual in whom this deeper consciousness first became a supreme, all-pervading influence, that redecmption means but the advent of such a disposition and its inward adoption as our very life blood, then only is Christianity really and thoroughly understood. (Vol. I, p. xv.)

Many details of Strauss' critique have been rejected by later scholars. He thought, for instance, that the Gospel of Matthew was older than that of Mark; the current view is that Matthew copied from Mark and also used a lost document called 'Q' which included a collection of 'sayings' or 'logia' of Jesus. Nevertheless his essential conclusion that we cannot treat the first three Gospels, much less the fourth, as factual accounts of historical events has come to be accepted by perhaps the majority of theologians, both Protestant and Catholic. Many would agree with Rudolf Bultmann that *'Gospels are expanded cultic legends'* (his italics).[12]

If the Gospels are not reliable sources for what Jesus said and did, it becomes doubtful whether he made any claims to be divine or rose from the dead. If these matters are doubtful they infect with uncertainty the traditional doctrines that Jesus was the Son of God, that there are three Persons in God, and that there is life after death. These doctrines were formerly supposed to have been revealed by Christ. Today many theologians distinguished two concepts of revelation. They reject the idea that God, either through the lips of Jesus or in any other way, reveals to us true propositions about himself or the supernatural. But they retain a notion of non-propositional revelation. God manifests himself in the universe as a whole, in the life of an individual, and in a special way, even if not in an absolutely unique way, in the life (however obscured, now, by the mists of time) of Jesus. These theologians would feel unable to defend traditional Christian belief if that belief is construed as the believing of a set of propositions like the creed; but they would question such a construction. Christian belief can be seen, and is more profitably seen in today's world, as a non-propositional trust and confidence in God.

This approach is well illustrated by Maurice Wiles. He wishes to hold on to the proposition that there exists a personal God, but finds it is no longer a 'viable possibility' for us to accept 'the doctrine of the unique incarnation of God in Jesus Christ'. Our world view is not one in which it makes sense either to assert or to deny that Christ's death had 'an objective effect altering the status of men as sinners'. Since, however, we can still admit 'the underlying reality of the world's ontological dependence upon God' and 'the profound importance of those occasions when a man acknowledges and responds with his full self to all he has come to know of God and of God's purposes for good', we can also hold that

> it is supremely through Jesus that the character of these purposes of God and the possibility of this experience of grace has been grasped and made effective in the world. If we speak of him as unique and of his claims as universal, the appropriate meaning to be given to such affirmations would seem to be two-fold. They bear witness to the radical nature of the transforming effect in the lives of those who have responded to him; and they express the conviction (which only time can test) that he will continue to fulfil that role in the future, however different the conditions of life may become.[13]

The theologians abandon propositional beliefs because they do not believe the New Testament narratives; and it may be worth while to emphasise that their chief grounds for thinking the narratives false are *a priori* and philosophical, not historical. There is no list of persons executed under Pontius Pilate on which the name of Jesus fails to appear; there is no record that followers of Jesus put about stories of his resurrection which were investigated and found to be untrue. The theologians accept Hume's argument about miracles; and they have a general view of the nature of reality according to which it is not possible that any particular sequence of historical events could have the unique, universal, once-and-for-all significance which propositional formulations of Christianity have attributed to the life and death of Jesus.

But if we turn from modern theology to modern philosophy, it looks as if the theologians have fled the field while the battle was still hanging in balance. For philosophers are by no means agreed that Christian belief cannot be propositional. In this century Hume and Kant have been held to be largely wrong on non-religious philosophical issues, and their views on religious issues cannot be regarded as above question. Among English-speaking philosophers today a significant number are not only practising Christians but Christians whose belief take propositional form; unlike many theologians they can recite the Apostle's Creed without a blush.

It would be wrong to say that modern theologians have no friends in philosophy. D. Z. Phillips is an example. Like Schleiermacher he offers an interpretation of the Christian doctrine of immortality which detaches it from the idea of continuing to exist after death. Phillips does not mention Schleiermacher. He professes to derive his ideas chiefly from the twentieth-century Austrian philosopher Wittgenstein. He owes to Wittgenstein the notion that what appear to be true or false statements about a life after death are really pictures which are operative or inoperative in people's lives, pictures by which the believer lives and from which he draws sustenance.[14] But he looks back to Schleiermacher when he equates immortality with 'dying to the self' and seeing that 'all things are a gift of God, that nothing is ours by right or necessity'. Phillips is careful to say that to speak of everything as a gift of God is not to commit oneself to 'the existence of the Giver'; he says:

> In learning by contemplation, attention, renunciation, what forgiving, thanking, loving etc., mean in these contexts, the believer is participating in the reality of God; this is what we mean by *God's reality*.

Phillips takes to task both Christian philosophers who argue that religious utterances say something true, and atheists who argue that they say something false or meaningless.

Phillip's position, sometimes known as Wittgensteinian fideism, has failed to win much philosophical acceptance.[15] Richard Swinburne has recently produced three fair-sized volumes purporting to prove that the existence of God is 'more probably than not'. Kai Nielsen and J. L. Mackie have thought it worthwhile to publish books arguing that belief in a personal God is groundless or false. Swinburne argues that what Phillips says about religious language, at least if it is intended as an account of what has actually been meant by 'the vast majority of theists down the past two millenniums' is false. Nielsen, says that Phillips and those who think with him 'unwittingly have created a new or at least a radically altered language-game with Christian terms and an atheistic substance'. Mackie, besides endorsing these views of Phillips, remarks that the 'clarity and honesty' of more traditional arguments for theistic belief are 'a welcome contrast to the evasiveness and oscillations between mutually incompatible views in which some recent theologians have taken refuge from criticism.'

The situation is complicated by the fact that there are at present two quite separate philosophical traditions in the Western world. In the nineteenth century English-speaking philosophers tried to keep in touch with developments on the Continent, and Jowett, Bradley and Bosanquet in different ways offered Hegelianism to English readers. At the end of that century, however, Bertrand Russell repudiated the German tradition and reverted to the pre-Kantian type of philosophy known as Empiricism which has always been particularly congenial to the British. Besides being an excellent all-round philosopher, Russell was probably the most brilliant logician since Aristotle, and also commanded a lucid and pleasing prose style. The principal nineteenth-century German philosophers, in contrast, were ignorant of logic and their style is extremely difficult for English readers. Since 1900 professional philosophy in English-speaking countries has been characterised by Empiricism, logical sophistication and a striving after a smooth, natural style, combined, since the work of the Oxford philosophers J. L. Austin and Gilbert Ryle, with a belief that we can still learn from Ancient Greek philosophy. On the Continent, in contrast, there has been a much more continuous development of the tradition of Kant and Hegel. The thread which guides this tradition is the so-called idealist notion that the world is not something which exists independently of our experience of it; at least insofar as our understanding can grasp it, it is a product of our thought. Completely objective truth, for this tradition, is a will o' the wisp. The task of the philosopher is to explain how we can do without it, and this task is tackled in a highly technical way with a vocabulary far removed from that of ordinary thought and speech. Incredible as it may seem to laymen, between English-speaking and

German- or French-speaking philosophers there is now almost complete mutual incomprehension. Whereas there is only one world of science or history, there are two worlds of philosophy. It is no exaggeration to say that during the last quarter century, only one Continental philosopher (the Jesuit M. Régnier) has attended the main British philosophical event of the year, the annual Joint Session of the Aristotelian Society and the Mind Association, while at the biennial Congress of French-Speaking Philosophical Societies I have twice found myself the only person for whom English is the mother-tongue.

Christianity being a philosopher's religion, this state of affairs has implications for theology. Modern Protestant theology came from Germany and is largely based on the Continental philosophical tradition. Catholic theology too, in the last fifty years, has come to rely increasingly on the philosophy of Continental writers like Heidegger. On the other hand in the English-speaking world in general the English-speaking philosophical tradition is dominant, so the theologians, whether Protestant or Catholic, find it very difficult to communicate with the educated people around them. Hence the exasperation voiced by Mackie and felt, I suspect, not only by many atheists but still more by many believing Christians. Underlying the disagreement between propositionalists and anti-propositionalists is the gulf between these two philosophical traditions.

4

In what follows I do not wish to quarrel with those Christians who prefer to see their faith as primarily or even exclusively non-propositional. Acrimonious feuding between Christians who wish to retain doctrinal propositions and Christians who do not seems to me to do no service to the cause of true religion. I shall try, however, to show what can be said, from the standpoint of a philosopher with some smattering of history, in defence of traditional Christian belief construed propositionally. Moreover while the existence of a personal God is a doctrine which cannot be omitted, it is shared by Jews and Moslems, and my concern will be more with the peculiarly Christian doctrines of the Incarnation and the Redemption. It seems to me that philosophers have often got bogged down in the issue of whether God exists. Nobody is going to be brought to an opinion on that issue simply by philosophical argument, and the argument is sometimes spun out so artificially and tediously that one wonders if the Philosophy of Religion is a genuine discipline at all. Perhaps the philosopher has nothing useful to say about religion unless he burns his boats and treks into the jungle of theology proper.

To the natives who dwell in that jungle – the theologians – that is naturally an alarming prospect, and we need not be surprised at their trying to convince these intruders with their sophisticated dialectical weapons that the jungle contains nothing that could interest them, no propositions. But I shall suggest that religious thinking is not so resistant to philosophical enquiry as has been supposed.

The modern theologian's feeling that there can be no cognitive or propositional religious beliefs has philosophical roots deeper and more extensive than any I have yet mentioned. It arises out of the fact that for several centuries philosophers have concentrated on one part of our thinking. Descartes and Leibniz, Frege and Bertrand Russell were all mathematicians. Kant and Spinoza were competent in the physical sciences. These philosophers and their successors on both sides of the Channel take our thinking about mathematics and physics to be the best kind of thought we can attain to, and the kind to which all other thinking should approximate. Modern metaphysicians tend to assume that the concepts employed in it, the concepts of space, time and causation, are the only ones through which understanding is possible. Modern logic is a study not of reasoning in general but of mathematical reasoning. Modern philosophy of language, at least prior to Davidson,[16] is a philosophy not of ordinary discourse but of the discourse of scientists. These philosophers operate, of course, at a high level of technicality and abstraction. They have no direct effect on ordinary educated men. But they have a powerful indirect effect. They are like solar storms and events in the upper atmosphere, which are not directly perceivable from the ground but nonetheless influence the weather which is.

What has either been ignored by philosophers or defeated them is our practical understanding of our own behaviour and the behaviour of people around us, something which in fact occupies our minds a good deal of the time. It is obvious that we have what might be called psychological concepts: concepts of mental and moral capacities, activities and states. But there is no agreed and satisfactory philosophical account of them. Philosophers either assume, or at best offer quite simplistic arguments to show, that we conceive mental states as causes and effects of physical events. They assimilate our practical thinking about persons to our theoretical, scientific thinking about things. As a consequence they are unable to produce a coherent account of a human being as a being who is at home in both worlds, the world of physical things and the world of intelligent, purposive agents.

The concepts employed in religious thinking are of the psychological kind. God is a person; the relationship between men and God is interpersonal; the principles imposed by Christianity are moral ones; the destiny offered to believers is a kind of life. So much, perhaps, is obvious; but I shall be suggesting that certain elements in Christianity which today seem specially mysterious, the notions of the dependence of the world in general and of men in particular upon God, of the deleteriousness of sin and of salvation through Christ, belong to practical or psychological thinking. They are more puzzling to us than they may have been to our ancestors because we have been taught that scientific understanding is the only sort of understanding possible and that spatial, temporal and causal relationships are the only relationships of which we can have any idea. I shall find it necessary to describe at some length ways of thinking other than the scientific; ways which might be thought to be the business of philosophy, not theology, but which philosophers have neglected or found too much for them.

Perhaps they really are too much for anyone who is limited to purely philosophical resources. Christianity, on the other hand, offers a unified picture of man as a member of the two worlds. Perhaps the dual nature of man is in fact understandable only in the light of the Christian doctrine of the incarnation of God in Christ. We think we apply the concept of a person to Christ; it may be that we derive it from him.

CHAPTER TWO
The Existence of God

I

An educated atheist is unlikely to be convinced that God exists by the arguments of theists, and an educated theist is unlikely to be convinced that there is no God by the arguments of atheists. We should not be in a hurry to conclude that the existence of God can neither be proved nor disproved. To start with we should recognise that different kinds of proposition are proved in different ways. Euclid proved that if a triangle has two equal sides it will also have two equal angles. It is not too hard to prove that however large a number you take, there is a larger number which is a prime number. The proofs of propositions like these are purely theoretical; they are carried out, so to speak, in the armchair; and the conclusions follow from the premisses with perfect logical rigour. It is quite different to prove that Uranus has rings, that there is a virus which causes pneumonia, or that there are particles just like electrons except that their electric charge is positive. In these cases you have to make observations with expensive equipment or carry out complicated experiments. It is different again to prove that nationalising the means of production will not automatically produce prosperity, or that the causes of a war were rather economic than political, or that Dreyfus was innocent or guilty. Issues like these are not settled either by theoretical reasoning or by empirical investigation; proofs tend to be cumulative, that is, they consist of several distinct grounds for belief which are separately indecisive but mutually reinforcing;[1] and what seems to be a proof to one person may not be accepted as adequate by another. A person who will not admit that there are pneumococci, or that there is no highest prime number, is unreasonable. We do not expect everyone to be able to prove these things himself, but everyone can ascertain whether a satisfactory proof exists. On the other hand it is characteristic of the kinds of proof that are offered in history books, deliberative assemblies and courts of law that it is a matter for judgement whether or not to accept them.

Whether God exists is not a question in science or mathematics. We may expect that reasons for answering it one way or the other will be of such a kind that it is matter for judgement how conclusive they are. And there is a further factor. Unlike questions in mathematics and science, unlike many questions, even, in history, the question whether God exists has practical implications. The God of Christianity is a person who, whether we like it or not, stands to us in an intimate personal relationship. He imposes on us an exacting code of behaviour towards each other; he requires us to belong to a visible society of people not all of whom are outstandingly likeable, the Church; and he demands that we should love him personally and acknowledge him publicly. Belief in the Christian God goes with a whole pattern of life. It is like belief in a political system or belief in your spouse. There may be theoretical arguments for the system of parliamentary democracy or strong empirical evidence against the constancy of your spouse; but these do not of themselves suffice to ensure conviction because it is part of being convinced to have a disposition or desire to order your life in a certain way. This is even truer of Christianity, and Christians believe that we can have the desire and disposition only by the grace or generosity of God.

That is, they think that believing in God requires faith. The word 'faith', however, is one to which people attach different meanings. When, in a non-religious context, we say 'You must just have faith' we mean a kind of belief that all will be well for which there is no rational justification. By 'faith' in a religious context the non-believer will often understand a quite irrational feeling of conviction. The believer is not likely to agree with that, but even among believers there are divergences of usage. Paul often uses the Greek word we translate as 'faith' to cover confidence in God and hope: so *Romans* Ch. 4. Calvin seems to be following this usage when he defines faith as:

> A firm and certain knowledge of God's benevolence towards us, founded on the truth of the freely given promise in Christ, both revealed to our minds and sealed upon our hearts through the Holy Spirit. (*Institutes* III.ii.7; the promise referred to is Heaven.)

But faith can be contrasted with the other so-called theological virtues of hope and charity, and believing that God exists is a matter of faith in this narrower sense.

How should this narrower sense be explained? There is, in general, an intimate relationship between knowledge or belief and behaviour: we cannot hold a belief which is not reflected somehow in our behaviour, and all behaviour, all intentional action and inaction, is an expression of belief. Religious beliefs are the beliefs expressed in a person's behaviour insofar as that behaviour has religious significance. An action will have religious significance, even if it is not an obviously religious act like praying, if it is done for some religious motive such as love of God or fear of God (or even hatred of God). A person's religious beliefs together make up his faith. Now to say that faith is given by God is not to say that a person's religious beliefs are planted in his mind by God. It is clear that they come into his mind in the same way as other beliefs: he gets them from his parents, his companions, his reading, his reflection on his experience and so forth. The claim is rather that it is only thanks to God that he can act on these beliefs, that they are operative within him.

To hold in this way that we need faith to believe God exists is not to admit that the belief can have no rational grounds. A Christian will want to say that Christian behaviour is not alien to the rest of human life or unnatural for us but a development of what is natural. If that is right, religious beliefs should not be conspicuously less rational than other beliefs on which we act.

If anything they should be more rational, and they should also be integrated with the rest of our knowledge.

I said that a rational argument for religious belief should be cumulative. We can distinguish at least three kinds of ground for accepting the existence of the Christian God, all of which, I think, are necessary.

First, nobody will become or remain a Christian if he finds the Christian way of life repugnant. It is necessary to find the combination of Christian belief, Christian ethics and the social life of the Church satisfactory: you must think you would be the better for it, and that if not all Christians, at least some are happy, wise and good. Secondly a man can admire Christianity and think it makes people good and happy, yet be unable to accept it because he sees insuperable theoretical difficulties in believing that the universe depends on a benevolent, personal creator. A Christian must at least be satisfied that there are no compelling philosophical arguments against the existence of God. I think that for most people something more positive is needed: most Christians would say that we cannot make sense of the universe except by supposing that it was created by God. Finally a man might covet the Christian way of life and also think that the universe needs a first cause, yet not be a Christian because he cannot believe that this first cause has ever intervened in human history or shown any interest in men. Christians hold that there is empirical evidence in human history of a series, culminating in the life of Christ, of interventions in human affairs by a superhuman person. Most Christians have themselves had experiences which they can best explain by saying there is a God who cares for them.

There are, then, three kinds of ground for belief in the Christian God: empirical evidence, in history and in the individual's own life, for the existence of a benevolent supernatural person; philosophical arguments to the effect that we have to posit a creator to explain the world; and a total impression, itself based on a variety of considerations, that Christianity is a good thing. To say that in practice the most important ground is the third, is not cynicism but orthodoxy. Christians hold that God is present, and even revealed, in the body of Christians alive now. Next in importance is probably the experience of God in the individual's personal life. Neither of these things, however, can usefully be discussed in a book like this. I shall concentrate on the theoretical or philosophical arguments for and against the existence of a creator, though I shall also say something about the empirical evidence in history.

2

> There are temporal phenomena in the world. And some other phenomena are causes of those phenomena. Now it is impossible that one set of temporal phenomena should be caused by another, and that the series should go on *ad infinitum*. No intelligent person can believe such a thing... So if there is a limit at which the series of temporal phenomena stops, let this limit be called the eternal.

In these words Al-Ghazali formulates what for many reflective theists is the basic ground for thinking that there is a God.[2] The sequence of events which constitutes the history of the universe must have a beginning. That beginning calls for explanation. And the explanation can be provided only by something non-physical which has no beginning, which exists without ever having started to exist. Instead of talking about a series of events people sometimes say simply that the universe cannot have made itself; the idea is the same, that physical reality must depend on something outside it.

Why? What has been offered is less a formal argument than a line of thought; what are the principles which underlie it, and which might serve as premises for a formal argument?

The theist should take care not to make it a principle that everything needs a cause distinct from itself, since he will then invite the question 'What is the cause of God?' or as Hume puts it, 'How shall we satisfy ourselves concerning the cause of that being, whom you suppose the Author of Nature?' On the other hand it is arbitrary to say simply that everything except God needs a cause. If we stop at God, says Hume, 'and go no farther, why go so far? Why not stop at the material world?'

These difficulties seem to have been recognised by Ghazali, who observes: 'If there can be a temporal existent which has not been brought into existence by anyone, then the world itself should be such an existent.' What the theist must say is that anything of a certain type, anything which is material, or temporal, or which begins to be, needs a cause, and that the series of causes cannot be infinite. The first thing of this kind, then, will have to be caused by something radically different, something not material or non-temporal.

The theist may fairly be asked what sort of entity a non-material or non-temporal cause could be, and how it could cause things which are temporal and material. I shall defer considering these questions, however, to Chapter Three. Here I wish to concentrate on the two principles which are emerging as premisses. One is the principle that any *physical* object or event must have a cause; the other is the principle that the series of causes cannot be infinite. It is these principles that critics of our argument usually first dispute.

Their strategy with the first is simply to challenge it. Mackie, whose *Miracle of Theism* is perhaps the best recent critique of theistic arguments, confines himself to saying:

> Though we understand that when something has a temporally antecedent cause, it depends somehow on it, it does not follow that everything (other than God) *needs* something else to depend on in this way ... There is *a priori* no good reason why a sheer origination of things, not determined by anything, should be unacceptable (pp. 92, 94).

This seems to me weak. According to the now unfashionable Steady State cosmological theory, an atom of hydrogen just pops up in any region of empty space which is more than about a foot across. Given a universe which is already, so to speak, a going concern, we might accept this as a law of nature. But it would be a very different affair to accept a law that a universe should pop up or have a 'sheer origination'. The notion of such a law is incoherent. A natural law says what is natural for things that already exist. Existence is not natural for anything, and to suppose it might be a natural law that a universe should exist is to commit precisely the error of the Ontological Argument.

How can anyone seriously maintain that things might just pop up? It is significant that Mackie himself accepts a general scepticism about causation. His book *The Cement of the Universe* (Oxford 1974) is the best defence that has yet appeared of the view that there is no more to one thing's causing another than its being followed by that other thing. This view derives from Hume, and it is probably shared by many who have found unimpressive the theistic argument we are considering. If there is indeed no genuine link between cause and effect, if events merely come about and are never truly brought about, it is not too difficult to believe that an event might occur completely out of the blue, with no antecedent whatever. The theist, however, has good philosophical grounds for rejecting this view of causation. He must be careful not to say that every change which takes place is brought about by the causal action of some material object. But he should hold that one way of understanding an event is to see it as the effect of this kind of causal action, and equipped with this notion of understanding he can require that if an event cannot be understood in this way it should be understandable in some other way. The beginning of the universe, of course, could not be understandable as the effect of causal action, and the theist will wish to say that there occur events which are not due to causal action upon us by other things whenever we act freely and intentionally. The refusal of most atheists (Mackie is among them) to allow that there might be occurrences which are not the effect of prior causal action in the sphere of human conduct, renders particularly weak their insistence that there might be uncaused events in the universe at large.

The position is different with the second principle. That there could be an infinite series of causes is current philosophical orthodoxy, and attacks on this orthodoxy meet with smart resistance. Many theists therefore allow that every event in the history of the universe might have been caused by a prior event, and fall back on the position that the whole infinite series still calls for explanation.[3] As against this Hume says: 'In such a chain ... each part is caused by that which preceded it', and claims that once we have a cause for each part of the chain we need not look for a further cause of the whole chain.

> Did I show you the particular causes of each individual in a collection of twenty pieces of matter, I should think it very unreasonable, should you afterwards ask me what was the cause of the whole twenty. That is sufficiently explained in explaining the cause of the parts. (*Dialogues*, ix.)

I suspect that many people who have thought that there might be an infinite series of causes – that the universe might have existed for an infinitely long time, during which there have been infinitely many Big Bangs and Big Crunches – are people who have failed to distinguish two ways of understanding the claim that every event might have been caused by an earlier:

(1) There actually *is* no event which *might* not have been caused by an earlier.
(2) There *might* be no event which *is* not actually caused by an earlier.

The difference between these is like that between:

(3) There is no one courting Penelope who might not marry her (none of the suitors is a non-starter).
(4) It might be that there is no one courting her who will not marry her (polyandry is an option).

In fact, (1) asserts merely that no finite number is the largest number of events possible; (2) says that the number of events might be infinite, i.e. greater than every finite number.

The argument for theism we are considering allows that (1) is true but declares that (2) is false. How is the issue to be decided? The theist can admit that there are series or sets of mathematical entities such as numbers or fractions with infinitely many members. But there are at least three reasons for doubting whether they could be infinitely many physical objects like stars or actual physical events like Big Bangs.

First, it is hard to see how the properties of an infinite set of mathematical objects could be shared by a set of physical objects or events. For example, the number of members an infinite set has is unaffected by the addition or subtraction of one. There are as many odd numbers as even numbers, and there are still as many odd numbers not counting the number 1 as counting it. But suppose there were infinitely many pairs of gloves. Then if we threw away one right-hand glove there would still be as many right-hand gloves as left. To believe that this is a genuine possibility puts, I think, some strain on our credulity. Or imagine a vast camping ground on which there are many tents, and suppose that no tent is empty and that no two tents contain the same number of campers. As I said just now, there are infinitely many finite numbers. Hence if there could be infinitely many tents it could also be the case that no tent had more than a finite number of campers (even though none is empty and no two have the same number of campers). But surely under these conditions however many tents there are, there must always be at least one with at least that number of campers.

Perhaps it will be objected that I am just spelling out the agreed properties of an infinite set and asserting that such a set is impossible; and this, surely, is to beg the question. My reply constitutes my second argument that any set of actual things must be finite. The reason why sets of mathematical entities can be infinite is that they are sets of possibilities. When there is nothing in the specification of a set to limit the number of members it can have, its possible membership is infinite and unaffected by the addition or subtraction of one. Consider, for example, the number of times a train might stop between London and Edinburgh (as every traveller knows, this is not, of course, limited by the number of stations). The number of stops it might make is unaffected by the number is has already made; however often it may have stopped before Peterborough, the number of possible stops in the rest of the journey remains the same. The set of finite numbers is infinite because it corresponds to a set of possible classes of sets. We can classify sets by the number of members they have. All sets which each have only one member would go into one class, sets with two members go into a second, sets with three members into a third, and so on. Clearly the number of classes of this kind that there can be is infinite and equal to the number of finite numbers. But if infinity attaches to the *possible* membership of a set when its possible membership has no upper limit, there can be no infinite set of actual things. To suppose that the number of stars might be an infinite number like Aleph (the number of integers) is the same kind of mistake as supposing it might be an imaginary number like the square root of minus one. The number of members a set might have should not, of course, be conceived as a set of actual things that might be put into the set, like the set of persons who have been proposed for a club and are awaiting election.

Thirdly, the thesis that there might be an infinite set of actual things cannot be given a clear and rigorous formulation. 'It is possible that every suitor will marry Penelope' is equivalent to 'Penelope might marry A and B and C ...' where A, B, C etc., are all the suitors there are. So the claim 'It is possible that every event has a predecessor' should be equivalent to 'There might have been an event before A and B and C ...' where A, B, C etc., are all the events there have in fact been. But this does not say that the number of events might be infinite; it says merely that (whether it is infinite or finite) it might have been greater than it is. 'There might have been more events than there were', of course, is itself ambiguous between: 'There might have been at least one event in addition to all the events there actually were' and 'It might have been the case both that a certain set comprised all the events that occurred, and also that an additional event occurred'. The first may be conceded by someone who holds that any set of actual things must be finite; the second is self-contradictory.

I conclude that the concept of an infinite number has no application to the actual, physical universe. Physical things are finite, so is the whole set of them, and so is their whole history. Friends of the infinite may, perhaps, feel my argument is a little unfair. 'Perhaps there *are* just as many stars not counting Sirius and counting it' they may say; 'If so, how wonderful and beautiful that would be. You theists gib at the idea, but that is because the universe surpasses your narrow powers of comprehension. You often tell us that this or that doctrine which *we* cannot understand, such as the doctrine that God is both three and one, is above our comprehension. You have a name for such doctrines: you call them "mysteries". Why should not we be allowed our mysteries too? That the universe has existed for an infinitely long time is a mystery.' This enthusiasm for mystery is a healthy sign, but it is not legitimate to claim a doctrine as a mystery until it has been shown not to be a muddle. Meanwhile the consequences of rejecting finitism are not, it seems to me, altogether beautiful.

If you shuffle and deal a pack of cards infinitely often, then every possible hand will come up not just once or twice or many times but infinitely often. If the amount of material in the universe is finite, but the universe has existed for infinite time, the material being shuffled, perhaps, at each of an infinite series of Big Bangs, we must be prepared to accept that over that infinite time there have been infinitely many planets exactly like ours, with indistinguishable night skies, indistinguishable weather patterns and indistinguishable human inhabitants leading lives indistinguishable from ours. If the universe is infinite in extent, with infinitely many stars or galaxies, then at this moment (insofar as the Theory of Relativity allows us to speak of simultaneity here) we may have infinitely many replicas ploughing through identical lives. This prospect seems to me not beautiful but bleak.

3

If the universe had a beginning, there is a *prima facie* case for postulating something outside it, something non-physical, which has no beginning, to account for it. We cannot do this, of course, without having any idea at all what the explanatory factor would be like; but the theist suggests it is a kind of person, a kind of conscious, purposive agent as contrasted with a mindless causal agent. Taking this line he will have at some stage to defend the concept of a non-physical person against the charge of incoherence. But there is another doubt that presents itself, perhaps, more immediately. The suggestion is that the universe has been produced by a person on *purpose*: does it show any signs of purposiveness?

It is common to distinguish between arguments from the universe to God on the ground that the bare existence of the physical world needs explanation, and arguments based on evidence in nature of design. The lines of argument, cannot be wholly separate for the reason just given: if the cause of the universe is a person, we must suppose the universe was produced for a purpose, and it will tell against this supposition if there is no convincing purpose it seems to serve.

In point of fact, the way things are in the universe has been appealed to both by advocates and by critics of theism. There is only one plausible purpose for the universe. If God is nonphysical he can hardly have made the universe for his own benefit. What good could it be to him? He must have made it for the benefit of some or all of the physical objects in it. But objects like stars and stones cannot be benefited; the only possible beneficiaries are living organisms, and of these perhaps only sentient or even intelligent ones. The question, then, is whether the universe looks as if it was made for the benefit of living things like these. There are three possibilities. It may be so well adapted to their benefit that we have an additional reason for thinking there is a God; it may be so badly adapted that we have reason for thinking there is no God; or the adaptation may seem consistent with the hypothesis of a God without lending any positive support to it.

The fact that sentient and intelligent life actually exists is a good ground for taking up at least the third position, and saying that the degree of adaptation is consistent with the idea of a purposive creator. It puts the onus of proof on anyone who favours the second position: such a person will have to argue that life, though possible, is so gratuitously unpleasant that we cannot suppose the world is the work of a creator, who, besides being purposive, is supremely powerful, wise and good. To this task Hume addresses himself (*Dialogues*, x). The following words are famous:

His power we allow infinite; whatever he wills is executed: but neither man nor any other animal are happy: therefore he does not will their happiness. His wisdom is infinite: he is never mistaken in chusing the means to any end; but the course of nature tends not to human or animal felicity: therefore it is not established for that purpose ... Epicurus' old questions are yet unanswered. Is he willing to prevent evil but not able? Then he is impotent. Is he able, but not willing? Then is he malevolent. Is he both able and willing? Whence, then, is evil?

For the purposes of this discussion it is usual to distinguish between what are called 'physical' and 'moral' evil. Physical evil is evil directly chargeable to the person, if there is one, who produced the universe: nastiness inherent in the natural scheme of things. Moral evil is nastiness attributable to men and any other creatures there may be who are morally responsible. Hume lists four sources of physical evil which, he claims, a competent creator could, and a nice one would, have removed:

(1) Our sensitivity to pain.
(2) The fact that all events take place in accordance with general laws, and God does not intervene to remedy troubles arising from natural processes by miracles or what Hume calls 'particular volitions'.
(3) Our indolence; our lack of appetite for mental and bodily labour.
(4) The unpredictable excesses of nature. Though storms, droughts, earthquakes etc., presumably have causes, we do not know when they are going to strike, and it would be better if they never struck at all, if the weather, for instance, were always just right for our crops, our holidays etc.

Since no one, so far as I know, has suggested any further improvements to the universe, I shall concentrate on these.

How much weight can (4) carry? The human race started, we may suppose, in a small way in a small area or in a group of small areas. These could not have been areas very hostile to human life; they were probably very favourable to it. Men did not first appear on the open sea in unstable boats, or in the frozen heart of Antarctica. There are localities now, in spite of all we have done to wreck the environment, where life is easy and pleasant. Men starting in such places could have ventured out with circumspection. They need not have produced too many children too quickly. They could have acquainted themselves with the hazards of areas for colonisation before moving in. Today we have ships which are not easily destroyed by storms, and vaccines against diseases. These remarks may sound heartless and unrealistic. It is certainly hard to imagine that men as we know them could have controlled their numbers or evolved a high technology without calamities. But why not? I do not think it is clear that it is because of the nature of primordial matter and not because of how our remote ancestors decided to live.

Point (3) is hard to take seriously. It seemed valid to Hume because Hume took qualities of character to be causal factors which were themselves causally determined by our physical make-up. They are not. So far as indolence is concerned, though a man's physique has some bearing on his capacity for sustained effort, more important factors for most of us are how we were brought up and whether we really try.

Point (2) might simply be rejected by a Christian. Hume takes it for granted that everything happens in accordance with natural laws because he has argued elsewhere that there are no miracles. I shall be considering that argument below; at this point it is enough to say that most Christians think miracles have occurred in the past and that God intervenes in the course of nature even now. Someone who did not think that would hardly make petitionary prayers. The Christian view, then, is that the system is not one of absolute regularity, but God does sometimes remedy evils by 'particular volitions'. Sometimes he does this unasked, sometimes in response to prayer.

This reply, of course, will not impress anyone who agrees with Hume that there are no miracles. To such a person we may put another consideration. The regular course of nature is interrupted by human actions. We are ourselves getting more and more efficient at guarding against and controlling the effects of natural processes. It could be that God wants the universe to be conducted increasingly by particular volitions, but to be conducted in this way through men. Hume apparently favours a mixed system of general laws and voluntary interventions, but one where the interventions are directly by God. I think a better mixed system would be one in which the inhabitants of the universe gradually assume responsibility for the interventions themselves.

Hume's point (2) should be distinguished from a point about divine interventions more often urged today. If a human being sees another human being about to suffer some great evil, and is able to intervene and prevent it, he has a duty to intervene and is wicked if he does not. Now men, it argued, often suffer great evils through no fault of their own or of any other man. A child playing in what appears to be a safe place might have an unforeseeable accident which sentences it to a life of pain or imbecillity. If there is a God such as Christian believe in, he will have foreseen this and could have prevented it. Why, then, did he not prevent it? Either he is wicked, or there is no God such as Christians describe.[4]

This argument is not intended to show that the universe is too unpleasant to have been made for our benefit; it is an independent argument against the existence of a benevolent God. It is convenient, nevertheless, to consider it here. It rests on the assumption that the obligation to prevent harm to human beings applies equally to other human beings and to God. Is that assumption correct?

I do not see how it could possibly be correct. We, it may be granted, have a duty to save each other's lives. If God had a duty to save everyone's life, how could we have a race of mortals at all? Is God supposed to make a universe which gives rise to mortals, and then stop any of the mortals from dying? Or should he have made a universe which does not give rise to mortals in the first place? In that case, there would be no purpose in having a physical universe. Such a universe can exist only for the benefit of living material objects, and living material objects are mortal.

If we say that God has no obligation to save the lives of the old and frail, why should he save the lives or health of playing children? We are already admitting that God cannot intelligibly be supposed to be under the same obligations as men. If he were, and lived up to them, life as we know it would be impossible and there would be no room for human obligations. If we start saying that God should ensure that nobody has his life cut short or his health impaired except through his own folly or the wickedness of other men, we are pulling principles out of the air.

It may be added that the duty of men to save other men from injury itself deserves some consideration. From what does it arise, and how far does it stretch? Everyone agrees we have an obligation to our friends and relations. It is less clear that we have to go to trouble and expense to save our enemies or people we have never heard of, such as nameless children in distant countries. The idea that we are obliged to help everyone seems to have come in with Christianity, and it is also a Christian doctrine that all men are, in a strong sense, brothers.

I come finally to Hume's complaint about our sensitivity to pain. This is based on a philosophical view of the nature of pain which he shared with his predecessor Locke. Locke and Hume thought that feeling a bodily sensation like pain was the same sort of thing as hearing a bang, seeing a flash, or smelling a smell. In his *Essays Concerning Human Understanding* Locke tells us that:

> The infinitely wise Author of our being... has been pleased to join to several thoughts and sensations a perception of delight... [He has also] annexed pain to the application of many things to our bodies, to warn us of the harm that they will do. (II. vii.3–4.)

That is, when we feel a sharp object entering our flesh, or we feel the temperature of a piece of red hot metal, God brings it about that we also feel pain. Hume's point (1) is that this is disobliging of God, and the same benefits could have been secured by annexing stronger sensations of delight to things which do us good.

It is fairly clear that this view of the nature of pain is mistaken, though important physiological facts about pain are still under investigation, and a fully satisfactory account is perhaps not yet available. When something cuts or burns us, however, the experience of pain is so related to our awareness of the thing as something to be avoided that it is very doubtful whether we could have the latter without the former. It also seems that how intense pain is, or how much we mind about it, depends partly on our state of mind or on what we do. People are more resistant to torture if they are convinced of the cause in which they are suffering. Childbirth can be acutely painful; but by mastering and using techniques of breathing and relaxation women have managed to give birth with nothing worse than discomfort. We may note, thirdly, that some of the worst pain is attributable directly or indirectly to the voluntary actions of men. Human torturers hurt people more than any cancer or abscess. And painful as these ailments may be, we must bear some responsibility for creating unhygienic conditions, for leading unhealthy lives, and for treating comparatively painless diseases which would otherwise be fatal until they are overtaken by diseases which are no less fatal but more painful. Hume's programme of replacing sensations of pain by stronger sensations of pleasure elsewhere is not worked out. As things are, insensitivity to pain is an extremely dangerous handicap. When our own contributions have been discounted, it is difficult to prove that the sensitivity we have is greater than would have been expected from a kind but competent creator.

Hume concentrates on physical evil, and it certainly seems at first that evil for which men are morally responsible cannot be used as evidence against a wise and good creator. But if some men freely choose not to do evil, might not such a creator have limited himself to making men like this, men such that they always freely choose the good?[5]

Mackie, who is a leading exponent of this line of argument, recognises that it rests on the assumption that free will is compatible with causal determination; indeed, on the assumption that our free choices actually are determined by our physical make-up and the physical state of the environment that stimulates our senses. If this were not the case, what could God do to ensure that only good men exist? A Big Bang, or a planet just before morally responsible action starts, in a world where only good men exist, need be no different from our own Big Bang or our own planet just before the appearance of Homo Sapiens.

This being so, the theist may reply that free action is not compatible with causal determination. That position does not beg the question in favour of theism; it has been espoused by so staunch an atheist as Flew (and I defend it in Chapter Three, s.3). Mackie argues against it but I do not find his argument convincing. Until a proof that it is untenable is forthcoming the theist may say that God could indeed have made only men who chose right, since the men he actually made could all have chosen only what was right; but God could not have made only men who could not help doing what was right.

I have been considering attempts to show that there is too much evil in the world for it to have been made for our benefit. Some people seem to feel it cannot have been made for our benefit, not because it is too unpleasant, but because we are too insignificant a part of it. So far as we know for sure, there is life only on this planet, and there has been sentient life of good quality here only for a few million years. But the diameter of the universe is at least 10^{20} times that of the Earth, and it has existed at least for 10^4 million years. Is it not naive to say that all these millions of years have rolled past, and all these millions of huge stars exist, for the benefit of so little? If the universe was made for organisms like us, is it not scandalously wasteful?

I do not find this line of thought at all forceful. So far as the size of the universe goes, the only good objection to the hypothesis of a creator would be that it is too small. It would be hard to believe in a niggardly creator. But it seems absurd to say the universe could not be made for us because if it were, the creator would have been recklessly extravagant. The same consideration applies to time, but here there is a further consideration. It is not at all clear how long the universe will last. What if intelligent life continued, not necessarily here but somewhere, for $10^{10^{10}}$ years? In that case, instead of saying God has wasted time, someone might object that he has rushed through the preliminaries with indecent haste. Whereas, given organisms of a certain size, we can ask what the minimum desirable size for the universe might be, I am not sure we can raise any sensible questions about what would be a desirable time-scale. If the universe had come to an end thirty seconds after the first appearance of life, that would not look like design, but that has not happened, and once even a single living thing has had a decent life-span, enough has been accomplished to render intelligible the production of a universe. It is absurd to say it is worthwhile to make a universe for, e.g., 10^{15} beneficiaries, but not for just one beneficiary. Why 10^{15} rather than $10^{15''}$? No number is absolutely large.

A theist has to say there is no overwhelming evidence in the universe that it was not produced by a benevolent creator; he does not have to say that there is evidence it was so produced. This has nevertheless been argued in two slightly different ways.[6] Christians in the Middle Ages were much impressed by uniformities in nature. The planets, for instance, always move in pretty much the same paths at the same speed. To them this suggested a sort of divine inspector monitoring their movements. Since the seventeenth century we have come to associate regularity more with mindlessness, but someone today might feel (especially if all is going well) that the universe is so beautiful and convenient that it must be the work of a divine artificer. It was this line of thought that Hume most wanted to oppose but his opposition is amateurish. To form an opinion on whether the odds are really against a universe in which we can thrive, we have to consider what we are told by modern scientists. It seems to me hard to form an opinion, not least because scientists tell us something different not just every few years but every few months.

At present scientists look back no further than the Big Bang, an as yet unexplained event which took place perhaps fifteen thousand million years ago. They recognise four basic forces: gravitation, electro-magnetism and the so called 'strong' and 'weak' nuclear forces. These differ greatly among themselves in strength, and there is no logical necessity that there should be so many of them or that they should have either the absolute or the relative strengths they have. If, however, they had been more than slightly different, or if there had been a different ratio of particles of different kinds (positive and negative, light and heavy) immediately after the Big Bang, the universe could not have developed in such a way as to support any form of life we can imagine; there would have been no galaxies or stars, no heavy elements like carbon and iron, no periods of peace and stability.[7]

It seems to me quite natural that people should find these considerations pointing their minds towards a personal creator. But it might be rash to lean heavily on them. At any moment scientists may succeed in explaining the Big Bang and exhibiting it as just one member of a series of cosmic expansions and contractions; they may also find a theory which will unify and explain the four forces which are now taken as fundamental. And even if no such explanations are forthcoming, before concluding that the universe was produced on purpose it would be necessary to say what the probability is of there being these forces and this distribution of matter in a universe which pops up by chance. Are the odds infinitely against or only slightly? For myself I find the notion of universes just popping up so repugnant that arguments based on what they could be expected to be like are superfluous.

4

The philosophical argument developed in s. 2 purports to show that there is a person independent of the universe on whom the universe depends. What I described as empirical reasons for believing in God are grounds for believing, not that there is a creator of the universe, but that there is a superhuman person who knows about and intervenes in our affairs. The strongest reasons for thinking this probably lie in an individual's own personal experience: he has had prayers answered, been consoled in trouble or what not. Such evidence, however, is too private for other people to take advantage of it; is there anything of a more public character we can appeal to?

Christians may want to point to three things: the history of the Jews, the life of Christ, and the history of the Church. I shall say a little here about the first and third of these, and rather more about the life of Christ at a later stage; but before I start I ought to consider a general challenge to this kind of argument. We are asking whether, to put it bluntly, the existence of God can be proved by miracles. I have already mentioned a famous argument by Hume which is sometimes supposed to show that it can never be reasonable to believe that any miracle has occurred.[8] What is this argument, and does it invalidate any reasoning from empirical evidence to the existence of God?

Hume defines a miracle as:

A transgression of a law of nature by a particular volition of the Deity, or by the interposition of some invisible agent.

We need not quarrel with this definition. In considering, however, whether it can be reasonable to believe a miracle has occurred, we must distinguish four cases:

(1) An amazing occurrence is witnessed by someone who has independent reasons for thinking there is a God.
(2) An amazing occurrence is reported to such a person.
(3) An amazing occurrence is witnessed by someone who has no independent reason for thinking there is a God.
(4) An amazing occurrence is reported to such a person.

Christians usually consider miracles in the context of case (2). It is taken for granted that God exists, and reported miracles are cited to show that Jesus of Nazareth was sent by God, or that God favours some particular Christian doctrine or denomination. Whether Hume's argument shows that it is never reasonable to believe a miracle in case (2) is extremely important for the question how much historical value we can allow the Gospels; but the question at issue here is whether it can be reasonable to believe a miracle has occurred in case (4).

Hume does not consider any cases where we ourselves witness a possible miracle – cases (1) and (3); he confines himself to believing on testimony. Moreover he omits to distinguish cases (2) and (4), so that it is unclear whether he hopes to show only that an agnostic can never reasonably accept a miracle-report, or that this can never be reasonable even for a theist. What he says is that it will be reasonable to believe a miracle-report only if it is

> attested by a sufficient number of men, of such unquestioned good sense, education and learning, as to secure us against all delusion in themselves; of such undoubted integrity, as to place them beyond all suspicion of any design to deceive others; of such credit and reputation in the eyes of mankind, as to have a great deal to lose in the case of their being detected in any falsehood; and at the same time attesting facts performed in such a public manner, and in so celebrated a part of the world, as to render the detection unavoidable.

And he adds:

> There never was a miraculous event established on so full an evidence.

A Christian might, it seems to me, say that Hume's requirements are reasonable, but that given independent grounds for believing there is a God, they sometimes *are* met, notably in the case of the resurrection of Christ. Hume's doubts about this case, it might be urged, are due to provincialism. Hume implies that the apostles were deficient in education and learning, that Jerusalem was a remote provincial town, and that the Jews were an ignorant and barbarous nation. In this he reveals the complacency of eighteenth-century society and the limitations of eighteenth-century historical knowledge. We do not consider upper-class education a necessary condition of being a good witness, and Jerusalem in the first century AD seems no more barbarous or provincial than Paris in the eighteenth.

Hume himself either allows or should allow that belief in a miracle can be reasonable in case (2). Some of his followers seem to want to amend his argument to rule this out. In doing so they destroy its plausibility. The discussion moves from the sphere of common sense to that of academic fencing. Rather than pursue it through its increasing complexities, I confine myself to two observations.

First, a sceptic may ask how, when a natural law seems to be transgressed, we are to decide betwen these two hypotheses: (i) the law is incorrect and should be replaced by a more complicated law (ii) the law is correct, and a supernatural person has intervened. Considerations of design usually play a part. The same question could be asked about an unusual structure we find in the desert: how do we decide whether it is a natural phenomenon, the product of some hitherto undiscovered natural process, or the work of vanished human hands? In practice it is not too hard to reach an opinion.

Secondly, Hume says we should accept testimony to a miracle only if it would be even more of a miracle for the testimony to be false. He himself glosses this remark in the reasonable way we have seen; but someone might think that this condition can never be fulfilled. For there would be nothing miraculous about a number of people having hallucinations, or setting out, for no apparent reason, to spread a lie. This might be unlikely, but it would contravene no physical law. I think we have here a drift towards radical, and therefore illegitimate, scepticism.

Any time I see something I may be deluded or suffering a hallucination. But unless I have some definite reason for thinking I am – unless I have taken a hallucinogenic drug or am watching a conjuring show – I must discount this possibility. That what I see conflicts with what I believe to be a law of nature is not in itself sufficient reason for thinking it is not really happening. For it is only by accepting the testimony of our senses as to what is happening that we arrive at knowledge of natural laws in the first place. The possibility, then, of natural error does not make it unreasonable ever to believe that a miracle has occurred in case (1).

But similar considerations apply in case (2). For our knowledge of nature is based not only on our own observations but on those of others which are reported to us. If another astronomer or field entomologist reports something surprising, unless we have definite grounds for thinking that he was deluded or that he is trying to deceive us, we must accept that the phenomenon really occurred. In general, when we have good reason to think that another person has good reason to think an event occurred, we too have good reason to think it occurred, though it does not follow that we *feel* any conviction. We may suspect that a rival savant who was carrying out a tricky observation made a mistake. Men often do. But it is not legitimate to invoke such generalities about human nature in scientific controversy. All we can do is repeat the observation – and that, in the case of a rare phenomenon like ball lightning, may be impractical. The point may be put like this. The reliability of our senses and of witnesses are empirical matters which, in a way, admit of investigation like any other empirical matter. But in another way they are privileged, since they have to be assumed in all investigations, including the investigation of themselves.

So much for case (2); what of case (4)? Here Hume's conclusion is more attractive. If one does not already believe that there is a supernatural person who takes an interest in human affairs, invoking such a person to explain something one has not witnessed oneself but merely heard about is a desperate move which reasonable people will be extremely reluctant to make. If, indeed, I had had a blow on the head, and on regaining consciousness I found everyone in the world declaring there had just been a spectacular theophany, that might impress me more than hearing a voice from a burning bush all by myself. But to believe in God simply on the strength of the miracle reports actually available would be rash indeed. That, however, is not what theists ask agnostics to do. At most they suggest that hearsay evidence of the miraculous can form part of a cumulative case for Christian belief.

This could be evidence of some isolated event; but in fact Christians wish to see a large-scale intervention in history which is not altogether discontinuous with the natural order of events. A little way back I mentioned the history of the Jews, the life of Christ, and the history of the Church. To the Jew, the second and third are irrelevant, but to the Christian, though the three can be considered separately, they form parts of the realisation of a single divine plan, and the first and third have to be understood through their relation to the second. These three things, it may be claimed, stand out from history like a range of mountains such as the Alps or the Pyrenees. The peaks of the Pyrenees, treeless and rocky, are different in kind from the plains around Toulouse, but there is no sharp line at which the plains end and the mountains begin. The Christian will see the history of Israel as the foothills leading up to the decisive intervention that consisted in the coming and work of Christ; and the subsequent history of Christianity not, indeed, as a gradual subsidence into the original condition of mankind, but as an elevated plateau extending out from the peaks.

Does human history really show signs of the action of a mountain-building supernatural force? The evidence for the early history of the Jews is scantier than we could wish. The familiar Old Testament narratives of the life of Abraham, the liberation of the Jews from Egypt and their receiving of the Law are not confirmed (even if they are not contradicted) by archaeology or other historical sources, and many scholars think they give us no information whatever about what happened to the Jews before they finally settled in Palestine round about the twelfth century BC.[9] On the other hand the evidence for the recent history of Christianity is too plentiful to be easily digested. We should not be deterred, however, from trying to reach an estimate.

We may choose what time we like for the first appearance of the Jews in the clear, cold light of non-mythical history; from that first moment they are distinguished by a tenacious and exclusive monotheism, coupled with a practical and ruthless conviction that the one God has specially chosen them. There is nothing like this outside the Jewish tradition – to which Christianity and Islam, of course, belong. There is no other popular monotheism at all. Still less is it seriously believed that God has communicated directly with a people. Nor has any other nation preserved its sense of identity for so long, and that in spite of the fact that for most of their history the Jews have been without a territory of their own. How are we to account for this? Did there just happen to appear, among the lower caste inhabitants of thirteenth-century Egypt, a leader with fertile religious ideas, and did these ideas by themselves confer on the group of his followers the property of being indestructible? Jews and Christians who hesitate to say that the Pentateuch narratives are true will still insist that God must have been working within the new-born people. But would a purely internal mode of operation, we may wonder, have been sufficient? After all, we are material objects, and knowledge comes to us through our senses. Perhaps Jews have believed for thousands of years that God spoke to their ancestors because he did: who can say how long the effects of such a communication might last? Perhaps the Jews are still with us because God promised to be their protector, and God does not take back his promises. If the narratives of Genesis and Exodus did not exist, it would be necessary to invent them.

Let us now turn from the early history of the Jews to the other side of the mountain-crest, the history of Christianity. During the last two thousand years a civilisation has developed which, so far as we know, differs from anything else history can show in two related ways. First, it is scientific. We employ inanimate sources of energy, not just slaves and beasts, and we use artificial aids to our senses to study nature. Secondly, it is world-wide. People can speak to each other by telephone or radio from almost anywhere, an event in one place can be known everywhere in a few hours, we have a single educational curriculum, so that everyone has pretty much the same set of ideas and the same knowledge. How has this happened? If there has been no such civilisation before, why has it arisen now? It arose around the Mediterranean, and it is primarily European. What, then, do we find around the Mediterranean, and especially in Europe, in the last two thousand years, which we do not find earlier or elsewhere? We find Christianity. It is needless to debate whether individual ecclesiastics aided or impeded the general movement. Everybody in the movement grew up in a Christian atmosphere, imbued with Christian ways of thinking about the natural world and about how we ought to live.

Although there are plenty of people to deny it, I think that modern civilisation is due quite clearly to Christianity. Science is possible only if people believe that nature is ultimately intelligible and domitable, and it is the Christian doctrine that God created the world for our benefit which has done most to establish that belief (in the teeth, it may be said, of very recalcitrant surface appearances). Science also needs patronage and financial support, and this has been provided by the Church and by Christian rulers. As to the world-wide character of our civilisation, Christianity has always been a missionary religion, and despite some lapses, has generally been a force against racial hatred and oppression. All these points, controversial as they are, could be supported by strong and ample argument. Can the theist show, however, not just that modern civilisation depends on Christianity, but that Christianity could not have generated it without the help of God? That may seem difficult, especially as in some parts of the world life is probably worse today than it was two thousand years ago. On the other hand the disturbance to the course of history which starts in the Eastern Mediterranean in the first century AD is so violent and appears so irreversible that it is not absurd to look for a non-natural origin.

To this we may add that Christianity is still here. In the rich countries of the West many people ignore certain traditional precepts which wear an austere or dusty look, such as those enjoining church-going or forbidding adultery. Even in these countries, however, there are still plenty of sane, educated and intelligent men and women who try to keep all the rules, and even some who adopt the self-denying lives of ministers of religion, monks and nuns. In other countries where Christianity is persecuted, Christians put up with life as second-class citizens and sometimes with imprisonment and suffering. What draws people to Christianity and sustains them in it? 'That is a mystery', the non-believer may say. 'We do not fully understand it now, but we may when psychology is more advanced.' But we can understand it perfectly well now if we suppose that Christianity was instituted and is still animated by a supernatural person.

This brings us to the central issue of the life of Christ. If the Gospels are to be believed, he claimed to be the Son of God, voices from the sky acknowledged him, blazing light transfigured him, and after he had been put to death he reappeared in an immortal form and ascended into heaven. Whether the events related in the Gospels really happened, and whether we can view Christ as an actual incarnation of God, are not questions to be tackled here; I shall consider them in Chapter Four. Here we are still examining reasons for thinking there is a God at all. If Christians appeal at this stage to evidence of divine intervention, it is important to remember that the intervention is not supposed to consist of sporadic and isolated wonders, a miraculous parting of waters here, a dead man's coming to life there; it is a supernatural transformation of the natural order. If the early history of the Jews is seen as pointing forward, and the history of Christianity as pointing back, to a certain set of historical events, and if the Gospels can be accepted as a substantially true account of those events, then I would claim that we have good evidence that there is a supernatural person who intervenes in our affairs.

I do not say that many people would be led to belief in God simply by these historical considerations. Most people would need some assurance from their own experience. Such assurance could take various forms. If a person did not merely hear of a miracle but witnessed one (case 3) that would supply the element of personal experience. Some contemporary philosophers, unlike Hume, seem to think that miracles can be ruled out *a priori*. Peter Winch in a recent British Academy lecture (*Proceedings* 1982) suggests that while a miracle story might be intelligible as a fairy tale or a move in a religious language-game it 'would in fact *make no sense*, considered as a narrative' (p. 349, *cf*. 352); it would be literally nonsensical. Winch, however, seems to be relying (like some other neo-Wittgensteinians) on a questionable theory about meaning. This is that whether a sentence like 'On the third day he rose again from the dead' – or, another controversial example, 'I am now dreaming' – is intelligible depends not on whether it is constructed in a grammatically correct fashion out of genuine words, but on whether we can specify situations in which it can correctly be used. I shall not criticise this theory here since no ordinary person doubts we can understand miracle stories. Moreover, distressing as it may be, miracles are still actually reported.

A much commoner thing than witnessing one, however, would be to have associated with people whose lives are founded on religion, and who seem to draw from it strength which could not come from a delusion. There are individuals, families and communities which give the impression that something supernatural is working though them and lighting them up. Thirdly, and commonest of all, a person can feel a response from something outside himself to his prayers or thoughts about God. He may feel that God is speaking to him, or cheering him up, or that God has done some special thing for him. The belief that another person has spoken to one in one's thoughts is by itself unverifiable, and it is hardly rational to base one's life simply on such feelings. But they become important as soon as they are related to the beliefs of others and to what we know of human history. That is an aspect of a matter to which I shall be recurring: a human person is essentially a member of a society. But perhaps nobody could believe in God if he did not, at least occasionally, have some private reassurance as well.

I have been careful to say that the empirical grounds for believing in God are grounds for believing there is a supernatural person. They are not of themselves grounds for thinking that this person is the God of philosophy, the creator of the universe. There might well be many persons much more powerful than we who intervene in human affairs. These persons might even be material, though longer lasting and stronger than men. That the person who was worshipped by the Jews, who helped Christ, and who sustains the Church is the actual creator of the universe is something Christians believe chiefly because the Jews, the Church, and above all Christ himself, tell them so. The two lines of thought we have been exploring, the theoretical and the empirical, come together in the person of Christ.

5

The arguments we have been examining purport to make it reasonable to believe that there exists a God; they do not, by themselves, provide any reason for thinking that God is unique. It may seem unlikely that the universe is the work of a committee. But why should there not be a plurality of non-physical persons who exist without ever having come into existence? Why should not several of them take an interest in human affairs? Christians believe that there is only one God, but this belief is not, so far as I am aware, supported by any very persuasive philosophical argument.

In the Preface to his *Catechism* Gregory of Nyssa (335–94) appeals to what is now called 'the identity of indiscernibles'. If there were two Gods, there would be nothing to distinguish them from one another; for both would be superlatively powerful and intelligent non-material persons. But if there is nothing to differentiate them, they would not be two but one. The same argument is used by Ghazali, Aquinas and Spinoza,[10] but today looks a little slick. Why should there not be a number of different persons who are all different individuals, though they are exactly alike in every respect? Aquinas and perhaps Spinoza thought that what makes two qualitatively similar material objects different is being composed of different parcels of matter, and this principle of differentiation would not be available to non-material persons; but this view of what makes material objects different seems to be arbitrary and erroneous.

An ordinary Christian might say that if there are more Gods than one, then the divine revelations on which we rely have been deceptive or misleading. While I feel that to be so, I am unable to point to any reported utterance of Christ which explicitly rules out the existence of other unoriginated persons besides his Father; and it might be argued that he was proceeding on the 'need to know' principle: if it makes no difference to how it is best for us to behave whether there are Gods other than the God of Abraham, there would be no point in revealing their existence to us.

Monotheism seems to have developed not through philosophical reflection but because Gods other than the God of Abraham proved unable to deliver the goods. Challenged by Jewish priests, or Christian missionaries, they failed to protect their images or their worshippers. εἰς κοίρανος ἔστω, Aristotle quoted from Homer: 'Let there be one ruler only.' One God is enough to account for the universe and for human history; perhaps it is a mistake to look for arguments to show that there are no more.

CHAPTER THREE
A Non-material Personal Creator

I

It would be vacuous to say that the physical universe depends on something non-physical outside it, if one had no idea whatever what that thing might be or how the universe might depend on it. The theist, as we have seen, is not in that position. He thinks the universe depends on a person, and the notion of a person he employs here is one he has acquired in his commerce with other human beings and applies also to them. But this being so he may be asked whether this notion will do the work required. Could there be a non-physical person? If so, could such a person be responsible for the existence of the universe? Inability to answer these questions would not by itself show that the universe does not depend on a non-physical creator; but it would plunge that belief into an embarrassing darkness. Christians hold not only that God made the universe to begin with, but that he keeps it going[1] and knows everything that happens in it; they also hold that each human being or human soul is the product of a distinct act of creation. These ideas too need investigation.

If God is not a material object I think it follows that his existence must be non-temporal. The notion of non-temporal existence (the first indisputable appearance of which is in Plato's *Timaeus*) is hard to grasp, and has never attained a place in basic Christian teaching. It is not used in the creeds or in any of the main Christian prayers. It can be found, however, in Augustine, Boethius, Anselm and Aquinas, and there are great theoretical difficulties in supposing that God's existence is temporal.

These difficulties arise from the nature of time. Time attaches primarily to physical change, and to other things only insofar as they are bound up with change.[2] Some philosophers hold, I think rightly, that time is actually an aspect of change. Anyhow, changes go on for stretches of time, and things which undergo them exist for stretches of time. Physical events stand in temporal relations to one another. Take any two events, and one will be earlier than, later than, or simultaneous with the other (given, Einstein reminds us, a frame of reference). If God is not composed of any sort of material, he cannot be subject to any kind of physical change, or interact with anything, or be involved in any physical events. That being so, he cannot be said to exist for any number of years or minutes. Neither can it be correct to say he existed in the past or will exist in the future. As Plato puts it, ' "is" alone is properly attributed to him' (*Timaeus* 37–8) and this 'is' or 'exists' is tenseless: it does not, like the 'is' in 'That leaf is yellow', refer to the time of the speaker's utterance. We can properly use tensed verbs only in speaking of events or states of affairs that stand in temporal relations.

In some ways the conclusion that God's existence is nontemporal is welcome. Given that he is unoriginated, if his existence is not timeless he will have existed for an infinitely long time, and I have argued that there cannot be an infinite time-stretch.

Even if the notion of infinitely prolonged existence is coherent, Schleiermacher declared it was unendurable. Recent philosophers have disagreed about whether he is right, but for my own part I at least find the notion daunting. If God's existence is timeless, the question of boredom cannot arise.[3]

It might be feared that the notion of timeless existence is open to objection from the opposite side, that it is too short. Boethius in a famous passage (*Consolation of Philosophy* V.6) tries to explain it in the words 'the complete possession of endless life all at once (*simul*)'. This seems to replace an infinitely prolonged existence by one collapsed into a single instant. But the term 'simul' is itself temporal. A timeless existence is neither infinitely long nor instantaneous; it neither drags nor flies.

But can we really make any sense of the notion of timeless existence?[4] Are there, indeed, any tenseless verbs? Every sentence seems to contain a verb which, by grammatical criteria, is past, present or future, even sentences in languages where the verbs, unlike European verbs, have no tense-inflections.

Two and three are timelessly equal to five. I have seen it suggested that the propositions of mathematics are true not timelessly but at all times. Two and three make five now, made five at every moment in the past, and will make five at every moment in the future. I think we can construe in this way scientific statements like 'Copper sulphate is blue' or 'Whales are viviparous', but not mathematical ones. What could a person mean who said 'Two and three will make five at 7.15 this evening.'? His words, taken seriously, would seem to betray a deep misunderstanding. Similarly temperance is timelessly different from asceticism, and if all Cretans are liars and I am a Cretan, it follows timelessly that I am a liar. The timelessness of these truths, however, will not suffice to justify the suggestion that God's existence is timeless. For these truths seem to be not so much about the actual world as about the relations between our ideas or thoughts, whereas God is supposed to be an actual person existing independently of our thoughts. These truths, moreover, are necessary truths. A proposition of mathematics, if true at all, is true necessarily. There has been much debate about whether propositions about God should be construed as necessary or contingent. My opinion is that they are neither. Necessary truths are about our ideas, contingent truths are about physical things, and God is neither a physical thing nor a mere idea.

A number of recent writers have claimed that even if the notion of timelessness is not wholly without application, it is incompatible with that of a person. A person is a conscious, purposive agent. Nelson Pike maintains that a timeless being could not create anything or act in the world. His opinion is followed, among theists, by Swinburne, among non-believers by Richard Sorabji. Swinburne's acceptance of Pike's argument, however, may be partly due to a misunderstanding of the issue. He says 'God's timelessness is said to consist in his existing at all moments of human time – simultaneously.' That is not what I have just said, and it would be self-contradictory, since simultaneity is a temporal relation.

But is it the case that if God is responsible as a personal agent for some change in the world, his activity must be temporal? Suppose he restores Lazarus to life, and Lazarus is restored to life in 28 AD: does it follow that God's restorative action was in 28? That would certainly follow if God acted causally in the world and restored Lazarus by some kind of causal action, such as wiring him up to an electric battery. This action would not only be temporally related to Lazarus' revival, but itself be temporal. If, however, God is not a material object, he cannot be responsible for events in the world through acting causally. How, then, is he responsible? That will be discussed shortly, but so long as it is not through causal action, we cannot infer, because God was responsible for Lazarus' revival in 28, that God in 28 was responsible for Lazarus' revival.

Christians hold that the events for which God is responsible occur because and when he wants them to occur. Suppose, then, that first a lunar eclipse occurs and then a solar; and suppose that God is responsible for both: need the theist suppose that God's desire that the Moon should be eclipsed occurred before his desire that the Sun should be? No. 'Things happen when God wants them to happen' means not 'their happening is simultaneous with his wanting' but 'their happening is simultaneous with the things he wants them to be simultaneous with'. He desires that the Moon should be eclipsed before the Sun; he does not desire, before the Sun is eclipsed, that the Moon should be eclipsed.

But is not any desiring or willing an event in time? Any physical process is in time, and so is any beginning or end of such a process; but the position over mental processes like desiring or willing and believing or knowing is not so clear.[5] We are able to date our beliefs and desires in two ways. First, and most important, we date them by our behaviour. We desire a certain outcome when we act in order that it may come about, or abstain from doing something that might prevent it. Similarly the motorist knows or believes that the light is against him when he stops or abstains from driving on for the reason that it is against him. Secondly, our thoughts seem to be correlated with events in our nervous system. When the motorist sees the red light, his eyes and his brain are affected by it. When he decides to move forward, some sort of electric charge passes from his brain to the arm or leg he moves. This second way, however, of dating thoughts is hardly ever used in practice, and is not infallible. For the motorist's eye and brain might be affected by the red light, but it would still be incorrect to say he had *seen* it, or *knew* that it was red, if he did not act because of it (or, in the exceptional case, in spite of it). Strictly speaking, then, the time even of human thoughts is the time of the related behaviour; the thoughts are not in time of themselves; and the second method of dating thoughts cannot apply to God because he is non-corporeal.

Our own thoughts are related to physical events in two different ways. If I act intentionally the time of my desire or decision to act is the time of my acting, but the time of my acting depends on my desire. I leave the house at six o'clock because that is the time at which I choose to leave; I want my departure to be simultaneous with the striking of six o' clock. Insofar as God's desires are related to physical events in this way, we may say that his thought is a source of temporal relations rather than itself temporal. But it is different with my belief that the clock is striking six. Although the time at which I believe this is likely to be the time at which the clock really is striking six, the clock does not strike because I know or believe it is striking; rather I know it is striking because it strikes. Now Christians hold that God knows of everything that happens: nothing escapes him. If this knowledge is like our knowledge of the things we perceive, it may indeed be held to be temporal.

Exactly how God knows the things he knows is a question

to which too little thought has been given. There seems to be a tendency to conceive his thought on the model of the appearance of a lot of pictures on a closed-circuit television screen, and to suppose that he is so splendid that these pictures just occur without any apparatus, rather as when he creates something that thing just appears out of nothing without any apparatus. Since the appearing of pictures is a temporal process, if we use this model we naturally suppose that God's knowledge is at times, and the next step is to wonder if God remembers things, that is, pictures them after they have happened, or foresees them, pictures them before they have happened. If God's knowledge is temporal, it seems impious to think events ever take him by surprise: surely he must foresee the future before it happens. So we saddle ourselves with a doctrine, not just of omniscience, but of omni-prescience; which causes us trouble when we consider God's foreknowledge of the voluntary evil deeds of men.

This way of conceiving God's thought ought to be rejected from the start as bad philosophy. Picturing will not do as a model for any kind of thinking, divine or human. The doctrine of divine omniscience, that nothing is hidden from God, is deeply entrenched in Christianity; but this kind of knowledge can be timeless or take its time from the thing known: God sees me poisoning your cough-medicine when I am poisoning your cough-medicine. The doctrine of divine omniprescience has commanded a respectable following, but the scriptural authority for it is weak. The First Vatican Council quoted *Hebrews* 4.13 ('All things are bare and open to his eyes') and added 'those too which will occur through the free action of men', but that is hardly implicit in the text (Denzinger 3003, *cf.* also 626).

Not all our knowledge is like my knowledge that the clock is striking six; some of it is like my knowledge that I am standing up when I stand up intentionally. This knowledge is not dependent on the things known. When we act not just intentionally but consciously, awareness of our action is involved in our action, and hence in our choice or decision to act. It seems to me that this is where we should seek a model for God's knowledge of what is happening in the universe; he knows because he is responsible. But this suggestion can be developed only when we have some positive account of how God is responsible for what happens: all I have said so far is that it is not through causal action.

Before I come to that, one last point about timelessness. Those who insist that action, desire or knowledge must be in time are often motivated by a deep-seated feeling that a person must be some kind of temporal being. This feeling springs from a misunderstanding of our notion of a person.

The word 'person' can be used as a variant for 'human being': we can say 'Socrates is a person and Socrates II is a horse'. But the notion of a person which is supposed to cover God is not a concept of a specific sort of thing, like the notion of a gorilla or the notion of a chair. It is the notion of a conscious purposive agent, and such an agent, unlike a merely causal agent which is mindless and purposeless, is one that can be benefited or harmed. The point is one to which I shall return, but I here state it baldly and dogmatically: we apply the notion of a person, we think of a human being or of any other entity as a person, in acting to benefit or harm it. I hope to show that we need not think of something as material or temporal in order to think of it as capable of being benefited or harmed; and if that is right, there will be no incoherence in holding both that God is a person and that he is timeless. What is not possible, what is mere playing with words, is to maintain that God is a person while being totally indifferent to him.

2

Christians say that God *created* the universe. By that they mean not only that God produced it but that he did not produce it out of anything that was already there. The word 'create' is used to rule out a certain model for the origin of the universe. Things like chairs, men and clouds come into existence and are produced, but they arise out of other things like pieces of wood, ova, water, and they are produced by the action, intentional or mindless, of causal agents like carpenters, parents and the sun. I use the expression 'causal agent' here in a strict sense to signify, not just something which is somehow responsible for something else, but something that brings about a change in a material object by acting causally upon it; by pushing or pulling or heating, for example. The only thing which can act upon a material object in this sort of way is another material object. Hence to think of anything as a causal agent is to think of it as material. God not being material, he cannot be a causal agent in the strict sense of the term; neither (Christians maintain) was there anything already there out of which the universe arose.

How, then, did God produce it? The question springs automatically to our lips, but if we think that God really did create the universe, we cannot expect a straightforward answer. For 'How did he produce it?' normally means precisely: 'Out of what materials, by what causal action?' That is what we want to know when we ask our host how the delicious pudding was produced. If the universe was created, this 'How was it produced?' question cannot be asked. What, then, do we want to know? At the least we want to know how a person can be responsible for something without being responsible for it as a causal agent.

As a generous and affectionate nephew I might buy a television set for my aunt. Since I should not have bought the thing *but for* her, she is, in a way, responsible for the purchase. She is responsible, we might say, as a beneficiary. This type of responsibility will seem at first very slight. My aunt may justly disclaim any responsibility for the buying of the television set: 'I never asked him to buy it: it is entirely his responsibility.' But in what way am *I* supposed to be responsible? Certainly I am the causal agent who made the syllables 'I'll take that one' ring out through the shop. But my responsibility goes beyond that. I should not be responsible in the way my aunt holds me responsible now if I had caused the syllables to ring out under the influence of hypnosis or drugs. We are *morally* responsible, as we call it, only for changes which we not only cause, but cause knowingly and intentionally. We are morally responsible not for all our causal action but for such of it as is voluntary, that is, a fulfilment of our desire or will. But what, then, is it for action to be a fulfilment of the agent's will?[6]

We are inclined to conceive the will as a special psychological capacity the function of which is to ensure that we actually do what our consciences or intellects tell us is best. If we operate with this conception of will we shall think that there are acts of will which cause movements in our limbs, and we shall say that intentional action, action for which we are morally responsible, is action caused by such acts of will. Locke and Mill took pretty much this line. But although the notion of an act of will goes back, as I said earlier, to the Old Testament and still has defenders today, it is open to objections. In the first place, it looks as if an act of will should itself be an intentional act. Otherwise we shall hardly be responsible for the behaviour it causes. But if intentional action is action caused by an act of will, and exercising the will is itself an intentional act, we are faced by an infinite regress of acts of will. Some philosophers think this difficulty can be overcome. Others are unconvinced, and in any case there is the further difficulty that there just do not seem to be any such occurrences as acts of will are supposed to be.

Most philosophers today dispense with traditional acts of will and say instead that an act is intentional if it is caused by the agent's desires. In this theory great emphasis is put on the genuinely causal character of the relation between action and desire. But it seems that the only thing which can strictly speaking cause a physical event is another physical event. Since bodily movements are physical events, if they are caused by desires it will follow that desires must be identical with physical events. Hence this theory commits its adherents (and they are mostly delighted to be so committed) to a fundamentally physicalist account of man.

I shall not argue against such an account here, but it seems to me preferable to say that an agent acts intentionally if he acts for the sake of some objective. To desire something is to have it as an objective, and my action is a fulfilment of my desire if it is for the sake of something which is an objective to me. The weight of the claim that an agent is non-causally responsible is taken by the preposition 'for the sake of'. I am really responsible for my action when my action is really for the sake of some outcome I desire, and does not merely result in it as a matter of fact.

But the notion of an objective is that of a benefit. The objective for which I act is the benefit for which I act; so the person non-causally responsible for the action is the person for whose benefit it occurs. The point is obscured because we talk of acting for the benefit of other people. I sign a cheque in favour of the television shop for the benefit of my aunt. But I act for my own benefit too. To act as a friend is precisely to make another person's objectives your own, that is, to make the other person's being benefited a benefit to you. A kind person is one to whom such action is good. All action for which I am non-causally responsible is action for my benefit.

I suggest, then, that the theist should conceive God's responsibility for the universe on the model of our responsibility for causal action for which we are morally responsible. In the way in which my action on the cheque is a fulfilment of my will, the going on of physical processes generally is a fulfilment of God's will. It is not caused by his *act* of will, since there are no such acts, but it is for his objectives.

This suggestion must be prepared for attack from two sides. An atheist might object that it could explain at most only the movements of physical things, and what needs explanation is the existence of those things in the first place. A Christian might fear that the proposal is pantheistic, or at least that it makes God the soul of the universe. I shall take these objections in turn.

It would be wrong to think that if God created the universe he must first have created a lot of bodies or particles, and only afterwards set them in motion. Modern physics has no use for the notion of a completely motionless, unchanging particle. Besides, there can be no time without change; the universe can have existed only for as long as there has been change.

But is there not at least a conceptual distinction between change and the objects which undergo it? Modern physics has no clear distinction. Its waves (unlike ocean waves) are not waves *of* anything, and its particles (electrons, quarks etc.) are hardly corpuscular. We must acknowledge a distinction of a kind between material objects and changes. But we cannot say there are these two sorts of entity, objects and changes, as we can say there are two sorts of animal, sheep and goats, or two sorts of change, alteration and locomotion. Sheep and goats both exist, alteration and locomotion both take place or occur, but locomotion and sheep do not both either exist or occur. This shows that the distinction between objects and changes is of a very peculiar sort. I think it is less a distinction between kinds of things than between ways of thinking and speaking about things. If we ask ourselves what there is in the world, we find ourselves listing sorts of material object. But if we try to form an idea of the actual existence of the things that exist, we find it consists in the going on of change.

We think that it is one thing to be responsible for movements and another for the things that move because we ourselves have direct responsibility only for the movements of our limbs. When I write my fingers move because I want them to, but they do not exist because I want them to, and they continue to exist even when I cease to write and fall asleep. That, however, is because our voluntary movements are imposed on other natural movements, including movements of molecules and atoms, rather as when we throw a stone into a pond, the waves from where it falls are imposed on the waves already in the pond. But if God is responsible for the natural movements, he will be responsible for the existence of our limbs. Or, it might be more correct to say, for the existence of the material in them; we ourselves, in moving voluntarily, have a responsibility for their existence as hands, fingers etc.

I am suggesting, then, that God's creative act is simply deciding that certain processes should go on. The going on of these processes will constitute the existence of physical objects. In his *The First Three Minutes* Steven Weinberg says:

> In the beginning there was an explosion. Not an explosion like those familiar on earth, starting from a definite centre and spread-

ing out to engulf more and more of the circumambient air, but an explosion which occurred simultaneously everywhere, filling all space from the beginning, with every particle of matter rushing apart from every other particle (p. 3).

The theist would be rash to suppose that all future cosmologists will give this account of the beginning of the universe, but it illustrates my suggestion that we conceive creation as a willing that something should happen, rather than as a willing that something should simply exist.

If the universe has existed only for a finite time, it is natural to speak of it as having a beginning. It need not have a beginning, however, in the same way as an ordinary movement or process. In the way in which there is an event which is the starting of my journey to Paris, there probably cannot be an event which is the starting of history. For my starting for Paris is a switch from my being at rest to my being in motion, and therefore presupposes an earlier time when I was at rest. When, however, a body moves from one place to another, though the time for which it is moving is finite, there is no first moment at which it is in motion. It is not in motion, obviously, when it starts, and there is no first moment after it starts. For every instant at which it is moving, there is an earlier instant, rather as for every fraction greater than $\sqrt{2}$ there is a smaller fraction which is still greater than $\sqrt{2}$. The history of the universe is like the history of such a movement if we leave out the body's starting to move. The universe has existed only for a finite time, but there is still no first instant at which it existed, and there is no primal starting up of things. Change has been going on for the whole time for which the universe has existed.

Christians claim not just that God created the universe in the first place, but that he sustains it or keeps it going. Against this it may be objected that no explanation is needed of a thing's staying in existence. Rather, we should want an explanation of its ceasing to be. Once a thing exists, we expect it to keep going until something interferes with it. The objection has a certain validity, but not against the Christian position. It is true that no *causal* explanation is required for a thing's continuing to exist.

Causal explanations are of change, not of staying unchanged. But God's will does not function as a causal factor, any more than does a human will. The continued action of a human agent (unless physicalism is true) is not caused by his beliefs or desires. It can nevertheless be explained by them in a non-causal way: we can say for what reason or purpose he continues to write or saw or cook. It is equally proper to explain the continued existence of the universe in terms of God's purposes. If there were no God there would be no explanation of why physical processes generally continue, and we should have to regard their continuation as a brute fact. But nothing prevents us from looking for an explanation, provided it is teleological in form and not causal. The Christian may be wrong but he is not incoherent in saying that the universe continues to exist because God so desires. It may be noticed that on this view God is responsible not as a man is responsible for the continued existence of a cobweb which he could destroy and does not, but as a man is responsible for the continuance of a walk he is taking or a song he is singing.

Whereas the non-believer may feel that appealing to voluntary action as a model for creation is inadequate, the believer may think it is dangerous. If God is related to physical processes generally as we are related to the voluntary movements of our limbs, will it not follow that God is the soul of the universe, or that physical things make him up in the way in which our limbs make us up?

Philosophers give two very different accounts of the human soul and its relation to the body. Some hold that body and soul are not two parts or components, but merely two aspects, of a human being. Considered as a material object which interacts causally with other material objects, a man does not possess but is a human body; considered as a person with consciousness and moral responsibility he does not have but is a soul. This is the view I shall myself develop in Chapter Five. It would certainly be pantheistic and incompatible with Christian belief to make God the soul of the universe in this way.

Other philosophers, however, maintain that soul and body are not just two aspects of a single thing but two distinct things.

They conceive a human soul as a person which in itself is non-material but which, while we are said to be alive, acts through a material object called, on that account, a 'human body'. As Swinburne puts it. 'A person has a body if there is a chunk of matter through which he makes a difference to the material world, and through which he acquires true beliefs about the world.' I see nothing to stop a Christian from saying that God is responsible for physical processes throughout the universe in the way in which these philosophers must suppose my soul is responsible for my limb-movements.[7]

Talk about souls apart, I am a material object not just because my limbs move as I want but for two further reasons. I can be morally responsible only for changes which are (directly or indirectly) caused by movements of my limbs; and I can be aware of occurrences for which I am not morally responsible only if my sense-organs are correspondingly affected. Neither of these further conditions holds for God. He does not know things in the way in which we know what we know by perception, and there is no part of the universe which has to play a causal role in connection with every change for which he is morally responsible.

3

It is generally held that living organisms developed naturally out of inanimate materials. By ordinary physical processes there arose complex molecules, monocellular organisms, and eventually such astonishing material objects as chimpanzees and men. If that is correct, is God's creative activity exhausted by his responsiblity for physical processes? Do life and consciousness come about automatically? Or do they call for some further explanation? There seem to be three possibilities. Some people say that consciousness (and *a fortiori* life) is reducible to physical factors; some people say that it cannot be reduced to them but can be accounted for by them; Christians mostly say that it is neither reducible to nor explainable by physical factors, but is due in a special way to God.

The ablest advocates for the first of these views support it by appealing to cybernetics.[8] We speak of computers in psychological language. We say they remember things, acquire information, calculate and so forth. Modern computers are sometimes so complex and programmed in such a way that it is impossible to follow every mechanical step in their functioning, and pretty well mandatory to use such terms. Originally people thought they knew what 'remember', 'learn', etc., mean as applied to men, and they applied them to computers in a lighthearted and metaphorical way. The present suggestion, however, is that we explain what they mean as applied to men in terms of the conditions under which they are applied to machines. Men think in exactly the sense in which computers think. Computers for their part think insofar as they can perform functions which when performed by men are taken to show thought.

This suggestion has been the subject of a great deal of technical discussion, into the details of which it would be inappropriate to enter here. It is no more impossible in principle for intelligent agents to be composed of wire and silicon than it is that they should be made of flesh and bone, no more incredible that they should be produced by soldering irons or microphotography than that they should be produced by sexual intercourse. If, however, anything is to think, it must act for reasons and purposes. I shall argue shortly that the same action cannot be both for a reason and causally determined. If that is true it is impossible that anything like a computer should think. Besides, to be conscious of itself a thing must not only act for reasons but understand for what reasons it acts. Very few people will accept that anything like a computer understands why it does what it does. It is easy to construct a machine which will type out sentences like 'I am conscious', 'I know why I am doing this', but we are inclined to consider this as no more than an amusing trick.

That human artifacts can think, that they know what is going on and can themselves exercise a control over events at will is not a new idea. It is the idea which powers the ancient practice of idolatry. The Judaeo-Christian view has always been that human artifacts, however beautiful or ingenious they may be, are all as a matter of fact blind, deaf and powerless to help us.

People today will break away from that tradition at their peril.

The reasons for doubting that statues, robots and other artifacts can think are equally reasons for doubting that human consciousness simply consists in very complicated processes in the brain. In the past many reflective people thought that consciousness is not simply reducible to or identical with any nexus of physical processes. But since it seems to occur only when a certain degree of complexity is reached, and since thoughts are correlated with events in the nervous system, they thought consciousness is a peculiar additional process or state which is causally dependent on these events in a way science had not yet quite succeeded in explaining. Meanwhile consciousness was to be compared, as an early critic put it, to 'the foam thrown up by and floating on a wave ... a mere foam, aura or melody, arising from the brain but without reaction upon it' (Shadworth Hodgson, *Space and Time*, London 1865, pp. 279–80). This view (sometimes called 'epiphenomenalism') is now out of fashion. It is hard to see how anything can be caused by a physical process except another physical process, and it would be perverse to identify consciousness with some special process which eludes detection by scientists, rather than with the processes open to psychological and neurological examination.

We should try to free ourselves from the assumption that consciousness or life itself must be either a physical process or a non-physical one. The expression 'living thing' is applied not only to men and the higher animals, but also to plants and micro-organisms, and for them life can be connected with certain processes of reproduction and chemical change. For human beings, however, there is more to being alive than just having certain processes take place. We think that some of the processes which take place in us and in the higher animals at least are *explainable* in a certain way. Processes like the digestion of food and the healing of wounds do not merely result in benefit to us; they seem to occur *for* our benefit. And more important than this, we think that when we act voluntarily or intentionally, the movements of the limbs we use are to be explained in terms of our reasons and purposes. If we call this sort of explanation 'teleological', then a conscious being, a person with beliefs and desires, is one whose beliefs and desires provide a teleological explanation of his or her bodily action and inaction. Hence life, at least insofar as that includes consciousness, is not so much a matter of special non-physical processes as of the occurring or going on of physical processes in a special, teleologically explainable way.

That being so, if life is due to God, processes go on in this way because God want them to. Does this require any further creative desire on his part besides the desire that natural processes generally should go on? That depends, I think, on whether the same thing can be both for a purpose and causally determined. Is it possible for any movements of my arms and legs to occur for some purpose of mine, say the purpose of getting to London or of avoiding an on-coming lorry, and also for these movements to be the inevitable result of the stimulation of my eyes, ears and nervous system by the rest of the physical world? If so, no special creative activity on God's part will be needed for the existence of life.

Philosophers are divided on whether a movement can be both purposive and causally determined.[9] It looks at first as if it cannot. How can I be said to have acted voluntarily in going to Paris or rescuing you from the sea when your boat capsized, if the movements of my limbs were all rendered inevitable by the action on me of other physical objects? In a closed, deterministic system later states are determined by earlier. If we form part of such a system, my movements in travelling or rescuing will have been determined since before the formation of the solar system, and how, in that case, can I be held morally responsible for them? Philosophers, however, have shrunk from saying that purposive movements cannot be causally determined, because that would make them discontinuous with other processes which go on in the world. To say they are not causally determined is to say that they are not mere continuations of earlier processes. And being discontinuous with earlier processes, they will mark off the organisms in which they occur from the rest of the contemporary world. We shall be discontinuous with the air in which we live or the water in which we swim in a way in which a mountain, for example, is not discontinuous with the rest of the planet or a cloud with the rest of the atmosphere.

It seems to me that this is a consequence we should rather welcome than fear. I find repellent the idea that there should be no objective basis for separating me off from the rest of the world, and there will be no such basis if all our behaviour is causally determined. We may suppose that where there is a certain degree of complexity there will be sentience, belief and desire (whether these are identical with physical processes or epiphenomena). Where there is consciousness it will divide up the world into objects which have a practical significance, which militate for or against the satisfaction of desires. That is, the beliefs and desires will be about such objects. The consciousness which corresponds to my brain or my body will consist of beliefs and desires about men, trees, lorries, rivers, beaches and so on: it will divide the world into these objects. But a different consciousness would divide the world up differently. There is, perhaps, a complexity in the region of space which at present includes my body, three quarters of my typewriter, and three sevenths of the brain of the person in the next room; or, if you like, in the matter or energy which makes up these things, among others. The consciousness corresponding to that complexity will divide the world up into objects of which I have no conception, like blarves and spintles. (Blarves are living things related to the consciousness I am imagining as human beings are related to my actual consciousness, and all the material at this moment in the River Thames forms part of the material, at this moment, in some spintle.) Clearly there will be no objective ground for saying that the world consists of men and the objects they recognise rather than blarves or any of the other perhaps infinitely many species of observer competing for the same regions of space and particles of energy.

The supposition that a movement can be both purposive and causally determined undermines our existence as distinct individuals; but does not the contrary supposition undermine the laws of nature? Not exactly. The laws of nature are the laws in accordance with which causal agents produce effects. They say what happens when one object acts on another in a certain way. It is in accordance with the laws of nature that if we are pricked we bleed, and if we are put into a fire we burn. It is not, however, a law of nature that a change in an object cannot occur unless it is rendered inevitable by the action of some other object. That is at best a heuristic methodological principle: the scientist seeks to explain changes by such action, and the explanation such action provides is what we call 'scientific explanation'. Neither does the scientist have to suppose that such an explanation will always be forthcoming. It cannot be a scientific principle, it can only be a philosophical principle, that scientific explanation is the only valid form of explanation. If what I have just said is correct, to maintain this is to maintain the philosophical thesis that life as we conceive it does not exist.

If purposive agents are marked off from the rest of the world by the fact that some of the processes which go on in them go on *for* their purposes, God will be responsible for their existence insofar as it is because he so desires that these processes do in fact occur for their purposes. But how, in that case, do I have a life of my own? Suppose that my hand moves in order that I may drink, in order that the liquid in the glass may go down my throat. If my hand moves merely because God wants it to move, what ground is there for saying that *I* exist as a purposive agent? If it moves because I want it to move, I exist as a purposive agent, but how can my existence derive from God?

The answer, I suggest, is that the movement has a double explanation. Insofar as it occurs in order that the liquid may go down my throat, it occurs to benefit and nourish the organism to which this throat and this hand belong, and we can say it occurs because I want it to occur. But it also occurs (the theist may hold) in order that I may exist as a purposive agent. This could, like the liquid's going down my throat, be an objective of mine, but only if I have the concept of a purposive agent and apply this concept to myself – conditions which, as we shall see, are not easily fulfilled. Before my existence as a person is an objective to me, however, it can be an objective of other people: of my parents and, the theist will wish to say, of God. Insofar as the movement occurs for the sake of this objectivity of God's, it occurs because God wants it to occur.

If this account is to leave God responsible for my existence as a person, the explanation in terms of his purpose must take precedence over the explanation in terms of mine. My hand, we must say, would not move in order that the liquid might go down my throat if it did not move in order that I might exist as a person. That should not be too difficult to accept, once it is admitted that physical processes in general occur because God want them to. Just as it is not a brute, inexplicable fact that physical processes in general go on, so it is not a brute fact that some processes go on in order that specific changes may come about. Given that the movement of the infant's hand in reaching for something is not a mere continuation of processes going back in time to before it was conceived, we want some explanation of that movement. And the explanation cannot be found simply in the infant as a purposive agent because the existence of the infant as a purposive agent is something which itself calls for explanation. There has not always been this agent; and its existence is not independent of the movements we wish to explain. It is attractive, therefore, to posit some further agent that wants it to exist.

But why is it or how is it (we may wonder) that this agent's wishes get fulfilled? A puppet-maker like Giapetto might want his puppet to be a purposive agent capable of moving in order to drink; but while Giapetto can make his puppet's hand approach the glass, the puppet remains his puppet, and does not come to life. Why, then, when my hand moves because God wants it to move, do I come to life? The difference between the cases is that the hand of Giapetto's puppet moves because Giapetto acts on it causally: since causal determination is incompatible with purposiveness, it follows that the puppet's hand cannot move in order that the puppet may drink. But when my hand moves, it is not acted on causally by God. 'That' it may be said 'perhaps ensures that you are alive. But it cannot make you a living person distinct from God: your life will be God's life.' In a way, as I shall insist in a moment, the

Christian accepts this: the Christian holds that no creature can have a life completely separate from God. On the other hand my hand is not God's hand. God is not nourished, or benefited in any other way, by the liquid's going down my throat. If my hand really does move in order that the liquid may go down my throat, that ensures my existence as a purposive agent distinct from God. All that is needed for my existence as the person with this hand is that this hand should move for the benefit of that person.

The question, then, is whether an explanation of the hand-movement in terms of nourishing or otherwise benefiting me really does apply. If my hand moves because God wants me to exist as an agent which acts for purposes like getting nourishment or pleasure from drinking, does it follow that my hand also moves for some such purpose? What, we may reply, would it be like if my hand moved for God's purpose but not for any purpose of mine? We should then have to imagine complicatedly structured chunks of matter going through elaborate dances just as if they were living organisms because God so wishes, yet not in fact being alive. But if that were so, God would be unable to create life. For what more could he do than he is already doing? Say 'Let there be life'? But we are already supposing that he wants there to be life, since we are supposing the movements occur in order that, as he desires, there may be living things. If they could occur without there being life, his desire would be stupid and his creative action vain.

In fact, however, what the theist explains as being in order that I may exist as a person is not just the moving of my hand but the moving of my hand already conceived as purposive, the moving of my hand in order that the liquid may go down my throat. That sounds complicated when stated in theoretical terms, but the point is easily grasped in practice. As I shall try to explain later, a person who has achieved self-awareness and moral responsibility will act not merely to bring about specific changes in the objects around him but in order to be a certain sort of person. That part of my behaviour which you explain as action in order that I may be, say, an attentive husband or a hard-headed business man is action you already conceive as being for the purpose of benefiting my wife or outreaching my rivals. Action for a particular purpose can occur because the agent desires precisely to act for that purpose. The theist may claim that it can also occur because God wants it to occur. Our existence as persons will then depend on God insofar as our purposive action occurs because he wants it rather than because we do.

It is one thing to say that I and God are two distinct agents, another to say that my life is completely separate from his. Christians will want to make the first of these assertions but not the second. Paul says: 'It is no longer I that live, but Christ lives in me' (*Gal.* 2.20). The reference to Christ, of course, belongs to the New Testamant. But it is an idea which goes back to the deepest roots of Judaeo-Christian thought that the creation of life is an intimate and personal affair. In the Old Testament it is the breath of God which gives life:

> [Things] wait all upon thee ... Thou takest away their breath, they die and return to their dust. Thou sendest forth thy spirit, they are created. (*Ps.* 104.29–30.)

In Christianity the breath of God becomes the Holy Spirit.

On the account I am proposing it could be said that God creates us as persons by acting within us. Although this notion may at first seem alarming, I think it will help us to understand Christian belief about salvation. Many theologians, past as well as present, have wished to represent salvation not as something on top of creation and discontinuous with it, but as a development and completion of it. If this strategy is to succeed, the conception of creative activity with which we start must be a fairly rich and complex one. The considerations I have been advancing will become clearer, I hope, when I return to them in Chapters Six and Ten.

There are a couple of consequences, however, which I should note here. First, if purposive movements are discontinuous with the rest of what goes on in the universe, God will not be responsible merely for the first appearance of life. He will have a separate responsibility for the appearance of each purposive individual. Christian writers regularly say that the creation of each human soul requires a separate creative act, but they speak less confidently about animals. An idea which may bother some is that if the souls of animals were created by God in the same way as our souls, they like us would be immortal. I do not think that would follow, and it seems to me that if the movements of an animal are really purposive, God must be responsible for the animal's existence in the same way as for ours.

The second point follows on from this. If God is responsible for purposive movements, then it is not because of any physical necessity that we and other organisms make movements which result in our escaping destruction, our being strengthened by nourishment, our having children. There would be no causal obstacle to a living organism's reaching for what is damaging to it, or to males and females consistently avoiding each other. That being so, questions about evil and design arise. The practical principles on which God wants an organism to act will, in a way, determine what is good for that organism. The things God wants it to pursue and shun will be, respectively, good and bad for it, and the best thing for it will be a life of pursuing the former and shunning the latter. But this need not accord with our ideas of good and bad. It is imaginable that we and other living things should have been endowed with natures such as, so far as we can form an opinion, we should prefer not to have; what God has fixed on as the best thing might turn out to be a kind of life which seems to us repugnant.

In actual fact that is not so. The natures we and other animals have are consistent with the idea of a wise and benevolent creator. But there is no room for sentimentality. Each living things tends to make the efficient use it can of the organic parts it has, in order to survive as a purposive agent and produce young like itself. This results in conflict. P. T. Geach is among Christian writers who have been impressed by the amount of pain which animals inflict on one another.[10] Can God, it might be wondered, desire the good of both foxes and chickens? It may be replied that any student of natural history, whatever his religious views, will try to see the inclination of foxes to apparently random killing as somehow beneficial to them; and it is perhaps better for the chicken to be aware of the fox as a source of harm and object of terror, than to have no idea at all of what is going on.

4

The Bible opens with an account of creation. It is sometimes said, indeed, that it opens with two, the first running from *Genesis* 1.1 to 2.4, and the second from 2.5–25. That is incorrect. *Genesis* 2.5–25 alludes to the creation of heaven and earth but there is no description of it. There is an account of the garden of Eden which looks forward to the account of the Fall of Man in *Genesis* 3, and a description of the formation of Adam and Eve which also looks forward to the Fall but the primary purpose of which is to make clear the divine institution and the importance of marriage. The only account of creation is in *Genesis* 1.1–2.4.

In recent years this account has acquired a grotesque prominence. Science has proved that since the Big Bang there have elapsed more than ten thousand million years. But *Genesis* says that God made the world in six days. What a howler! Yet Christians declare that *Genesis* is divinely inspired and still read it in church on solemn occasions as if it were true. To some people this seems to cast a severe doubt on the rest of Christian belief.

It is not at all clear that the authors of *Genesis* intended their audience to think the world was made in six days. They clearly wish to break the creation into parts, and the audience is meant to marvel at each part in turn; but we do not have to suppose that the order of exposition and meditation is meant to reflect a temporal order. There is a tradition going back at least to Philo (*Creation* 26) and still preserved in Anselm (*Cur Deus Homo* I.18) that God created the universe all at once. If the authors of *Genesis* really thought of creation as taking time, what kind of time-intervals can they have had in mind? The 'days' cannot have been sunset-to-sunset periods, since the sun was not made till the fourth day. Were they, then, twenty-four hour stretches of absolute time? To credit such a notion to people living in a more or less clockless society is fanciful indeed.

As to inspiration, it is an ancient Christian doctrine that the Holy Spirit spoke through the prophets. That there was the same inspiration for the Law, i.e. the first five books of the Bible or Pentateuch, is said in only one of early creeds collected in Denzinger (46). But in any case it is one thing to hold that the Holy Spirit inspired Moses or whoever wrote *Genesis*, another to say that the writings of inspired authors contain accurate information about astronomy, geology, pre-history or, for that matter, history.

That second opinion could hardly have been held before quite recent times. Modern scientific research starts in the seventeenth century with the invention of microscopes and telescopes. Before then it would have been impossible for anyone to maintain that the Bible supplies us infallibly with information we seek by such research. Scientists like Galileo, not churchmen, were the first people to construe the Bible as containing answers to scientific questions. Always easily provoked, churchmen then set themselves the desperate task of defending these supposed answers against mounting scientific evidence. That the authors of the Bible had no conception of the questions occurred to neither party. Something similar goes for history. Most of the Old Testament goes back to a time when people had quite different ideas from ours of what kind of truth is recoverable from the past. To see that we should first reflect on how far our knowledge even of things which happened in our neighbourhood a few years ago depends on diaries, newspapers, photographs etc.; and then ask ourselves what idea a person in Palestine in 1200 BC or even 600 BC could have had of knowledge of events not in living memory. Clio took up her abode in Greece in the fifth century BC, but her summer holidays in north-western Europe were rare and brief. For a thousand years most of those Christians who heard *Genesis* read aloud must have had the same view of the past as its authors.

It is hard to think that inspiration makes people inerrant in fields of non-religious knowledge of which they have no conception, and hard to accept the picture of how it works offered in Leo XIII's Encyclical of 1893:

> By supernatural power the Spirit so moved and excited the authors of scripture to write, and so stood beside them while they were writing, that they both correctly conceived in their minds, and faithfully desired to write, and aptly expressed with infallible truth, all those things and only those things which he commanded (Denzinger 3293).

If someone in 1893 had claimed to write something because the Holy Spirit was standing beside him and exciting him, Leo XIII would have been the first person to ask 'How do you know? What makes you think it was the Holy Spirit and not your imagination?' The experience which the words I have quoted suggest would be a major intrusion of the mystical, a serious disruption of a man's life. I do not say it could not occur, but a man who passed through it would want not only to convince others but to satisfy himself that it was genuine. In point of fact, Leo's description is not wholly inappropriate to the prophets. Jeremiah in 1, 1–10 describes how 'the word of God' came to him, how he hesitated to accept the call, and how he was reassured. There is no indication, however, that *Gen.* 1. 1–2.4 is inspired in this way.

Two rather different things are said about it by modern scholars. Some assign an early date to it, but say it is typical of creation myths current in Mesopotamia at the beginning of the second millennium BC. The Enuma Elis is often mentioned as a parallel. I think, however that the unbiased reader who compares the two will be struck more by their difference than by their resemblance. The Enuma Elis begins:

> When on high the heaven had not been named, firm ground below had not been called by name, naught but primordial Apsu, their begetter, (and) Mummu Tiamat, she who bore them all, their waters commingling as a single body; no reed hut had been matted,

no marsh land had appeared, when no gods whatever had been brought into being, uncalled by name, their destinies undetermined – then it was that the gods were formed within them.[11]

The next ninety lines contain a detailed description of the newly-formed gods ('four were his eyes, four were his ears, large were all four hearing organs' etc.,) and their first quarrels with their parents. Creative work proper begins (lines 105–142) with the producing of storm-winds and monsters, 'the Viper, the Dragon and the Sphinx, the Great-Lion, the Mad-Dog and the Scorpion-Man, mighty lion-demons, the Dragon-Fly, the Centaur', apparently as munitions for the divine wars. It is not for another four hundred lines, and still in the context of divine feuding, that anyone turns his attention to constructing the sky and the heavenly bodies. In contrast with this Genesis begins:

> In the beginning God created the heaven and the earth. And the earth was without form, and void; and darkness was on the face of the deep. And the spirit of God moved on the face of the waters. And God said 'Let there be light'; and there was light.

In acknowledgement of the difference many scholars date *Gen.* 1.1–2.4 to the latest possible date, the years following the Babylonian captivity. It does not, however, proclaim an origin among sixth century priests any more than among nomadic patriarchs of twelve hundred years earlier. All we can say with confidence is that it represents speculation about the origin and nature of the universe by intellectual leaders of the Jews.[12] Nothing in it seems to me inconsistent with the belief that God helped the people concerned to speculate in an intellectually humble but disciplined and persevering way, and aided or strengthened their judgement.

CHAPTER FOUR

The Divinity of Christ and Historical Truth

I

The position that there is a single person who has always existed and on whom the universe depends may be called 'bare monotheism'. It is not a position in which it is easy to rest. The monotheist will want to know more about what the one God is like and how he regards mankind. Is he aware of us? Does he care what we do? Can we get into communication with him? If no answers to these questions are forthcoming, the belief in God has no practical significance and becomes shadowy.

Christianity offers answers which at first sound definite enough. God is indeed aware of us. He has shown his concern for us by sending us Jesus Christ. We can communicate with him through Christ. Christ is at once our teacher and our saviour. On examination, however, these answers prove to be problematic. There is disagreement about what and even about how Christ teaches; and there is quite sharp disagreement about how he saves.

The Jews of his day were hoping God would send them what they called a 'Messiah'. The word means 'anointed one', kings were anointed, and the Messiah they looked for was a royal figure who would liberate Israel and inaugurate a peaceful, prosperous and perhaps world-wide kingdom. The name 'Christ' is the Greek equivalent of 'Messiah', and Christians hold that Jesus was the Messiah God sent; but contrary to the reported hope of his followers he did not restore the kingdom of Israel.

The traditional Christian view, which goes back at least to

Paul, is that the human race had been delivered over, bound hand and foot, to sin, death, and after death, extinction or misery. We were labouring under a load of crime and spiritual deformity which separated us from God, condemned us to death, and placed us in the power of evil spirits. In pity at our plight God sent his Son, a divine being, to take the form of a man as Jesus of Nazareth. By accepting crucifixion Jesus obliterated our guilt, reconciled us to God, and made it possible for us to live on after death in unending happiness. He saved or redeemed us in the way in which someone might secure the freedom of a slave or the pardon of a prisoner under sentence.

Today this view meets with resistance on several counts. First, people find it hard to believe that but for Christ we should all be sinful and guilty. It may be pointed out that before the coming of Christ some people led heroic or saintly lives, and there have been plenty of villains since his coming, even among Christians. The position, as we tend to see it, is that all men go wrong occasionally, though some are worse than others, and if you do a bad act that need not fill you with despair. You can try to repair it, or, failing that, shrug it off and forget about it. Next, the idea that wrong-doing should involve us in punishment beyond the natural consequences of the crime, in particular that it should expose us to eternal torment, is deeply repugnant. People think that if the universe is indeed controlled by a benevolent God, there cannot possibly be such a place or state as Hell. Hence there cannot be any redemption from Hell. Finally, though people are not so convinced that there is no such place as Heaven, they are unenthusiastic about the idea. Many seem to hope that death is the end. Conceiving eternity as infinitely extended time, they find the prospect of eternal life terrifying. If, however, we have to survive death, then again if the universe is controlled by a kindly God, he will make eternity as bearable as possible for everyone. There is no need for a special redemptive act. God has only (as Anselm's Boso observed, *Cur Deus Homo* I.12) to practice himself that forgiveness and charity he keeps urging on us.

These reflections lead to a different view of what Christ has done for us. The happiness and advancement of mankind depend largely on moral qualities and ideas. It is necessary to recognise the basic dignity of the individual, and also the duty of every man to help his neighbour. We must be tolerant and forgiving. We must make peace and freedom our ideals, and try to eliminate cruelty, grasping selfishness, superstitious fear, rule-worship, and everything else that depresses the human spirit. Christ revealed all this in his teaching and example, and thereby transformed our lives in this world, here and now. If he freed us from sin and Hell it was by making us see that the burden of guilt and the eternal punishment it seems to entail are illusory. Those who interpret our redemption in this way usually concentrate on moral qualities but, as I said earlier, our science and technology, which have done so much to relieve human suffering, are indebted to Christianity. Christ omitted to give any specific directives about experiment or research; still, it is largely thanks to his influence that people abandoned the belief, fatal to those activities, that the natural world is controlled by spirits that must be approached by priests offering sacrifices.

This modern view is edifying, but has two fairly obvious inconveniences. First, a discontinuity opens up between this way of understanding Christ's achievement and the way the first Christians understood it; for they clearly thought their guilt and peril not illusory but real. The usual reply is that this discontinuity is really an advantage: it keeps our faith alive and constitutes a true continuity which runs deeper than any mere verbal agreement.

> Time and again, continuity with the past is preserved by shattering the received terminology, the received imagery, the received theology ... Only that man is in genuine continuity with past history who allows it to place him in a new condition of responsibility ... Only in the decision between faith and unbelief can petrified history even of the life of Jesus become once again living history.[1]

This answer may be satisfactory for Germans: 'A faith', says Heidegger, 'that does not perpetually expose itself to the possibility of unfaith is no faith but merely a convenience.'[2] It rests, however, on an idea at which many English-speakers will jib: that what is important for religious beliefs is not to be true but to be arrived at in the right way (ideally, perhaps, by 'a leap through which man thrusts away all the previous security, whether real or imagined, of his life')[3].

A second awkwardness of the new way of thinking is that it does not cohere too well with surviving religious practice. Christians call themselves Christians on the ground that Christ did more than anyone else for the human race. Did he really? What about Socrates? What about the religious leaders who came after Christ, such as Paul and Martin Luther? Would he not have lived in vain but for them? And even if Jesus is the figure of decisive importance, he lived two thousand years ago; why this obsession with him now? Why these weekly or even daily meetings in his honour in special buildings preserved for the purpose, at which our most respected senior citizens preside in fancy dress? Perhaps it will be said that only if we read and meditate on the life of Christ will the Christian ideas and virtues work in us. That life is an irreplaceable source of inspiration. But that is strange. Why cannot Christian ideas and virtues be imparted for their own sake, without reference to Christ? Besides, all this church-going and praying, if Christ is a figure like Socrates only more influential, savours a little of that superstition which it is supposed to have been one of Christ's merits to have resisted.

The question whether the traditional view is morally and theologically acceptable is important. But I think it must yield precedence to the question of the reliability as historical records of the New Testament writings. This has, indeed, been disputed. Many theologians reacted to scholarly criticism of the New Testament by saying that the historical facts about Christ are of no relevance to religion. Some go so far as to represent a separation of theology from history as theologically mandatory. 'Faith should not seek security in historical data' E. P. Sanders begins a recent book.[4] The Reformation insight that salvation comes to us through the word of God in Scriptures, and that the Scriptures must be their own interpreter, forbids any appeal to historical facts lying behind the scriptural text. It seems to me doubtful, however, whether this is a wholly accurate reflection of the thinking of the Reformers. When the Thirty-nine Articles uphold 'the sufficiency of Scripture for salvation' they oppose the Scriptures to the teaching of the Church and the General Councils; it would no more have occurred to Cranmer or Jewel than to later Anglicans like Fleetwood to oppose the Gospel narratives to the actual events of Jesus' life. Käsemann seems to me closer to Heidegger than to Luther when he says:

> Nothing is settled about the significance of the Resurrection tidings for me personally, simply because the evidence for the empty tomb has been shown to be reliable. The handing on of relatively probable facts does not as such provide any basis for genuinely historical communication and continuity.[5]

For Käsemann it is neither possible nor desirable to aim at a completely objective appraisal of historical facts. This despair about objectivity and rationality is surely the negative aspect of a clinging to that German idealism of which Heidegger said:

> It was not German idealism which collapsed [beneath a pincer-movement of Marxism and Positivism]; rather the age was no longer strong enough to stand up to the greatness, breadth and originality of that spiritual world, i.e. truly to realise it, for to realise a philosophy means something very different from applying theorems and insights.[6]

Those who have less nostalgia for this kind of idealism may agree with Samuel Sandmel:

> Can the theological interpretation be logical, acceptable and persuasive if the factual basis is questionable? The candid answer must be a forthright no.[7]

Sandmel is referring to the Old Testament, but his words surely apply still more to the New. If Christ really walked on water, rose from the dead and said 'Before Abraham came to be, I am' it is inadequate to represent him merely as standing to Judaism as Luther stands to Mediaeval Catholicism:

> On the one hand was the artificiality of a hair-splitting and barren erudition, on the other the fresh directness of the layman and the son of the people; here was the product of long generations of misrepresentation and distortion, there was simplicity, plainess and freedom.[8]

Conversely if Jesus was in actual fact a Protestant reformer, or, as Geza Vermes more plausibly suggests, a typical, pious, first century Jewish exorcist, it seems extravagant to believe that he, and he alone, enables us to enjoy after death eternal happiness with God.

Can the Gospels, then, be treated as authentic historical records? It is probably true to say that a majority of professional scripture scholars think that is not an open question. Their task, as they see it, is to explain how, given that hardly any of the events recorded really happened, our documents could have come into being. For this enterprise they have developed various techniques of which it is usual to distinguish three. There is 'source criticism', the attempt to find written sources behind the Gospels. There is 'form criticism' which seeks the origins of bits of the Gospels (classified by their form as legends, exhortations etc.) in the needs of early Christian communities. Finally 'redaction criticism' is the project of showing how original stories have been embroidered and otherwise altered for theological purposes. In the course of pursuing these lines of research critics distinguish a Palestinian and a Greek Church and claim that different elements were evolved to fit the wants of these different people.[9]

It may seem temerarious indeed to attack a whole discipline, an entire academic industry. I do not think, however, that we are obliged to regard the historical question as closed in the way the scholars would wish. We must bear in mind that the falsity of the narratives is not a conclusion of the discipline but an assumption on which it rests. For there is no evidence outside the New Testament for oral traditions, lost written sources, Greek or Palestinian churches or theological movements. These are postulated to explain how the Gospels came into being, *given that the events related did not take place*: if they did take place, no further explanations are needed.

And as it is, the basis for all these constructions is the New Testament we possess. Dibelius in words quoted approvingly by Bultmann describes the aim of the critics as

> to discover the origin and history of the particular units, and thereby to throw some light on the history of the tradition before it took literary form.[10]

But the discovery is to be effected simply by reading the New Testament. Hence the exercise has a circularity the critics themselves admit:

> The forms of the literary tradition must be used to establish the influences operating in the life of the community, and the life of the community must be used to render the forms themselves intelligible. [In short, New Testament criticism is] fundamentally indistinguishable from all historical work in this, that it has to move in a circle.[11]

Bultmann is echoed in our own day by Sanders: 'Historians always move in this kind of circle.'[12]

The idea that all historical work moves in a circle is derived from Heidegger who holds that all understanding generally moves in a circle.[13] Whatever may be thought of this as a philosophical doctrine (it has not been found enlightening by many English-speaking philosophers), the historian may protest that serious historical work does not move in anything like so contracted a circle as this.

The current orthodoxy about the Gospels presents a certain resemblance to a view which recently held the field among

English-speaking philosophers. This is that the senses of sight, hearing, touch and so on give us no direct access to material objects, but only to entities technically termed 'sense-data' which depend for their existence on human perception and are private to each perceiver. Leading professors who taught this theory were Bertrand Russell and G. E. Moore at Cambridge and A. J. Ayer and H. H. Price at Oxford; and Price went so far as to say that if anything in philosophy could be taken as proved it is that we do not directly perceive material objects.[14] This philosophical theory resembles the current theory about the New Testament in several ways. Whereas everyone has heard of material objects, only philosophers have heard of the sense data which are supposed to be the sole things of which we have certain knowledge, and whereas everyone has heard of Christ and Palestine in the time of Tiberius, only scripture scholars have heard of the kerygmata, sources and early Christian communities to which alone the Gospels are supposed to give us access. The philosophers found that once we recognise that sense-perception is in any degree fallible or that its reports can ever to the slightest extent conflict, there is no stopping short of the conclusion that it gives us no information about the physical world at all; and the Scripture scholars proceed in the same way with New Testament authors.

These similarities are not wholly fortuitous. The philosophical background to the scriptural orthodoxy, German idealism and phenomenology, is the Continental equivalent of the sense-datum theory. But there is a difference. The sense-datum philosophers never forbade the critical examination of the grounds for their theory. The issue of the truth of the Gospel narratives arouses much stronger passions. One might say that as the altars are neglected the odium theologicum burns all the more brightly. If Scripture scholars are asked why they think the Gospels give us no direct access to the life and teaching of Christ they are apt to raise the cry of fundamentalism. 'Fundamentalism' used to mean the position that God created the world in six twenty-four hour periods. Now it is coming to mean the position that God created the world, and to treat the Gospels as straightforward factual narratives like Nepos' life of Atticus or Josephus' history of the Jewish wars is fundamentalism indeed.

A. N. Sherwin-White allows himself this indulgence in *Roman Society and Roman Law in the New Testament* (Oxford 1963). Comparing the Gospels with the sources for Christ's 'best-known contemporary' the Emperor Tiberius he says (p. 188):

> The divergences between the synoptic gospels, or between them and the Fourth Gospel, are no worse than the contradictions in the Tiberius material.

I agree, and would be happy to defend the two following propositions. First, in spite of the eloquent remarks of Strauss in *New Life* s. 9, the authorship of the Gospels by Matthew, Mark, Luke and John has better than average attestation for first century documents.[15] Different authors of that age are attested in different ways. Strauss demands that the Gospels should be supported by a conjunction, not a disjunction, of these kinds of testimony.[16] Secondly, if we grant the Gospels their traditional authors, there are no events better attested in ancient history than the trial, death and resurrection of Christ. The discrepancies between the Gospel narratives are trifling.[17] Scholars, indeed, speak of two vast contradictions: John says Christ was crucified on the day of the Passover (14th–15th Nisan), whereas the synoptics say he ate the paschal meal the night before;[18] and though the angels at the resurrection tell the apostles to meet Christ in Galilee, when they do not go he meets them in Jerusalem. Far from a contradiction,[19] the second point seems to me a complete non-problem. As to the first, might Christ not have had reasons to eat the paschal meal a day early?

What really influences scholars is that the Gospels contain miracles and miracle (to quote Käsemann)[20] is 'offensive to the world view of the modern age'. Only this can explain the dogmatic statements, unsupported by any explicit reasoning, in which works of Scripture scholarship abound. Thus Bultmann in *The Synoptic Tradition* blandly declares that the women present at the Crucifixion are 'as little historical' as those at the empty tomb (p. 274). The guards at the tomb in *Mt.* 27. 62–6 are 'an apologetic legend' (p. 286); 'originally there was no difference between the Resurrection of Jesus and his Ascension' (p. 290); or his Transfiguration either (p. 259; though here Bultmann does indeed give us, not indeed a reason, but a bundle of authorities). Or to take a more recent example, E. P. Sanders says:

> All the sayings which attribute to Jesus the will to die *correspond so closely* with what happened and with early Christian doctrine that the case for their creation by the early church is overwhelmingly strong.[21]

If a prophecy is fulfilled, for Sanders it follows that it was made after the event.

2

If we believe (say for the reasons rehearsed in Chapter Two) that there exists a God able and willing to intervene in nature, we cannot reject a narrative simply because it reports such interventions. But we must still ask the Humean question: which is easier to believe, that there really were such interventions in Palestine in the first century, or that the New Testament narratives are false? Some scholars and theologians do not like to hear it asked whether statements in the New Testament are false, but if they wish to communicate with educated English-speaking people they must keep the words 'true' and 'false' in their vocabularies.

If the events related did not take place it looks as if we have to choose between two possibilities. As Pascal puts it:

> The Apostles were either deceived or deceivers. Either supposition is difficult. One does not just *take* someone to have risen from the dead. (*Pensée* 802, ed. Bruschvig.)

Strauss grasped both horns of the dilemma. He said that Paul certainly and the other apostles probably suffered from delusions. The standard counter to this is: how could a story of a resurrection, started by such people in so short a period of time (the conversion of Paul some three years later is surely a *terminus post quem non*) have escaped contradiction?

Strauss also claimed that John's Gospel is 'conscious fiction'.[22] People do, of course, write fiction innocently, with the best of motives, and Strauss wished on the whole to understand the Fourth Gospel in this way; but it is hard to read it as we read C. S. Lewis' Narnia novels, or even as we read the narrative passages in Plato.

But it is still harder, as Pascal observes, to accept the hypothesis of fiction which is not innocent but fraudulent in intent:

> Work it out in detail. Imagine these twelve men assembled after the death of Christ, forming the conspiracy to say he has risen from the dead. Thereby they are attacking all the powers. The heart of man is easily affected by levity, by change, by promises, by wealth; if just one of these men had been led to retract by all these inducements, and, what is more, by prison, torture and death, they were all lost. Follow that line of thought. (*Pensées* 801.)

A major objection to saying the apostles were deceivers is that history contains no record of a comparable deception. No individual or group has ever succeeded in persuading a substantial number of people for any length of time that a god has appeared among men and worked wonders. It is doubtful if anyone has ever even attempted such a fraud. In Herodotus I.60 we are told that the Athenian ruler Peisistratus tried to pass off a tall and beautiful courtesan as the goddess Athene, but many historians now believe the story too good to be true. If Christianity is founded on a hoax, such a hoax is without parallel in human experience.

It is a tacit confession of the force of these considerations that most sceptics prefer the hypothesis of unconscious fiction. They favour a Chinese Whispers theory of the gradual incrustation of tradition with myth, the gradual growth of legend. I have yet to see a coherent and credible version of this theory.

The opinion of the majority of scholars is that the Gospel of Mark was written just before or just after 70, that Matthew and Luke were written in the 80s, and that John was written in the 90s. It is granted, or rather insisted, that our gospels were preceded by written accounts of Christ's life and teaching, and in fact such accounts must have come into being as soon as missions began to be sent to places outside Jerusalem. Some evangelisation would be done by people who were not eye-witnesses, and very few of the new communities can have included eye-witnesses. At the same time the communities kept in touch, by correspondence and otherwise, with Jerusalem. Under these circumstances written accounts must have been unavoidable. We must also suppose that these accounts were subject to checking by persons like Peter and James who were in a position to know if they were substantially accurate or not. Did these persons countenance the insertion of miracles and theologically convenient utterances, the replacement of the original accounts of the resurrection appearances by fictitious but more impressive ones, and so forth? Then we are back at the hypothesis of conscious fraud. Or did the falsifications occur after the eye-witnesses were out of the way? The scholars are notably reluctant to commit themselves on the actual activity of the apostles between 30 and 65, but this seems to be their preferred view. It involves two monstrous improbabilities. First, we must suppose that between 30 and 85 Christians throughout the Mediterranean world lost or suppressed authentic records. Secondly we must suppose that in this period there existed persons who had the theological genius to concoct gospels containing a divine incarnation and redemption, who had the authority to get this theology universally accepted, yet of whom history preserves no trace.

It is this that the sceptic who applies Hume's test must hold to be more likely than that the miracles reported really occurred. I do not say that no reasonable man could take this option; only that it is not obvious or attractive. It is much more attractive to think that the gospels we have grew out of authentic but fragmentary written accounts without substantial falsification – and at an earlier date, the synoptic gospels at least reaching their present form before 70. We have only one real piece of evidence, apart from the evidence of Eusebius, for the origin of the gospels, namely the introduction to Luke:

> Seeing that many others have tried to draw up a narrative of the things that have been brought to fulfilment among us just as those who were originally eye-witnesses and servants of the word handed them on to us, I too have decided, after tracing everything back accurately, to write it down for you, most excellent Theophilus, as a consecutive narrative, in order that you may see the secure basis of the instruction you have received.

This makes perfectly good sense as something written in the early 60s, thirty years after the Crucifixion.

But surely the growth of miraculous legend is a familiar and widespread phenomenon. Is it? One would like to see some other instances, not of a false story gaining currency, for that happens every day, but of a story's being falsified in this particular fashion, by the accretion of miracles. It is often suggested that in the first century AD any tale of the marvellous was greedily swallowed. That is not quite correct. There was plenty of superstition, plenty of readiness to give money for charms and so forth. But we find hardly any belief in the kind of miracles attributed to Christ.

The best evidence is in Tacitus, *Histories* IV.81 (referred to by Hume). The Emperor Vespasian is there indeed reported as curing a blind man and a cripple in the way in which Christ is said to have cured people. It is significant that this story comes from Alexandria in 70. By 70 there is likely to have been a Christian community at Alexandria, and the miracles of Christ will have been spoken of. The episode Tacitus reports is an isolated one, it came as a surprise to the Romans, and it shows what we with hindsight might expect. When the story of Christ's miracles started to circulate we should expect imitations, but the crop of imitations would not be large, because convincing miracles are not easily worked. In this particular case a Christian miracle could have been fathered on Vespasian as a compliment.

Scholars have combed the Rabbinical writings for traces of a flourishing school of Galilean wonder-workers, but the yield has been meagre. Geza Vermes in *Jesus the Jew* (London 1973) offers only one name, Hanina ben Dosa, and Hanina too appears to have been active a generation after the death of Christ. The people from whom Christ's followers were drawn, the orthodox Jews of rural Palestine, seem, in fact, to have been singularly free from superstition and credulity. Hence critics who wish to show that belief in miracles was widespread throughout the Mediterranean world in apostolic times are usually forced to fall back on Lucian's *Philopseudes* (*The Lover of Lies*) and, Philostratus' *Life of Apollonius*. Since Bultmann and others refer to these writings without describing them, it may be worthwhile to say a few words about them.[23]

The *Life of Apollonius* was composed in the early third century, more than a hundred years after Apollonius's death, and it is doubtful how far it is intended as serious biography. However that may be, the idea that it represents Apollonius as a miracle-worker comparable with Christ is inaccurate. In eight lengthy books Philostratus attributes to Apollonius only two deeds which bear some resemblance to New Testament miracles. In IV.20 a demon leaves a youth at his bidding, and in IV.45 he raises to life a girl who is being carried out for burial. The first story is weakened by the information that no one knew the youth was possessed by a demon, and he was supposed to be suffering only from high spirits and drunkenness. As to the second story, Philostratus admits there was a doubt among the witnesses whether the girl was really dead or Apollonius found a flicker of life in her. In VII.38 we read that while in prison he took his leg out of the fetters and then put it back in, but the parallel between this and, say, the miraculous delivery of Peter in *Ac.* 12.6–10 seems to me remote. Philostratus certainly means to portray Apollonius as a supernatural being; but it is not his plan to do this by ascribing to him a series of acts that plainly contravene the laws of nature.

Lucian's dates are c. 125–180. His *Philopseudes* is a dialogue about the taste for tales of the supernatural. It contains a number of lively specimens, but they are probably parodies made up by Lucian, not genuinely current stories he has collected, and while charms, magic and ghosts figure prominently in them, the only thing at all reminiscent of the miracle-narratives in the Gospels is a reference to an exorcist in s. 16. Where diseases are thought to be caused by evil spirits (not such a very irrational belief in a society without microscopes), exorcism is a regular mode of treatment, and one story of exorcism is not evidence of a widespread belief in miracle-working. Lucian must have had some contact with Christians both in Egypt and in Western Europe, and it is noteworthy that he does not represent them as superstitious. He has only two references to them. In his *Alexander* he classes them as atheists along with the Epicureans; in *Peregrinus* he says it is easy to get money out of them.

The older critics held that the Gospels are completely mythical: they tell us nothing true at all about the historical Jesus. More recent critics are sometimes drawn to the idea that the Gospels might be right on certain cardinal points, though encrusted with legendary details. Wolfhart Pannenberg, for example, thinks the Resurrection may really have happened, but the Virgin Birth is a myth; he thinks it true that Christ's body was placed in an identifiable tomb which was later found empty, but false that the risen Christ appeared to anyone in Jerusalem. He is even prepared to believe in two Divine Persons but not three.[24] Some distinguished Roman Catholic scholars take a similar line. Raymond Brown,[25] for example, considers the accounts of Christ's conception and birth in Matthew and Luke to be legends composed because nobody knew when, where or in what circumstances Jesus was born. The accounts of the appearances and ascension of the risen Christ are also, it appears, either pious inventions or at least historically unreliable. But in spite of this it is not irrational to go on believing that Jesus did rise from the dead and that his origins were divine.

Such compromise positions seem to me very difficult to sustain. There are no satisfactory principles of criticism by which we can accept the testimony of the Gospels to one supernatural occurrence but not to another. It is hard to accept that a person has risen from the dead if the only evidence is an empty tomb and nobody has seen him restored to life. To say 'The reports of Christ's conception and birth are fictitious, but he might nevertheless have been conceived without a human father through the intervention of the Holy Spirit' is even more idle than to say *The Pickwick Papers* is a work of fiction but there might nevertheless have been a man named Pickwick who did everything Dickens says'. And in general, if the traditional doctrines are essentially true, if Christ was the Son of God and did rise from the dead, it is strange indeed that in the seminal documents of Christianity the truth should be so heavily overgrown with falsehood and legend.

3

If we decide that the Gospels are truthful records by people in a position to know the truth about the events recorded, it follows that Christ taught more or less what the evangelists say he taught; it does not follow that we can accept this teaching as true. To decide whether it is true (or, some would prefer to say, to decide how literally we should interpret it) we must reach a view on whether, as Strauss puts it, there is any supernaturalism in the person of Christ. That is partly because one thing he appears to teach is precisely that he is somehow unique and supernatural. But the rest of his theological (as distinct from his purely ethical) teaching is such that we might hesitate to take his word for it unless he was something more than a human being.

Christ teaches that God loves men personally and wants them, after they have died, to share eternal life with him. That there is some sort of after-life has been very widely believed, but as Plato observes, we cannot have clear knowledge of this without a divine revelation (*Phaedo* 85 c-d). That God loves all men is hardly apparent even in the Old Testament, and has probably never been believed by anyone outside the Judaeo-Christian tradition. People have thought that there are little tribal or domestic gods who, if they are properly worshipped, support their worshippers, but Aristotle is dubious about the possibility of friendship between persons so unequal as gods and men (*Nicomachean Ethics* VIII 1158^{b}33–6). Theologians who wish to represent the life of Jesus as a non-propositional revelation of divine love must consciously or unconsciously accept as true the propositions in which Christ describes his Father's nature.

How could he have obtained his information? Could thoughts have just, by divine decree, flashed into his mind? Perhaps; but why, then, should he have accepted them? All sorts of thoughts flash into our minds, and we do not accept them all. If God put thoughts (miraculously or non-miraculously) into Jesus' mind and Jesus believed they were true, God must either also have put arguments for them into Jesus' mind or given some sign that it was he who was inspiring them. If Jesus believed the theological doctrines he taught on the basis of rational argument, it is amazing that he did not give the reasoning. What sign, then, might God have provided? How could Jesus be sure which thoughts the sign was attesting, and how could he know that he was really receiving a sign and not just fancying one? The case of Moses, as described in *Exodus* 3, 1–6, is not parallel. According to *Exodus* Moses heard a voice which others could have heard if they had been there, and the divine origin of the voice was attested by the burning bush, something there for anyone to see. In the case of Christ, the only voice involved is that of Christ himself. It is revelations by Christ, not revelations to Christ, that are attested by miraculous signs. Christ never suggests he has received any private revelations of the Mosaic type; he claims to know the truth of what he says directly. The trail ends with him. In the case of Moses, if we believe that there really was a voice and a bush, what remains is to satisfy ourselves that the voice was of divine origin, that whatever produced it knew what it was talking about. In the case of Christ, it is the divine origin of his own voice that needs to be accepted.

How are we to decide? The Christian argument is simple and well known.

(1) Christ claimed to be divine.
(2) Either (a) he was mad, or (b) he was a fraud, or (c) his belief was rational but mistaken, or (d) it was correct.
(3) He was not mad or a fraud, and his belief could not have been rational but mistaken.
(4) Therefore his belief must have been correct; and this conclusion is supported by his miracles, and especially the Resurrection.

In this argument (2) seems to cover all the possibilities. What about (3)? The belief that you are the son of the Duke of Devonshire might be rational but mistaken, for instance if you were brought up as the son of the Duke, but had, in fact, been switched surreptitiously for Lord Hartington as a baby. The belief that you are divine, that, in the Gospel phrase, God is your private or personal father, is of a different character, and on the face of it must be either crazy or correct.

Could Christ, then, have been mad? The suggestion was made in his lifetime (*Mk.* 3.21; *Jn.* 10.20). The evidence against it is the same as the evidence against the supposition that he was a deliberate fraud, and is threefold. In the first place, the account we have of his words and actions shows him, as clearly as any account can show anyone, to have been sane and sincere. Next, his disciples seem to have been ordinary, reasonable men, without any motive or personal inclination to fanaticism. After his death they gave up the rest of their lives to spreading his teaching, and all or most of them were eventually martyred. It is incredible that they should have acted like this if Christ had been either mad or a deliberate fraud. Moreover it is clear that his chief opponents, the leaders of the Jews, did not really think he was mad or fraudulent. They took his claims seriously. Lastly, if he had been either a madman or a fraud, how are we to account for such things as his walking on the water, his transfiguration, his multiplication of the loaves and fishes? Above all, how can we explain his resurrection, except in the way indicated in (4), as a proof that his claim was correct? The only alternative is to suppose it the work of some fraudulent supernatural agent who wished to create the false belief that

Christ was divine. This too was suggested in Christ's lifetime, and his answer was to point to the character of his actions. Even evil spirits would hardly work against themselves; 'Every kingdom divided against itself becomes desolate' (*Mt.* 12.24-5).

In practice there has not been much controversy about the later stages of the argument. Those who reject the conclusion concentrate on (1). Now it is easy, of course, to say that Christ never claimed to be divine if you reject the historical character of the New Testament writings, as most of those who deny that Christ was anything more than a man actually do. Passages in which he seems to be making divine claims are dismissed as late insertions. Some writers, however, also question whether a claim to divinity is in the New Testament as we have it. Let me, then, give the evidence.

The most striking evidence is in the Gospel of John.

(1) *Jn.* 5.17–18. In reply to criticism of his curing people on the Sabbath, 'Jesus said: "My father goes on working right up to the present, and I go on working." On account of that the Jews sought all the more to kill him, in that he not only broke the sabbath but spoke of God as his own, personal father (*idios pater*), thereby making himself equal to God'.

(2) *Jn.* 8.56–8: '"Your father Abraham exulted that he might see my day. He saw it and rejoiced." The Jews then said to him: "You are not yet fifty years old; have you then seen Abraham?" Jesus said to them: "Amen, amen I say to you: before Abraham came to be, I am."' The emphatic use of the words 'I am' or 'I exist' (*ego eimi*), the name the Jews had for God, is reported also at 8.28, 13.19 and 18.5–8.

(3) *Jn.* 10.30–3. Jesus says, 'I and the Father are one.' The Jews understand this as a claim to divinity: 'Although you are a man you make yourself God.'

(4) *Jn.* 17.5: 'Now bestow on me beside you, Father, the glory I had beside you before the universe existed.'

(5) *Jn.* 3.35. John the Baptist seems to be reported as saying:

'The Father loves the Son, and has given everything into his hand.' If these words are really to be attributed to the Baptist, and are not merely a comment by the Evangelist, that Christ stood in a special relation to God was a doctrine being taught early in his ministry.

That the Gospel of John represents Christ not just as in fact supernatural but as making divine claims is admitted even by Strauss. That is one reason why scholars are keen to show it is late and unhistorical. I do not think that view of it can be sustained; but to show that the Synoptics too give Christ divine pretensions, I take some passages from Matthew.

(6) The Synoptics are agreed that it was precisely for claiming to be divine that Christ was condemned by the Jews: 'The High Priest said to him [Jesus]: "I put you on oath by the living God to tell us: are you the Messiah, the son of God?" Jesus says to him: "The words are yours. Moreover I tell you all that you will shortly see the Son of Man seated at the right hand of the Power and coming on the clouds of Heaven." Then the High Priest tore his clothes and said: "He has blasphemed. What need have we now of witnesses? See, you have now heard the blasphemy."' (*Mt.* 26.63–5, *cf. Mk.* 14.61–3, *Lk.* 22.70.) In his reply to the High Priest Christ makes two quotations, both of which he had used earlier, so their significance will not have been missed. The first is from *Ps.* 110: 'The Lord said unto my Lord, Sit thou at my right hand.' This quotation does not merely amount to a claim to be the Messiah; in commenting on it (*Mt.* 22.41–5) Christ had argued that it implies the Messiah is to be more than human. The second quotation is from *Daniel* 7.13: 'One like a son of man came with the clouds of Heaven.' Although in Daniel this figure is interpreted as the body of the faithful, the saints, Christ applies the quotation to himself in speaking to his disciples in *Mt.* 24.30, and so applied, it strongly suggests an individual that is superhuman. The point of these quotations, then, is to make it clear that Christ is claiming

to be more than a human saviour, and that is how the High Priest understood them.

(7) The claim to forgive sins (*Mt.* 9.2–5) was understood as a claim to divine authority.

(8) Christ claims to be greater than the Temple and master of the Sabbath (*Mt.* 12.6–8).

(9) Christ claims special knowledge of God: 'Nobody knows the Son except the Father; neither does anyone know the Father except the Son, and persons to whom the Son is willing to reveal him.' (*Mt.* 11.27.)

(10) Christ accepts the title of Son of God from Peter (*Mt.* 16.16) and, after walking on the water, from the other disciples (*Mt.* 14.33).

(11) Christ claims the position of Judge of the human race (*Mt.* 13.41, 19.28–9).

(12) When children hail Christ as 'the son of David' and the priests and scribes object, he quotes: 'Out of the mouths of babes and sucklings you have filled up your measure of praise.' (*Mt.* 21.16.) The quotation is from *Ps.* 8, the Septuagint version: 'O Lord, our Lord, how amazing is your name in all the earth! Your greatness is lifted up above the heavens. Out of the mouths of babes and sucklings you have filled up your measure of praise.' Since in the original passage the praise is of God, in applying these words to himself Christ claims to be God.

(13) The parable of the wicked husbandmen who killed not only the servants but the son of the owner (*Mt.* 21.33–46) is an adaptation of a famous poem about God and Israel in Isaiah (*Is.* 5.1–7). It implies, therefore, that Christ is not just the servant but the Son of God.

In *Jesus the Jew* Vermes argues at some length that Jesus never thought of himself as the Messiah, much less as someone divine. His argument, however, depends to a large extent on rejecting these passages. 'It is a very tall order' he says 'to expect anyone to accept as historical the dialogues between Jesus and the High Priest and Pilate' (p. 147); the reference to Daniel 'is derivative and can scarcely be ascribed to Jesus himself' (p. 184). *Mt.* 11.27 is to be removed 'from the lips of Christ' and accredited to 'the primitive Church' (p. 201). In the comparable *Mt.* 24.36 where nobody knows the day of judgement 'not even the Son', the 'honorific title "*the* son" is likely to have been introduced precisely in order to counterbalance the disturbing impression left by the saying as a whole' (*ibid.*; one wonders why the redactor who was willing to 'introduce' a non-authentic title did not simply omit the disturbing reference to Christ altogether). At the same time, however, Vermes claims that *Mt.* 16.16 and the parallel *Mk* 8.29, *Lk.* 9.20 report Christ as *rejecting* the title 'messiah, the son of God', and that his reply at the trial is deliberately ambiguous and equivocal between 'yes' and 'no' (p. 149). These are extraordinary interpretations. What is the point of reporting Peter's confession if Christ rejected it? If Christ did not consider himself either the Messiah or the son of God, why be evasive, and if the High Priest thought the answer evasive, why the cry of blasphemy?

Besides the evidence of the Gospels, we should take into account that of the rest of the New Testament. In those of their speeches which are recorded in *Acts* (2.22–36, 3.12–24, 4.8–12, 5.29–32, 13.17–41) Peter and Paul emphasise that Christ is the Messiah and that he rose from the dead, but not that he was the Son of God. A hasty reader might infer that the divinity of Christ was not a doctrine of the first years of Christianity. That is hardly a coherent speculation – we should have to suppose that *Acts* is historically reliable, and the Synoptic Gospels, at least, seem to be earlier than *Acts* – and a simpler explanation is to hand. The speeches reported are all public speeches to non-believers, to Jews and others who as yet know nothing of Christianity. The apostles may have thought it prudent to start with a concept familiar to their hearers, that of a Messiah, and lead them on gradually. The doctrine of the Resurrection was difficult enough; they might get nowhere if in their opening address they tried to explain the Trinity. The case of Stephen, however, suggests that from the earliest time the divinity of Christ was being taught to people who accepted him as the Messiah. Stephen is accused of blaspheming against Moses and against God, but it is difficult to find witnesses to prove it. The alleged blasphemy must have occurred in private instruction to initiates. The blasphemy against God can have consisted only in teaching the divinity of Christ. From the description of the trial it appears that Stephen's calling Christ the Messiah aroused indignation, but did not amount to blasphemy. It is only when Stephen says 'I can see the Heavens open and the Son of Man standing on the right hand of God' that the Jews stop their ears and make a rush at him.

Whatever they may have said in their opening addresses to new audiences, Peter and Paul teach the divinity of Christ in their letters to believing Christians. In view of the doubts recorded by Eusebius (*History* III.xxv.3), the apologist may hesitate to rest much on the reminiscence of the Transfiguration in 2 *Pet.* 1.16–18. 1 *Peter*, however, begins with an invocation to 'God the Father of our Lord Jesus Christ' who 'was known before the creation of the universe' (1 *Pet.* 1.20). The clearest passages in Paul are:

> He existed in the form of God, but he did not consider being equal to God a thing to be clung to; he emptied himself, taking the form of a servant and coming to be in the likeness of men. (*Phil.* 2.6–7)

> He is the image of the unseen God, the first-born of all creation. For in him were created all things in heaven and on earth, seen and unseen, whether thrones, dominations, principalities or powers. All things were created through him and towards him, and he himself exists before everything and all things are constituted in him. (*Col.* 1.15–17; my translation preserves Paul's characteristic but puzzling use of prepositions.)

Some New Testament scholars, partly because of these passages, say that these letters are late and spurious, but that is too facile a way of dealing with evidence which is embarrassing, and the doctrine is implied elsewhere. At *Rom.* 8.3 Paul says: 'God sent his own son in the likeness of sinful flesh'; see also 2 Cor 8.9.

Theologians mostly reckon it 'fundamentalism' to hold that Jesus himself or his immediate followers believed he was divine in an 'ontological' sense. I am not sure what non-ontological ways there are of being divine, but even theologians must concede that if the New Testament documents were historically reliable we should have to grant that Jesus claimed to be ontologically divine, and that being granted, the rest of the argument I sketched at the beginning operates.

It does not, of course, function all on its own. The doctrine of the divinity of Christ is intimately bound up with that of the redemption, and will not be accepted by anyone who cannot believe that God might try to save us by becoming incarnate at a certain time in history, or that the life and death of Christ can be seen as such an attempt. We have to consider the plausibility of Christian theological teaching as a whole. To some people it may, in the end, seem incredible that the author of the universe should empty himself and take the form of a servant. Since this doctrine goes with a view of human nature which is at least partly alien to a good deal of modern thinking, in the next three chapters I shall discuss that. I shall start with considerations which belong entirely to philosophy and move on to the more theological topics of our relationship with God and the possibility of life after death. Only after treating these topics from the standpoint of what I called 'bare monotheism' will I return to questions about Christ.

CHAPTER FIVE
Soul, Good and Evil

I

Christians have a conception of what they sometimes call 'the soul' which is fundamental to their beliefs about sin, salvation and life after death, and which seems alarming or puzzling to non-believers. I shall now try to make this conception clear.

The English word 'soul' is today seldom used outside religious contexts. It therefore appears to carry with it a load of theory. The non-believer may think that a soul is by definition a supernatural, non-physical being, created by God and immortal. If he thinks that is what 'soul' means, he will be inclined to say that there are no such things as souls. But 'soul' is descended from words like *anima* and *psuchē* which are not theory-laden in this way, and which express a notion with which we cannot dispense.

A human being, a man, is just as much a physical body as is a tree, an artifact, or an inanimate natural object like a star. By that I mean that a man has a certain mass, and can be affected by pushing, cutting, burning and other kinds of physical action. Moreover a man has, or consists of, organic parts such as head, trunk and legs; of quantities of material such as flesh and bone; of biochemical or physical constituents such as cells, molecules, atoms. We are composed of such things; so much I take to be uncontroversial. I suggest we define *having a body* as *being* a physical body in this sense. By 'George's body' (where we do not mean George's torso, his corpse, or the corpse he is now dissecting) we mean George himself, considered as a physical body. To describe my body is to describe the physical body I am, or to describe me *as* a physical body, that is, in physical terms. It is as physical bodies that men are causal agents; so to think of me as the causal agent responsible, say, for the squashing of the tomato, is to think of my body.

Besides being physical bodies and causal agents, men are conscious, purposive agents. They have knowledge or beliefs about themselves and other things, and they have desires and aversions. Sometimes a man's causal action is intentional. Sometimes we act on our beliefs, in furtherance of our desires. This too I take to be uncontroversial. I suggest we define *having a soul* as *being* a conscious, purposive agent, a person with beliefs and desires. By 'George's soul' we mean George himself, insofar as he has beliefs and desires and acts intentionally. To describe his soul is to describe the conscious, purposive agent he is, or to describe him as such an agent, that is, in psychological terms. To say 'He knows Greek' or 'He is bad-tempered' or 'He thinks it is snowing and is averse to going out of doors' is to describe someone as a soul or to describe his soul. Men are moral agents, that is, they are morally responsible for some of the changes they bring about. The notion of a moral agent is the notion of a thing with beliefs and desires, whose beliefs and desires are manifested in action. Hence to think of me as morally responsible for the consumption of the whisky is to think of my soul.

The notion of a soul which I have just explained meets all the needs of the Christian believer. In saying his soul is immortal he says that he himself, as a conscious, purposive agent, is immortal. When he says that our souls are more important than our bodies and deserve more care, he means that our moral and intellectual qualities are more important than our physical ones, and that it is better to become a wise and virtuous moral agent than a powerful causal one. When he says that our souls are made in the image of God he means that it is as conscious, purposive agents that we are like God.

The Evangelists, reporting Christ's utterances in Greek, occasionally put into his mouth a Greek word, *psuchē*, which is often translated 'soul'. This word did not have the theological connotations of our 'soul'. Sometimes it was used as a word for life. That is how it seems to be used in some passages in the Gospels, for instance *Mt.* 16.24–6. Greek philosophers, though they were divided on what philosophical account should be given of the human soul or mind, tend to use *psuchē* as if it were a word for a conscious, purposive agent. When they speak of the *psuchē* of a man they do not mean his life, neither do they seem to be referring to a property or attribute of the man, since they attribute properties to the *psuchē*, they seem to be speaking of an *aspect* of a man. Christ is not often made to use *psuchē* in this way, but the sentence 'My *psuchē* is disturbed' (*Jn.* 12.27) is equivalent to 'I am disturbed', or 'I am disturbed in mind', and in *Mt.* 10.28 the body-*psuchē* contrast is a contrast between the physical and the psychological generally. It is like the contrast in 'His body is enfeebled but his mind is as vigorous as ever.'

If the concept of my body is the concept of me as a causal agent, and the concept of my soul is the concept of me as a purposive agent, it may seem obvious that my body and my soul are one and the same thing conceived or described in two ways. Nevertheless the notions of a causal agent and a purposive agent are very different. If we wish to claim that they are indeed notions of a single thing we must explain how a single thing can be conceived in two such different ways. Many philosophers, without disputing what I have said in the preceding paragraphs, maintain that the notion of a human being is the notion of a pair of things. They maintain, in effect, that it is like the notion of a dagger, or even of a married couple. A dagger is a thing which you can hold, and which can penetrate flesh. But it consists of two separable parts, of which one, the handle, is grasped and does not penetrate, while the other, the blade, penetrates and is not normally grasped. The Joneses can properly be said to bear children and obtain money to support them; but it is only Mrs Jones who actually bears the children, and it may be only Mr Jones who actually earns any money.

Plato and Descartes are among philosophers who have held that a human being is a kind of marriage of a soul, which thinks and desires, and a body, which acts causally. Aristotle, in contrast, seems to have wished to sustain the fundamental unity of body and soul. As I understand him, a man is a person with beliefs and desires *composed of* flesh and bones, or *constituted by* arms, legs, sense-organs and so forth. That is the view I favour and it is supported by many orthodox Christian thinkers, but so far as I can see, there is nothing in Christianity to compel a Christian to take either side.[1] What is important is to have a good and clear conception of a conscious, purposive agent. For that purpose it will be useful to assign a strict sense to a couple of words we constantly use informally.[2]

By a 'reason' I mean something that can be introduced into an explanation by 'for the reason that'. The grass may dry *because* the sun is shining, but it does not dry *for the reason that* the sun is shining. On the other hand I might go to the beach for the reason that the sun is shining. What is given as a reason for action or inaction is given as an object of belief. It is given as something the agent knows, or at least thinks, even if wrongly. We can say that it was for the reason that Desdemona loved Cassio that Othello killed her, because though she did not in fact love Cassio, Othello believed she did.

By a 'purpose' I mean what can be introduced into an explanation by words like 'for the purpose of', 'in order that'. The sun shines with the result that plants grow, but not (we think) in order that they may grow. But men build greenhouses, plough fields, uproot weeds, sprinkle water and the rest of it, in order that plants may grow. The notions of desire and aversion are connected with that of purpose. To act in order that your pigs may become fat you must desire – if not as an end in itself, at least as a means to something else – this change in your pigs. If you refrain from drinking lest you become drunk, you must be averse to becoming drunk.

Not only does acting for a purpose involve desire; at least with human beings it is an essential part of desiring an outcome to act (unless there are strong reasons for refraining) to effect it. Desire and aversion must normally be reflected in behaviour. Similarly it is an essential part of believing that something is the case, to have that thing function as a reason. If I really believe at this moment that my sister is in California, if, so to speak, I now judge that proposition to be true and not false, then I must be acting or speaking either for the reason that she is there or (exceptionally) in spite of the fact that she is there.

Many philosophers use 'reason' to cover both beliefs and desires, and say that intentional action is action *caused* by reasons in this broad sense. As I pointed out in Chapter Three, if we say this we must identify beliefs and desires with events in the brain and take a fundamentally physicalist view of man. I would wish to contrast causal explanation with explanation in terms of a reason or a purpose. A causal explanation is intended to bring out the inevitability of the event it explains. An explanation in terms of a reason or a purpose brings out the voluntary character of the behaviour explained, and exhibits it not as inevitable but as intentional. The two sorts of explanation are quite different in kind. Both yield understanding, but seeing the intentional character of a man's action or inaction is a different kind of understanding from seeing the inevitability of a caused occurrence.

The notions of good and evil are closely related to those of desire and aversion. To desire an outcome for its own sake is to think it good, and to be averse to it for its own sake is to think it evil. Philosophers in the Empiricist tradition have tended to think that for something to be good is for it to be somehow a source of pleasure, and for it to be bad is for it to be a source of pain. This position (ethical hedonism) is now recognised to involve severe difficulties. It is better to say that to be good or evil is to be capable of playing a certain explanatory role. An outcome is good if we can understand action as action *in order to* effect it (or inaction as inaction in order not to prevent it), without attributing to the agent any ulterior purpose. An outcome is evil if we can understand behaviour as action or inaction *lest* it should come about, without supposing an ulterior purpose. Other things are called 'good' and 'evil' besides outcomes or changes we can try to effect or prevent; but the goodness and badness of these other things can be seen as derivative. An evil person is one disposed to bring about what is evil or to prevent what is good. Gold is good to possess and wine to drink if action can be understood as being for the purpose of acquiring the one or drinking the other.

2

What things are good and evil? In the first place, for sentient beings like us, certain sensations. The sensations of sex are pleasant; so are certain sensations of warmth and coolness, and some caused by drink and drugs. Unpleasant sensations include pain, nausea, and pangs of hunger and thirst. You can understand my moving from the fire to avoid being scorched, or staying in the sun so as not to lose its warmth, without attributing to me any further purpose.

Next, there is good and evil connected with utility. Most artifacts, such as axes, aeroplanes and houses, are designed to be used for one or more purposes. We also, of course, use parts of our own bodies like hands and eyes; and many natural organisms are useful or have useful parts. If something becomes less useful as a thing of its kind, if an eye becomes blind or a boat ceases to be water-tight, we say it is damaged. Other things being equal, damage is an evil which we want to prevent independently of any immediate need for the useful thing; and the repairing of damage is a good. Something may be described as harmful or dangerous if it is apt to cause pain or damage. That a thing should become more harmful is an evil, and that it should become less is a good.

These kinds of good and evil may be described, in a non-pejorative sense of the term, as 'egocentric'. There are also social goods and evils. We stand to other people in social relationships of various kinds. There are the family relationships of a husband, a parent, a nephew and so forth, and relationships belonging to larger societies like those of doctor, employee, priest. Although some of these, like that of parent or child, are partly definable in causal terms, in all societies they are conceived as carrying duties or obligations and rights. What the duties of a father are may vary from society to society, but it would be a strange society in which the causal relationship of being a begetter did not carry any duty or right. The doing of a social duty, tedious or inconvenient as it may sometimes be, is nevertheless a kind of intrinsic good in that it can be understood as an end in itself. In a society in which parents have a duty to educate their children we can understand a man's acting to make his children educated without attributing to him any ulterior purpose. The question 'Why are you educating your daughter?' is either foolish or rude. Equally where there is a social duty to refrain from some kind of behaviour, say brother-sister incest, that behaviour will count as an intrinsic evil.

Besides these social goods and evils there are certain interpersonal goods and evils connected with friendship and enmity. Social goods, goods connected with utility and goods connected with sensations may all be classed as 'first-level' goods or purposes. What I call 'interpersonal' goods are second-level. If you are my friend, if my disposition towards you is one of what Aquinas calls 'charity' and Polynesians 'concern',[3] that a first-level good should come to you, say that your roof should be repaired, will be a second-level good to me; and that you should experience pain or (where this is a social evil) sleep with your sister is a second-level evil to me. In the case of enemies, to which I shall return below, the opposite obtains: a first-level good to one is a second-level evil to the other and vice versa.

To complete this survey of goods we must note that when an activity is pleasant or enjoyable, engaging in that activity is a good or end in itself independent of (or, as Aristotle puts it, supervening on) any good derived from it.[4] In general any activity which we want to engage in or which looks like yielding one of the first- or second-level goods mentioned earlier may be expected to be enjoyable unless there is some special factor that stops us from enjoying it. Even mending a roof will be pleasant if it is not too laborious or dangerous or if the mender is not in the grip of some pain, grief or anxiety. But there can be factors – good weather is an example – which make an activity more enjoyable than usual; and there are certain types of activity which seem particularly pleasant. These may be brought under two principal (and not mutually exclusive) heads. It is pleasant to exercise a skill, say in playing a game, practising an art or even pursuing academic research; it is also pleasant to pursue second-level goals.

Corresponding to first- and second-level goods or goals are first- and second-level reasons. In general the presence of a source of harm is a first-level reason for action or vigilance to avoid the harm. A cobra in your bedroom is a reason for action to avoid being bitten; sharp rocks just under the surface of the water are a reason for not approaching in your boat. On the other hand the presence of something which is apt to confer a benefit is a reason for action to obtain the benefit. That the flask contains whisky is a reason for taking a swig. These are egocentric reasons; that someone stands in a social relationship to you can constitute a social reason for action or inaction. That I am your grandmother is a reason to you for visiting me in hospital when I have my hip operation.

Some philosophers question whether we can ever, strictly speaking, have a reason for doing something (as distinct from a reason simply for thinking something).[5] It seems to me that it is part of conceiving a relationship to carry a duty to regard it, on occasion, as a reason for discharging that duty; and it is part of conceiving a tiger, say, or a policeman as harmful or useful or beneficial in some way to regard its or his presence, on occasion, as a reason for certain behaviour.

The reasons just described are first-level reasons. But what is a first-level reason to me is a second-level reason to my friends and enemies. The presence of a cobra beside my bed is a reason to me for not getting out that side; it is a reason to my friends for acting lest I should heedlessly get out that side. In this case their action is likely to be verbal: they will say 'Look out, there's a snake by your bed' in order that this reason may actually function as a reason with me – in order that I look out because there is a snake there. In general a first-level reason R to a man A for doing X is a second-level reason to A's friends for doing something else, Y in order that, for the reason R, A may do X.

That sounds complicated when formulated in abstract terms, but I hope that the cobra example shows it happens naturally enough in ordinary life. We even take in our stride the case where *A*'s second-level reason functions as a reason for those who feel concern for him. If I have German measles, that is a first-level reason to your pregnant wife for not visiting me, a second-level reason to you for warning her not to visit me, and a reason to your friends for warning you to warn her not to visit me. We might say it is a third-level reason to them; but in fact I shall call it still 'second-level', and keep the term 'third-level' for a different sort of case to which I shall come in a moment.

But first, two further points about second-level reasons in my broad sense. One is that it seems impossible to be aware of other people as persons, that is, as beings with beliefs and desires, without acting for such reasons. Philosophers sometimes treat the concept of a person as though it were like the concept of a biological species – the concept of a porcupine, for example. They treat the concepts of believing and desiring as similar to concepts of physical processes or activities like gliding and melting; and they think we can apply these concepts to other people in the more or less idle and cold-blooded way in which we can say to ourselves at the zoo: 'That animal is a porcupine', 'That bird's beak is yellow'. Certainly we can *say* 'George is a person', 'George wants to go to London' in a spirit of idle indifference. But if what I said earlier about belief and desire is correct, *thinking* that George has a desire or belief (and hence thinking of him as a person) involves some understanding of his behaviour. Is this understanding compatible with complete indifference? It is notoriously difficult to give the content of a thought like 'Othello's action is killing Desdemona is for the reason that she loves Cassio'. Expressions like 'for the reason that' 'for the purpose of' do not have meaning, or their meaning cannot be explained, in the same way as expressions like 'to the left of'. I suggest that what makes it true to say 'Iago thinks Othello's action is for the reason that Desdemona loves Cassio' is that Iago is acting in order that Othello may act for this reason (or may not find out that she is not unfaithful).

That brings me to my second point. If it is only in acting for second-level reasons that we understand the behaviour of other people, and it is only in understanding (or trying to understand) their behaviour that we are conscious of other people as persons at all, we may suggest that acting for second-level reasons and purposes has a preeminent place among human goods. For we seem to be so constituted that interpersonal relationships are essential to our well-being. The pleasures of exercising artistic or theoretical skills are not, I think, independent of the pleasures of sympathetic understanding of other people. A man may say he would like to go off by himself and paint or study. But artists and scientists do not really live alone. Besides friends, relatives and servants they have colleagues, rivals and publics. The people who come closest to a life without human contacts have been religious persons who have hoped that by living apart from men they might get closer to God.

If someone thinks he could be happy painting or studying independently of interpersonal relationships he probably imagines himself at least as being conscious of these activities. I shall now contend that our consciousness of ourselves and our activities depends on our being conscious of other persons.

Many philosophers have thought that we are conscious of ourselves and of our own mental states by introspection.[6] Introspection they conceive on the model of seeing and hearing: they think it is using a kind of internal sense. Taking this view Descartes believed that we could form ideas of ourselves as persons without thinking of anyone else as a person, and I suspect that this view is still deeply rooted in modern Western thinking. It is the metaphysical basis of the political theory of individualism, according to which society is viewed as an aggregate of individuals, each of whom can exist and lead a satisfactory life more or less independently of all the rest.

Other philosophers reject the conception of an internal sense as ultimately incoherent, and I agree with them. Apart from anything else, the mental state of being aware of something cannot itself be an object of awareness of the same general kind. If we think of others as persons in thinking of circumstances and outcomes as reasons and purposes to them, we must think of ourselves as persons in the same way. We must be aware of ourselves as persons in understanding our behaviour; and that must mean being personally involved with ourselves. But how is that possible? I do not think we could take an interest in ourselves as persons if we had not first taken an interest in someone else.

I suggest we first apply the notion of a person to other people. We think of them as acting for first- or second-level reasons. We notice that sometimes in acting for second-level reasons they are thinking of *us* as persons. They want us to be aware of certain circumstances and act accordingly. Bit-by-bit I derive from other people an idea of the person they would wish me to be, a conception of the things they would like me to desire or be averse to and of the things they would like to have functioning with me as reasons. Most of us derive this conception primarily and chiefly from our parents. And having seen what sort of person others want me to be, I decide whether to be such a person or not.

'Do not swim in the bay' say my parents. 'It contains sharks.' I am aware of the sharks, then, as things they want me to be aware of, and to be aware of as reasons for not swimming. I have to decide not just whether or not to swim but whether to swim despite the sharks or abstain from swimming because of them. My eventual action or inaction will have the purpose not just of escaping harm or experiencing the pleasant sensations of swimming, but of behaving in a certain way and being a certain sort of person. It is insofar as I act for these sophisticated purposes that I am conscious of my thought and aware of myself as a purposive agent. And whereas a circumstance is a second-level reason when I act in order that someone else may act because of it, we may say it functions as a third-level reason when I act in order that I myself may act because of it (or in spite of it). The sunshine is a third-level reason to me for going out if I not only go out because it is sunny but think this a good and sufficient reason for going out and go out because the person who takes advantage of the sun is the sort of person I want to be.

This kind of awareness of ourselves and understanding of our behaviour is perfectly familiar to us in practice, and I shall suggest it is the key to several Christian beliefs that many people today find puzzling. Unfortunately it has been largely ignored or misunderstood by philosophers. Perhaps I may recapitulate five crucial points they dispute or overlook.

(1) Understanding human action is grasping its reason and purpose. This is completely different from causal understanding.
(2) The notions of belief and desire are explanatory: to think that a person has a certain belief or desire is to think his behaviour is for a certain reason or purpose.
(3) Being aware of someone else as a person is inseparable from having it as an aim to benefit or harm that person.
(4) Thinking of oneself as a person presupposes thinking of others as persons; we get our ideas of ourselves as persons from others.
(5) Thinking of oneself as a person involves acting in order to be a particular kind of purposive agent.

Acting for third-level reasons is, in general, pleasant. We all want to be aware of our own existence and to understand our behaviour. But I doubt if third-level action is an objective separable from second-level action, since I doubt if awareness of ourselves can ever be wholly separated from awareness of other people. I derive my idea of myself from others. When I decide whether or not to be the kind of person they want me to be, on what principles do I decide? How can I grade types of agent or sets of practical principles? I cannot say 'These principles suit *my* requirements; this type of agent satisfies *my* ideals.' For at this stage I do not yet have any concept of myself; one might say that there is not yet a properly constituted me to have requirements or ideals. No doubt if I have already accepted some principles I can judge that others harmonise or conflict with them. But what chiefly motivates us, I suggest, to be or not to be the persons others want us to be is love or hatred of those others. If we at first accept the practical principles of our parents, that is largely out of a desire to please them. It is not necessary, every time we act for a third-level reason, to have in mind some particular person we want to please or spite. But if over a period of time I did not think that my actions or predicaments were of any interest to any other person, human or divine, I doubt if I could retain a grip of my own identity.

3

Some people reject the idea that we can do evil altogether. They think that though we can do harm, it is not our own fault; it is always the consequence of being disadvantaged in some way or of sickness, provocation or stress. This view really does away with moral responsibility completely, since if we cannot be responsible for pernicious actions we cannot be responsible for good ones either. Other people, and it is this more moderate view I want to criticise, agree we can behave appallingly, but think that so long as this does not involve any physical changes in us, it does not involve any real change. We remain the same people, and we can always make a fresh start. If I treat my wife with cruelty and my children with injustice, *they* may be injured, but it is pie in the sky to suppose that *I* sustain any genuine damage.

This position is a kind of combination of physicalism and Christianity. On the physicalist side people think that physical changes and states are the only real ones, or at least that there can be no real change in a person without a physical change. On the Christian side they think that we should be endlessly forgiving, that we should never write anyone off, that people can redeem themselves at the last moment. These are certainly Christian thoughts, but they do not touch the question at issue, which is not whether the bad effects of evil-doing are remediable, but whether they are real in the first place. It may be that if an evil man repents and wants to behave well, he is as capable of doing so as someone who has never done wrong. But Christians add that if we behave badly enough we cannot repent without God's help. Evil destroys the capacity to want to do right. Unless this is accepted, the Christian account of salvation from sin will seem nonsense.

That evil-doing imparts a taint to the personality which we cannot easily purge away is not an idea peculiar to Christianity. It is taken for granted by the Jews of the Old Testament and by the ancient Greeks and Romans; perhaps only where Christianity is influential has it been seriously questioned. But what is its basis?

We think of ourselves as behaving badly chiefly in interpersonal relations: in harming others or omitting to benefit them. Failure through cowardice to help friends in danger would come under the second heading; so would failure through love of luxury or miserliness to help the destitute. Omissions of this kind are often contemptible but it is not easy to show that they are damaging to the agent. The first kind of bad behaviour may start with selfishness. It is selfish to do what is beneficial to yourself in spite of its being injurious to others. The word 'selfishness' suggests minor offences. But grave harm has been done in the past by landlords who selfishly deprived families of their homes in order to make more profitable use of the land or in order to have better hunting or shooting; and between married people a common form of selfishness which often inflicts deep wounds is having adulterous love affairs.

When selfish behaviour involves doing a serious injury to another person, it is usually necessary to deceive the other person or to render him or her unable to resist; it is necessary, in other words, to act precisely in order that the other person may not do what he or she has reason to do. If acting in order that someone else may act for reasons is friendly, acting in order that the other person should not so act is inimical. Whereas merely selfish behaviour is often inconsiderate, the agent hardly thinking of the persons affected as persons at all, inimical behaviour involves thinking of your victim precisely as a conscious, purposive agent. Lingering at the public house although your wife is lonely at home is acting in spite of second-level reasons, but hitting her or lying about your pay-rise is acting *for* second-level reasons, though in what may accurately be called a perverse way. It is because the blow is painful that you inflict it, because the pay-rise makes it reasonable for her to ask for more house-keeping money that you deny you have had it.

The disposition to act like this towards someone is what we call 'hatred'. Hatred tends to spread itself, and to spread itself in two ways. We hate those whom we have hurt, and it seems inconsistent to act in order to harm a person in one way and in order to benefit the same person in another. A youth enters an old woman's home to steal, and finding her there, he clubs her about the head in order to prevent her from summoning help; besides taking any cash he can find, he may well smash her china and foul her carpet. Secondly, if I hate you I will tend to hate your friends, and I will want my own friends to hate you and them.

Besides growing in this way, hatred involves cruelty. Whereas acting in spite of factors which make your action likely to cause pain or distress is merely callous, acting because of them is cruel. Cruelty spreads with hatred. If I am cruel to one person I will be cruel to others, and my cruelty is likely to infect those who associate with me.

I think it may be held that hatred and cruelty really do have a deleterious effect on us, not as first-level but as second- and third-level agents. Mervyn Peake's study in his Titus Groan trilogy of the deterioration of Steerpike's character unconsciously but convincingly illustrates this point. At a certain stage in his criminal career, after, in fact, his murder of his immediate master Barquentine, Steerpike undergoes or finishes undergoing a change (see especially *Gormenghast* Ch. 42). He is not conscious of the change, and his intellectual powers seem unimpaired. Something in him, however, has perished, and it is no longer possible for him unaided – the reader may feel that no natural power could now enable him – to become a normal human being again. Steerpike, of course, is a fictional character. Peake, however, had some experience of the Nazi extermination camps. It is wholly credible that the people who over a stretch of years gladly conducted atrocities in these camps, or in the camps of Solzhenitsyn's Gulag, were affected in a similar way. No Englishman of good education, we like to think, would behave like that. But education is no guarantee against being a malignant and vindictive spouse. Or take the bureaucrat who competes with a colleague not by open rivalry but by a long campaign of undermining the colleague's alliances, running down the colleague behind his back, setting traps in order that he may appear incompetent, depriving him of vital information at the crucial time and so on: will this specimen of civilisation emerge from the campaign totally unscathed?

But how is it possible to be changed by what we do? In any situation in which an agent can behave well or badly there are likely to be both reasons for and reasons against any course of action he seriously considers. Calypso offers Odysseus immortality but he is married to Penelope; my aunt is in hospital but my friend wants me to play golf. As a result of our choices in a series of situations where similar factors are at work we become disposed to attach more weight to some sorts of reason than to others. This is what it is to become a person, that is, a rational agent, of a certain type. People differ as persons when the same circumstances weigh differently with them. Everyone would agree that Amanda's being charming and affectionate is a reason for making love to her, and her being married to a friend is a reason for not making love to her. If to you the first reason outweighs the second and to me the second outweighs the first we differ as persons. In ordinary talk we might be said to differ in personality or character;[7] but these words 'character' and 'personality' express a person's nature, not as a living organism, but precisely as an agent for prudential, social and second-level reasons. We are born apt to avoid some sensations and seek others; but our abilities to act for social and second-level reasons depend both on our having concepts which are not innate – concepts of social relationships, of utility for all sorts of purposes etc., – and on being able to decide between conflicting reasons and act in spite of some because of others. As children we act in problematic situations under the guidance of others or more or less at random; to act of oneself, one has to develop into an agent of a certain sort.

Inimical or malignant action affects one's character. It also introduces a kind of incoherence into one's practical life. The father who hates his son lavishes money on his daughter although she does not need it because his son does. This cannot easily form part of a consistent programme of behaviour. While trying to injure his own son the malignant father still presumably, wants his friends to keep on good terms with their children. Hence his personality as a purposive agent is to some extent split. The damage is greatest to him when he acts in full consciousness as a third-level agent, that is, when he acts in order to be a person of a certain kind. It is a frightening decision to do something because it will cause harm in order to be a person to whom the fact that a deed will cause harm is a reason for doing it. I said that we recognise that our friends have ideas about the sort of persons they want us to be, and we accept or reject these ideas. Our friends do not as a rule want us to be malignant. Hence a deliberate choice of malignant action generally involves a certain rejection of one's friends. But the agent's position is particularly grave if (what is sometimes the case) the person he wants to injure wishes him well. In that case to injure that person he must try to destroy himself as a purposive agent.

A disposition of hatred towards someone is a bad state of character in that it divides the hater as an agent and in its worst form turns him against himself. In the long run it is also deleterious to the intellect. In the first place it confuses our sense of the practical significance of things. That cobras have a venomous bite is not always a way in which they are harmful; it is a way in which they are useful against enemies. This point cannot, perhaps, be pressed very far, but I think that in proportion as we hate people our vision of the world must lose that gem-like clarity which characterises the descriptions of Homer and the paintings of Fra Angelico.

Next, we saw that for an agent to have a certain character is for him to have certain principles for balancing pros and cons which guide his judgement of how it is best to act in situations where it is possible to behave well or badly. When a situation involves an enemy hatred will, of course, affect the agent's practical judgement. It might be better not to make love to the wife of a friend, but it is a good thing to seduce the wife of an enemy. In the long term hatred can hardly fail to distort a person's practical principles. No doubt bad principles also produce hatred, since they lead us to injure people; but the fact remains that hatred tends to dull or distort our moral perception, and make us genuinely unable to see that certain kinds of behaviour or particular actions are bad.

Thirdly, I said that we are really able to think that other people have beliefs and desires only insofar as we act to benefit or harm them. It is unpleasant and difficult to attribute innocent or benevolent thoughts to those we are harming; hatred inclines us to think they are selfish, malignant or stupid. Since they may in fact be none of these things, it makes us unable to understand them. It generates a cynical stupidity as regards other people which is disgusting or (when combined with power) frightening. And what of the hater's idea of himself? My grasp of my identity as a person, my assurance that it is *I* who have these beliefs and purposes, is rooted in my understanding and approval of my own behaviour. Actions inspired by hatred become increasingly compulsive and unintelligible to the agent, and his identity disintegrates.

If evil-doing leads to hatred and cruelty, and these things spread and injure the evil-doer as a rational agent, the next question is: how far can they be remedied by resources men have naturally at their disposal?

It is regrettably clear in practice that whereas friendship takes a long time to ripen and always remains a little precarious, enmity breaks out easily and is hard to extinguish.[8] Friends drift apart, enemies do not drift together. Vendettas are passed down like family jewels. It is true that hatred does come to an end sometimes. One of the two parties may admit to being in the wrong, ask for forgiveness and receive it, or a third party may effect a reconciliation. But this goes much against the grain. Everyone feels shame at admitting to being in the wrong. Nor is forgiveness a universal ideal: many people consider revenge a duty. Where that belief prevails, disinterested peace-makers may be few.

It is easy to say 'Of course if men become enemies they can

cease to be enemies'. This first law of pneumatodynamics, however, has long been suspect. Just as a young plant is more plastic than a mature tree so when we are young we can, up to a point, choose what sort of people we should like to become and try to become like that; but once we have become people of a certain kind it is hard to change. Bad behaviour is often described as a lapse or fall. The reason is obvious: it is easy to fall from a height, but it may be difficult or impossible to get back up again.

CHAPTER SIX

The Soul and God

I

The Christian view of sin may be summarised in two theses: that evil-doing has lasting bad effects on the doer's personality, and that it injures or displeases God. The first thesis is primarily philosophical, and was defended in the last chapter. The second is theological, and will be discussed here. We may start by trying to get a clearer view of how we are related to God. In Chapter Three I suggested that God creates living things in that those processes which occur for the benefit of particular organisms and which thereby mark off those organisms from the rest of the physical universe, also occur because God so desires and in order that such individual purposive agents may exist. It is now possible to develop this suggestion by comparing God's creative action with human action for second- and third-level reasons.

The resemblance to second-level action is clear. The parent is aware of the fire as a source of harm to the child, and wants the child not only not to be harmed but to move and abstain from moving in order to avoid harm. The parent's first desire is that the child should exist as an agent for first-level reasons. That is how God must be supposed to stand to all living creatures.

Our simplest second-level action is linguistic. We say 'fire', 'hot' or 'food' 'good', trying to make reasons for action known to the person concerned. Can God's creative action be regarded as linguistic, as a kind of speech? Those movements of an organism which are to obtain a benefit or to avoid a harm are correlatable in their parts and qualities with the object of pursuit or avoidance. When a lizard stalks and pounces to catch an insect, its movements are like a living representation, like a translation into bodily behaviour, of the insect as a reason for appetitive action. I suggest that insofar as these movements occur because God wants them to, they may be viewed as a speaking of God to the lizard, as God's making the lizard aware of the insect.

The obvious objection is that the lizard must first be aware of the insect before it can stalk it. But what is it for a lizard to be aware of an insect? The insect must affect its sense-organs before it starts to pursue, but having its sense-organs affected is only a condition of being aware. In general, awareness of a reason for action is neither temporally nor logically prior to desire and some kind of response. Perception and volition are not cause and effect but rather two aspects of behaviour which in itself is simple. With men, between seeing something attractive and grabbing for it a period of deliberating and refraining from grabbing can intervene; the lizard's awareness of the insect must surely be confined to the time of actual pursuit.

It will be remembered that Hume complains because God makes things painful. We need not say that God decides that water at one temperature will give pleasant sensations and at another pain. Rather he decides what things he will make a given organism aware of. The organism can be aware of things only as reasons for action; insofar as something is a reason for evasive or preventive action and the organism is made aware of it by and in such action, it is a source of pain. How could my awareness of the bathwater in hurriedly and violently withdrawing myself from it be other than painful?

But though God's creative action resembles our second-level action in some ways, it differs in others. A small point is that we are usually aware of reasons to other people through perception. God has no sense-organs; hence he can be aware of reasons for action to us only as we are aware of those reasons to others which consist in our own voluntary movements – as when we say 'Look out, I'm coming'.

A much more important difference is that when I make your reasons and purposes my own, though I identify myself with you as a purposive agent, I remain distinct from you as a causal agent. Not being a causal agent at all, God cannot be distinct as a causal agent from the living organism he creates. The causal action for which he is responsible is that of the organism. It is for this reason that we say that God acts in us.

Further differences flow from this. When I act in order that you may act, I may fail. My action – telling you, for example, that petrol is stored here – is separate from the action I want from you, extinguishing your cigarette. God's action, at least at this stage, cannot miscarry. The causal action for which he is responsible is identical with the action by the organism which he desires. The movements which occur in a parcel of material in order that that parcel may constitute a living lizard are the very movements the lizard makes in pouncing and fleeing.

Finally, when I act in order that you may act, I have to assume that you already exist as a purposive agent. God's action is creative of such agents. He does not make reasons his own which are already reasons for action to us; he decides what shall be reasons to us, and in acting in us it could be said that he himself animates us.

Where God's action differs from our action at the second level it resembles our action at the third. When you not only know that the sun is shining but know that you know this, and judge that the sunshine is an adequate reason for basking (either because you have no duties elsewhere or in spite of the fact that you have such duties); when you make this first-level reason your third-level reason and act in order to be a person who acts because of it, you are not separate from yourself as a causal agent. The action for which you are morally responsible is identical with the basking you desire from yourself. Above all, you are creatively responsible for your existence as a person to whom such sunshine is a reason for such action: you animate yourself.

Up to now I have been considering God's responsibility for our existence as first-level agents. He must be supposed to create us as second-level agents also, and in the same way. When a mother acts in order that her infant may act, her action also occurs because God wants it to occur and in order that the mother may exist as a second-level agent, aware of her infant as a person. It is possible to view her actions and her talk to the infant as a kind of linguistic act by God to make her aware of its existence as a purposive agent. She does not have to be aware of it as a living person before acting, any more than the lizard has to be aware of the insect as prey before stalking it. On the contrary, it looks as if the mother actually shares with God creative responsibility for the existence of the infant as a person, and makes it a person by treating it as one.

What of third-level action? I have just said that when you act for a third-level reason you are yourself creatively responsible for your existence as a person. You are responsible for your movements both insofar as they are for lower level purposes and insofar as they are in order that you may exist as an agent with these purposes. To that extent you take over responsibility from God. But God can still be responsible for your becoming conscious of yourself in the first place. I suggested that we first become conscious of ourselves as purposive agents through recognising that other people think we are persons and act in order that we may act. We understand that they want us to be agents of this or that kind, and we act to gratify this desire. Such action is a new departure. It is not ordinary second-level action, the purpose of which is to make other people act. We may suppose that it occurs not by chance but because God wants it to occur, and in order that we may exist, not just as purposive agents, but as agents conscious of ourselves. Insofar as our third-level action is for this purpose, initially at least it is rather God's responsibility than ours. Initially, because we can come to act in order to be conscious of ourselves; for one thing we can recognise that other people want us to be not only rational and purposive but self-aware.

If what I have been saying is right, among the people who are aware of us as persons and who want us to act for reasons is God. Of these people, in fact, God is incomparably the most important. Is it possible for men to come to know this? Can they not only know with moral certainty that God wants them to exist as conscious, purposive agents, but act to gratify this desire? In the ordinary way of things, that seems quite impossible. We can know about other people only by sense-perception. Since God is not a material object he cannot be perceived, and we cannot, therefore, know what, if anything, he wants of us. Christians maintain, however, that the ordinary way of things has been superseded by God's becoming incarnate in Christ. Through Christ's words and actions God reveals what he wants us to be, and through Christ we act to be this.

2

If we are related to God in the way I have just tried to describe, evil-doing is bound to offend God in at least two ways.

First, and most obviously, we injure God in a way in which children often injure their parents. A child can injure its parents without wounding or robbing them, without, you might say, affecting them as causal agents. It makes them unhappy by making itself unhappy. If God wants us to avoid pain, to have the satisfaction of fruitful activity, and above all to enjoy close personal relations with other people, if God originally created the universe and now acts in us for these purposes, a man injures God by leading a life which is worthless and ruinous to his health, and still more by coming to be on terms of hatred with other people.

There is a further parallel with parents and children. Although the activities of childhood have a certain charm, we are so constructed that we cannot remain children for ever. We grow up; and childlike behaviour in an adult is no longer charming. Moreover an adult is not a decayed child; a child is an immature adult. It follows that we cannot enjoy childhood properly without engaging readily in those activities of learning, assuming responsibility in small matters and so on which are a preparation for adult life. Children particularly distress their parents by rejecting these activities and clinging to childishness. Now Christ teaches that there is a life after death, and Christians believe – the comparison goes back to Paul, to 1 *Cor.* 13.11 – that human life as we know it here is a mere preliminary to this, standing to it as childhood to adult life. There are activities which prepare us for the after-life. These include, besides second-level action generally, religious acts of prayer, worship and meditation. If we neglect these activities, and still more if we do what will render us incapable of an after-life, our behaviour is bound to be distressing to God. (To complete the parallel it should be noted that as the children who prepare themselves best for adult life are not necessarily those who give most thought to it – much thought in childhood to money-making, sexual life and the rest can be stunting – so those who prepare themselves best for the after-life need not be the most conspicuous for religious observance.)

Someone might object that God's happiness ought to be so complete that nothing can ruffle it. Surely it is absurd to imagine God made unhappy by the actions of men. Against this, it seems vacuous to say that God loves us or wants us to be happy if he is not distressed by our making ourselves miserable.[1] The solution, a Christian may say, lies in Christ. God is distressed, but in the person of Christ. The measure of his horror at how we injure ourselves is that he sent his son to us in the form of a human being, and it was part of Christ's redemptive work to experience all the suffering human evil causes to a person who has unlimited love for all men.

I shall return to this suggestion later. Meanwhile there is a further and quite different way in which our evil-doing may be expected to offend God. God is responsible for physical processes generally, and for purposive action insofar as we are not responsible for it. If I drop a rock on my enemy, it falls because God wants it to fall. The strength and continued existence of my limbs, insofar as they depend on purely physical factors, depend on God. I therefore involve God in my crime; I make him my instrument in it.[2] Even when we act with deliberate malignance, our symbiosis with God remains. We merely use his physical action to act in the way contrary to that in which he would have inspired us to act if we had not taken over moral responsibility. If God continues to act in us when we do evil, and we are turning this action of his against his purposes, we should not quarrel with those Old Testament writers who speak of his awareness of our evil-doing not as distress but as anger.

3

Even if in sinning we injure God, it does not follow that we do so intentionally or even knowingly; and if someone does injure God intentionally, if he forms a hatred of God or Christ and acts in order to spite him, it is not clear that he thereby draws down on himself punishments beyond the natural consequences of his acts, from which he can be saved only by divine assistance. Does a Christian have to believe this?

Christians certainly believe that death is not the end for wicked men; after death they will be brought back to life to be judged. This is taught explicitly by Christ in *Mt.* 25, and professed by Paul in *Ac.* 24.15. Christ also teaches that the fate after death of evil-doers will be dire. In *Mt.* 25.41 he says he will say to them:

> Go away from me, accursed ones, to the eternal fire which has been got ready for the Devil and his angels.

The same message is conveyed in a series of parables, *Mt.* 13.50, 22.12–14, 24.51, 25.30, and is implied in a number of passages including *Mt.* 18.8–9, 23.33, *Jn.* 5.29. But what exactly is the fate? In *Mt.* 25.46 Christ is given the phrase 'eternal punishment'. In some of the passages just mentioned he speaks of a consuming fire, in others of exterior darkness. The talk of fire (echoed in *Rev.* 20.14–15) would be compatible with the idea that the wicked are rather obliterated than preserved in endless suffering, and *Jn.* 5.29, where we are told that the good will rise to life and the bad to judgement, suggests that eternal life will be reserved for the good. It would have to be reserved for the good if, as Paul regularly seems to imply, eternal life is a sharing in the life of Christ. In the parable of Dives and Lazarus (*Lk.* 16.19–31) the wicked are undergoing punishment after death in spite not only of a desire to be with God but of desire to benefit other men. The intention of this parable, however, is not to inform us about the details of life after death – Christ is simply using popular conceptions – but to introduce a message to the Jews about their present conduct: 'If they do not listen to

Moses and the prophets, they will not be convinced even if someone rises from the dead.' The parable of the unforgiving debtor in *Mt.* 18 suggests (verse 34), if it suggests anything at all, that bad men after death will undergo a finite period of purgation.

Because of this obscurity about the fate of the wicked, I do not think it would involve rejecting any fundamental Christian belief to hold that a person who dies hating God will eventually be blotted out. Anyone who disagrees will have to say how being blotted out and eternal misery differ. That will not be too easy. God's existence is non-temporal, and so, up to a point, must be the existence after death of men; a life of eternal happiness cannot be construed as a life of infinite duration. In 2 *Thess.* 1.9 the wicked are said to suffer 'eternal *olethron* from the face of Christ'. The Greek word *olethron* could be translated either 'ruin' or 'death', 'ceasing to be'; once the notion of time is removed, the difference between these translations becomes negligible.

Most Christians, nevertheless, think that the wicked will not be annihilated. There is less consensus about whether they can expect any punishment beyond the natural consequences of their actions. The early Christian writers seem less bloodthirsty in this respect than some of their successors. Irenaeus is not untypical and writes, in my opinion, with good sense:

> To those who keep friendship with God he will give communion (*koinōnia*) with himself. Communion with God is life and light and enjoyment of good things from him. To those who defect from God in their minds he gives their separation from him. Separation from God is death, and separation from light is darkness. Separation from God is a casting away of all the good things from him. It is by their defection, then, that they cast these things away, and being deprived of everything good they come to experience every punishment. God does not take the lead in punishing them; this punishment follows through their being deprived of all good things. Eternal and endless are the good things of God, and on that account the lack of them is eternal and without end: just as light is perpetual, and does not bring blindness, but those who have blinded themselves or been blinded by others are perpetually

deprived of the enjoyment of light. (*Against Heresies* V. xxvii. 2; PG 7. 1196–7.)

It might be thought that the language of Christ's warnings is too frightening to fit an after-life in which bad men experience merely the automatic consequences of their misdeeds. But in considering what those consequences would be, we must take into account the theological aspect of evil-doing. In the usual course of life a non-believer will not be aware of God, and when he does a bad act he will not know he is acting against God. If, however, it is true that God will judge everyone after death, that surely means that everyone will come to recognise his dependence on God and God's love for him. At that point the former non-believer will have either to accept God or to hate him. We may suppose that which he does will depend on how he has behaved towards other men, especially as God acts in and through other men. If he has loved other men, he will love God when he recognises him directly, and if he has hated other men, the persons he has hated and tried to harm will turn out to be so many masks God was wearing.

I argued that even hatred of a single other man is a serious evil. Hatred of God is a total calamity. It will involve systematic hatred of all God's creatures, at least insofar as they have turned out as planned. A person who hates God must hate the whole of inanimate nature and all people who love God. To such a person, consciousness of God's happiness and that of good men will be intolerable. He will wish, therefore, to remove himself as far as possible from them. There is no need to imagine God excluding sinners from Heaven; rather we should imagine him permitting them to escape at least some way from his presence.

A person who hates, wishes to injure the object of his hatred. The only way in which a man could injure God in an existence after death would be by harming himself. He would try to make himself miserable or to destroy himself, whichever would be most distressing to his creator. There is hardly any scope left then, for divine punishment. The evil-doer will want to inflict a kind of self-punishment. Since pain is an intrinsic evil to men, if it is possible to feel pain after death he will try to feel it.

It may be objected that this is not what Christ says in the Gospels. He does not say that sinners will condemn themselves or punish themselves, but that he will condemn them and hand them over to fire or darkness. The obvious reply is that Christ's aim is to warn us. Not much of a warning would have got through if he had told his hearers that they would get themselves into a state to prefer eternal misery to eternal happiness, since they would neither have understood him nor believed him.

But if a man does reach the stage of wanting to make himself wholly miserable, surely a truly merciful God would blot him out? This merciful God might if he was an Englishman. We count it a virtue to kill our faithful old dogs and horses as soon as we judge that their lives have become unpleasant. But what if God is an Italian? The Romans seem to think it wrong to kill even the starving cats that sun themselves on the ruins in their city.

Some Christians have believed that not only do unregenerate sinners undergo punishment after death, but the task of punishing them is entrusted to evil spirits. This belief does not seem to be in the New Testament. Perhaps the nearest approaches to it are in 1 *Cor.* 5.4–5 and 1 *Tim.* 1.19 where Paul speaks of handing people over to Satan to correct them. Paul seems, however, to be speaking figuratively, and if the passages are taken literally they do not attest the belief in question. The handing over is by Paul, not by God, and the punishment is not eternal but is supposed to be the saving of the people who are punished. 2 *Pet.* 2.4 and *Jude* 6 have fallen angels detained in dark storage-pits till the Last Judgement, and a belief in evil non-human persons runs pretty well through the New Testament (see *Jn.* 12.31, *Eph.* 2.2, etc.) but the notion of a Hell run by demons seems not to be there.

But is not the belief in demons by itself absurd enough? These demons are supposed to be, like us, created but, like God, non-material. I do not wish to enter here into whether the notion of such beings is coherent. It is hard to deny, however, that there are evil human beings. These certainly want to harm others. They like to cause pain and loss. But the greatest harm we can do our enemies is to make them become evil and malignant. Iago was well inspired in trying to make Othello hate Desdemona. The Greek word *diabolos* which we translate 'devil' literally means one who enjoys poisoning relations between friends. If an evil person knows about God he will try above all to poison other persons' relations with God. This, rather than punishment, is the main activity of Biblical demons (*Gen.* 3.1–5, *Job.* 1.8–12, *Mt.* 4.1–11, etc.)

The argument of this chapter and the last may be summarised as follows. If we leave God out of consideration evil actions still have lasting bad effects since they gradually fill us with hatred, and this is destructive of our personality and cannot easily be removed. But the Christian belief that the effects of sin are absolutely appalling rests on theological ideas: that God loves us and acts in us, that evil actions make us hate God, and that there is an after-life. If Christianity is true we not only have opportunities, but also stand in perils, of which non-believers are ignorant.

4

The *Genesis* account of creation is immediately followed by the story of Adam and Eve and the Fall of Man (2.5–3.24). This is no more conceived as history than the preceding section is conceived as astrophysics; it presents in narrative form reflections on the nature of man as a moral agent. But it has provided the basis for the Christian doctrine of what is called 'original sin'.

The first human beings, it is held, did evil, and thereby separated not only themselves but all their descendants from God. They made it impossible for men to get to Heaven, and according to some speculations caused life on earth to become much more unpleasant.[3] Those who have passed beyond treating the *Genesis* account as a rival to Darwin's in *The Descent of Man* may ask two questions. First, could human history really have got off to a better start? Secondly, is it not monstrously unfair that we should suffer for the misdeeds of our remotest ancestors?

As to the first question, the viciousness of human beings is quite surprising. The more we learn about other species the more exceptional our own appears. Wolves and chimpanzees seem to manage their affairs far better than we.[4] If an observer from Mars had visited the Earth just before men evolved he would have expected a very different species. It is not, therefore wholly unreasonable to think that the natural order must have been disturbed by an appalling moral catastrophe.

How could such a catastrophe have been avoided? When human beings first reflected on their behaviour and became aware of their reasons for acting, they must have had to decide what is a good reason and what a bad, and how, on balance, they ought to act. The *Genesis* story of eating the forbidden fruit of the Tree of the Knowledge of Good and Evil has suggested to some readers that the first men chose to follow their own judgement and set up their own system of values in defiance of God. But how could they have done otherwise? How could they have known what system God favoured? They could hardly wait for him to become incarnate and tell them.

Perhaps we can obtain a hint from the fact that the *Genesis* account of the Fall is carefully juxtaposed to a passage which emphasises the importance of marriage. The story of the formation of Adam and Eve (2.5–24) is not intended to suggest that human beings were made differently from animals; it is intended to lead up to the conclusion that a man has a closer relation to his wife than to any other material thing:

> On that account a man will leave father and mother and be united with his wife, and the two will be one flesh. (2.34.)[5]

Perhaps the first human beings should have acquired the essential knowledge through loving and acting to please one another. If they were in a state of innocence God will in fact have been acting in them and making them desire what was good and right for each other. On this view they went wrong through failing in love for one another. In Adam as portrayed we find first an uncritical compliance and then a willingness to sacrifice Eve when things got difficult.

'Natural faults' it may be said; 'a reasonable creator would have anticipated them.' But that is the point at issue. The traditional doctrine is that they were not natural. It is hard for us now to imagine someone without them, but Christians hold that Christ was conceived without original sin, and that means that his nature as a human person was unfallen. Christ was not compliant or unfaithful to his friends. His character had a force and beauty which even at this length of time from his death can inspire love strong enough to carry people though heroic conduct. A society where everyone was like Christ would have had a chance to develop as God wished; and the corruption of such a society would have been an unimaginable disaster.

On the consequences of the first sins the account in *Genesis* (unlike some later accounts) is largely naturalistic. Adam and Eve are not deprived of conditions of life or faculties very superior to ours. Neither need Christians say that human beings were rendered incapable of entering upon a happy existence after death. Whether or not they might have become capable of such an existence without any kind of Incarnation,[6] being material objects they can hardly have been naturally capable of it. But the idea that the sins of the first men affect us is deeply rooted in Christian thought.

> Through one man sin entered the universe, and through sin, death, and in this way death has come to all men, since all have sinned ... If by the fall of one man death came through that one to rule, all the more those who receive the abundance of grace and the gift of goodness will reign in life through the one person Jesus Christ. (*Rom.* 5.12–17.)

Underlying such passages is the idea that God views the human race as a unity. Painful as it may be to our individualism, the idea is well founded. Not only are we, from a biological standpoint social animals; I have argued that our intellectual life depends heavily on language and interpersonal relations.

It is a consequence of this that sin and corruption can be inherited. Goodness and badness of character are not physical properties and so cannot be transmitted via the genetic code. But ideas, institutions and customs are necessarily transmitted in societies and with more certainty than anything Mendelian. At the most elementary level we depend on our predecessors for our ideas of what a person is. I think it may also be held that as individuals acquire virtues and vices in the course of their lives, so do societies.

Conversely it is on the unity of the human race that salvation, in Christian thinking, depends. Not only is Christ the second Adam but eternal life is sharing in God's life. If we are all to share in the life of the same individual, God, we must look forward to being rather parts of an organism than members of a collection.

CHAPTER SEVEN
Life after Death

I

That death is not the end of us, that there is an after-life, is an integral part of Christian belief. Following Schleiermacher, Christian spokesmen today sometimes lay more stress on being united with God in this life – and that, perhaps, is of more immediate practical concern. Still, to the ordinary person the question whether there is a life after death seems not irrelevant to the planning of life now. Paul speaks for such ordinary people in a famous passage at the end of his first letter to the Corinthians:

> Since the message is that Christ has been raised from the dead, how are some of you saying that there is no resurrection of the dead? If there is no resurrection of the dead, then neither has Christ been raised. If Christ has not been raised, empty is our message and empty your belief. And we are found to be false witnesses about God ... If Christ has not been raised, vain is your faith, you are still in your sins; yes, and those who have fallen asleep in Christ are lost. If our hope in Christ is to have been for this life only we are the most pitiful of all men. (1 *Cor.* 15.12–19.)

Let us first look at the origins and basis of this belief.

The Jews seem to have been unusual in not having a long tradition of belief in a life after death. The earliest clear testimony to such an idea is in the mid-second century BC, when Judas Maccabaeus offer sacrifice for some recently dead Jews 'that they might be released from sin'. The historian comments: 'If he had not expected those who had fallen to rise again, it would have been superfluous and foolish to pray for the dead.' (2 *Mac.* 12.44–5.)

The belief at that time seems (see 2 *Mac.* 7) to have been in a bodily resurrection at least for the virtuous. *Daniel* 12.2–3 attests a belief of the same kind, and *Wisdom* 3–5 a belief in an after-life of some sort, not necessarily a bodily one:

> The souls of the just are in God's hand, and torment will not touch them. In the eyes of the foolish they seemed to be dead ... but they are at peace. (*Wis.* 3.1–3.)

Josephus (*Jewish War* II 154, 163) says that among the Jews a life after death was accepted by the Pharisees and Essenes but not the Sadducees.

Christian belief in an after-life is based primarily on the resurrection of Christ. That can be seen from Paul's words to the Corinthians and is obvious. The best possible proof that death is not the end would be someone's returning from the dead, and that is what we have in the Resurrection. The Resurrection established both that there is an after-life and that it can be bodily. Indeed, our ideas about the bodily aspect of it are based almost entirely on what the Gospels tell us about the risen body of Christ.

The most explicit recorded statement by Christ on the subject of life after death is probably this:

> The children of this era marry and are given in marriage. Those who are judged worthy to achieve that era and the resurrection from the dead neither marry nor are given in marriage. For they are no longer capable of dying. They are angel-like, and are sons of God, being sons of the resurrection. That the dead are raised is made clear by Moses in the passage about the bush, when he calls the Lord the God of Abraham and the God of Isaac and the God of Jacob. He is the God not of the dead but of the living; for to him all men are alive. (*Lk.* 20.34–9, *cf. Mt.* 22.29–32, *Mk.* 12.24–7.)

What Christ says definitely here is that there is an after-life at least for the virtuous; and he does not imply it has to be bodily in the way conceived by the seven brothers of 2 *Mac.* 7, since no bodily resurrection of Abraham, Isaac or Jacob has yet occurred.

The reference to the *Exodus* passage deserves some comment. Nineteenth-century German scholarship would not allow the Pentateuch to give us any information at all about the early history of the Jews; Abraham, Isaac and Jacob were wholly legendary figures. In 1929 Albrecht Alt proposed a more modest view which commends itself to many modern scholars: Abraham, Isaac and Jacob could have been real persons who had religious experiences, but they had three separate gods who belonged to separate ethnic groups and who were fused only in the twelfth century or thereabouts.[1] What should the Christian make of Christ's apparent acceptance of the Pentateuch account of the patriarchs as factually true? In *Jesus, God and Man* R. E. Brown refers to other passages to show that Jesus' scriptural knowledge, like his knowledge of biology and astro-physics, was no greater than that of his contemporaries. In the present passage, however, Christ does appear to be speaking with an authority that should rest on supernatural knowledge. The quotation from *Exodus* is not an argument for personal immortality; rather it tells us what the scriptural words mean to God. There is a still stronger implication of special knowledge in the reference to Abraham at *Jn.* 8.56–7 (quoted earlier). It is fortunate, then, that there are no compelling reasons to think the patriarchs legendary, and if they existed, they might just as well be interrelated as independent. Alt's theory was an ingenious surmise with no real basis beyond the Biblical text we have.

Besides the statement just discussed the Gospels record several other sayings of Christ which relate to life after death. His words on the cross to the repentant thief, 'This day you will be with me in Paradise' (*Lk.* 23.43) suggest a life which immediately follows death and does not have to wait upon an end of the universe as we know it now or a bodily resurrection. Christ often contrasts a life of suffering here with another life of unending happiness (*Jn.* 15.18–16.4, 21.18, *Mt.* 19.28–9, etc.) On several occasions, e.g. *Mt.* 13.41, 25.31–46, he speaks of what is clearly a judgement of the dead: a general judgement of all human beings at an undisclosed time in the future which will terminate 'this era'.

The later writings of the New Testament give us some idea of how this teaching was understood by the apostles. *Hebrews* 6.1–2 describes the resurrection of the dead as one of the 'foundations' of Christian teaching. The general resurrection was conceived as part of a remaking of the whole universe. Paul in *Rom.* 8.22 says: 'We know that up to now the whole universe has been groaning together in the pangs of giving birth.' 2 *Pet.* 3.14 looks forward to 'a new heaven and a new earth', a prospect which inspires the vision of the new Jerusalem in *Rev.* 21. The apostles, however, do not think they have to wait for the general resurrection for their lives after death to begin. In 2 *Cor* 5.8 Paul says we 'want to be exiled from the body and settled with the Lord'; similarly *Phil.* 1.23. The Apocalypse envisages martyrs and saints in Heaven before the end of the world.

The traditional belief of Christians, then, is that after death the virtuous will enter upon an unending life with God, and that in due course the whole material universe will be renewed and they will regain bodies. This belief rests primarily on the fact of Christ's resurrection, a fact the evidence for which we discussed in Chapter Four, and on the New Testament teaching just reviewed. It does not rest on philosophical arguments of the kind offered by Plato and Descartes.

Christian opinion is divided on whether arguments like those could ever prove that we shall or even can survive death. Aquinas offers two arguments which show, he claims, that life after death is possible. One is based on the fact that men desire to survive: it would be unwise and unkind of God to make men with this desire if it could not be fulfilled. The other is taken from a very obscure chapter in Aristotle's treatise *On Soul*, and purports to show that the concept of a thinker is from the start the concept of something nonmaterial or independent of any body. These arguments have not found universal acceptance. Many Christians who accept the immortality of the soul as an article of faith find the second argument, as an argument, unconvincing. It seems to me that Aristotle can prove only (what is clear to us from modern science fiction) that there is no particular kind of body a thinker needs; he fails to prove that a thinker could exist without a body at all. Moreover there is a risk, as Aquinas himself is aware, that if the argument succeeded it might prove too much, and destroy the unity of body and soul. As to the first point, it might be argued that the desire which all men have, and perhaps must have to retain a grasp of their identity as persons, is for a further period of temporal existence; whereas the existence we are promised after death should be mainly timeless.[2]

In view of the weakness of the proofs offered, many Christians follow Duns Scotus in holding that the possibility of an after-life is, in fact, unprovable.[3] But if Christians cannot prove that such a life is possible, they ought to be able to refute attempts to prove it is impossible; can they do this?

2

The best argument against the possibility of life after death is old and obvious. Our life now, even as conscious, purposive agents, depends on our bodies. Without limbs we cannot act, without sense-organs we cannot become aware of reasons for action, and without brains we cannot remember or understand anything. The proof is that damage to the brain impairs or totally destroys our ability to think and decide. If our mental life is suspended when we are badly battered, it is absurd to suppose it will start up again after we have passed through the crematorium.

I shall consider this argument later. First, however, I should like to examine a different argument which has been advanced more recently, and which some philosophers judge to be a clincher.[4] This turns on considerations about identity, and may be stated as follows. If Queen Anne has continued to exist since dying in 1714, there must now be a bodiless person who is the same person as the English Queen living in 1710, and as some bodiless person existing in 1800. But the identity of a person depends on the identity of his body. The man now courting my daughter in London is the same person as the man who stole my watch in Cairo ten years ago if and only if he has the same body – if the body of the London wooer is the same body as the body of the Cairo thief. That being so, the English Queen of 1710 cannot be the same person as any bodiless person now enjoying the beatific vision of God; and *a fortiori* a bodily person existing now cannot be identical with a bodiless person existing in 1800. In fact a bodiless person does not have enough identity to have thoughts assigned to him or her at all. A thought about roast goose in 1710 can be attributed to Queen Anne, and a thought about Sir John Vanburgh to the Duchess of Marlborough, because the first is correlated with a process in the Queen's head, and the second with a process in that of the Duchess. But there could be no basis for assigning thoughts to one bodiless person rather than another.

Those who argue in this way in fact hold two distinct theses about identity: (i) Bodies are prior to persons for purposes of identification on any particular occasion. To count the people in a room you must count the bodies, and *this* person has to be identified as the person with, or constituted by, *this* body; (ii) The identity of a person over a period of time depends on a certain kind of spatio-temporal continuity. A man identified in Cairo in 1970 is identical with a man identified in London in 1980 if there is a similar man at intervening places at intervening times, and these places and times make up a series which is continuous in the mathematician's sense of that word: the series is continuous like the series of real numbers or at least the series of rational fractions. These two theses are independent. We could accept that this person is the person with this body, but deny that the identity of a body over a period of time consists in spatio-temporal continuity. Conversely we could accept that identity consists in spatio-temporal continuity, but deny that bodies are prior to persons for purposes of identification. Either thesis, however, makes it hard to see how there could be a bodiless person, so I shall consider both.

The first seems to rest on a confusion about bodies. When

someone says 'Persons are identified by their bodies' or 'A person's identity depends on the identity of his body' we may ask him what he means by 'a person's body'. Outside theoretical discussions like this one, by 'my body' I should usually mean a certain part of my body, namely the trunk or torso; but thesis (i) does not concern torsoes. A medical student might mean 'the corpse I am dissecting', but nobody supposes that a medical student derives his identity from the corpse he dissects. The word 'body' can be used as a variant for 'material object'. In that sense, the planet Mars is a body and so am I. But when we use 'body' in this sense we do not say 'my body' or 'his body'. Moreover the notion of a body in this sense is useless for purposes of identification. We cannot just count the physical bodies in a region of space. What counts as one body must first have been counted as one planet or one man or one molecule. The notion of a physical body is in fact the notion of an aspect of a thing. A man or a planet is a body *considered as a massive causal agent*. A thing cannot be considered as a causal agent unless it has first been identified as something else. In philosophical discussions, as I explained in Chapter Five (s.1) 'a person's body' is best taken to mean 'a person considered as a physical body'. It is quite incoherent to say: 'A person derives his identity from himself considered as a physical body.'

Against this objection that the notion of a person's body which the argument depends on is confused, someone might say this. When Queen Anne dies, we are left with her body. Her corpse is surely the same body as her body when she was alive. So we have a coherent concept of a person's body which covers both the body of a living person and the body of a dead one. This reply merely involves a further confusion. 'The Queen's body' does not mean the same in 'The Queen's body is enfeebled, but her mind is as vigorous as ever' and in 'The Queen's body will lie in state for two days before being buried'. The genitive has a different meaning. In the first sentence, the phrase means, as I have said, 'The Queen in her physical aspect'. In the second sentence the genitive expresses that from which. The Queen's body is the corpse she has passed away into, or the corpse that has come into existence at her death. It is like the genitive in 'The ashes of my house', or, for that matter 'The Queen's ashes'. The Queen's ashes are the ashes into which her corpse has turned, or, if we are speaking of Dido, into which she as a living organism has turned.

We have no concept of a body which will permit us to say that this man is the man with this body, and the same man is the man with the same body. On the contrary, it is fairly obvious that the notion of a person is primary for purposes of identification and reidentification. The man wooing my daughter is the same material object as the man who stole my watch if he is the same person. The body you tripped over last night is the same body as the one you are now hauling out of the way if it is the body of the same drunkard. My hands are the hands which form part of me; that is why we call them mine instead of giving them names of their own and calling me theirs.

The second thesis is that for an object, whether a person or anything else, identified at one place and time to be identical with an object identified at another, is for a continuous series of intervening places to be occupied by similar objects at intervening times. This is a highly unattractive account. If identity over time is to reduce to these place-occupyings, each must be logically independent of all the rest, and if the series is to be truly continuous, there must be infinitely many of them. So we have to suppose there can be an actual infinite, a supposition criticised earlier, in Chapter Two (s.2). Moreover the place-occupiers will each have only an instantaneous existence. They will not therefore, be human beings, which necessarily exist for longer than an instant. So a man dissolves into a lot of momentary hominids, rather as a rainbow is dissolved by scientists into a lot of raindrops.

Advocates of thesis (ii) may be influenced by the thought that to get from Cairo to here by physical means I must pass through a continuous series of intervening places. But passing through them does not make me identical with the person here now. At most it makes me *be here* now. These passings-through do not account for my identity with the present occupant of this place; at best they account for my occupation of it, for my present place. A parallel may make that clearer. In order to become drunk you may have to drink a bottle of whisky. Your drinking, however, does not make you identical with one of the drunken men in the world; it simply makes you drunk. It accounts for your intoxication, not for your identity with any particular intoxicatee.

These considerations suggest not merely that spatio-temporal continuity does not constitute identity over time, but that nothing does. Nothing can make me identical with the person you met thirty years ago in Bombay, in the way in which begetting a child makes me a father or losing my hair makes me bald. I just am the same person or I just am not. Identity and difference are brute facts. But even if there is nothing which is what it is to be identical with the person identified in Bombay thirty years ago, is a continuous spatio-temporal existence a necessary condition of identity?

There is room for debate about that. If my watch is resolved into its component wheels and screws, and they are scattered for a time but later reassembled, we should probably say they were reassembled into the same watch and not into a new one like it; but we could hardly say that the watch existed throughout the interval. If a living organism could be resolved into its atoms, and those atoms reassembled (as in the film *The Fly*) we might say we had the same organism, though its existence was discontinuous. Existence for a person is a kind of life consisting in purposive activity, but our purposive activity at present is discontinuous.

The important question, however, is not whether our existence has to be continuous but whether it has to be temporal. We saw that a non-material person must be non-temporal, so if our existence must be temporal it follows at once that we cannot exist without bodies. A material object can exist only temporally, and I take it we are material now. Bernard Williams suggests that anything which is material is essentially material, and attributes to some believers in an after-life the view that being material is essential to us at some stages in our existence but not others.[5] Since a thing's essential properties are those it cannot lose without ceasing to exist, this view is self-contradictory. I grant that it is essential to human beings to start as material objects, but that is not to say that when we start we are essentially material. Williams might agree that it is essential to us to start as babies, but an infant human being is only temporarily, not essentially, a baby. Christians maintain that we can cease to be material without ceasing to exist. Williams offers no formal argument against this position. If it is correct, the question how dead people preserve their identities through time does not arise. They can be related to the temporal sequence of events only as God is.

To ask, in fact, how bodiless persons can be identical with corporeal persons living earlier is to ignore the way in which Christians actually think about the dead. Hamlet may ask, 'Is this ghost identical with my dead father?' but the ghost is visible and audible, a kind of causal agent. Dead persons normally come into Christian thinking not as causal agents but as moral agents or as beneficiaries. 'The person for whom I am offering this prayer is my dead father', says the Roman Catholic, or 'The person thanks to whose intercession my daughter has abandoned her life of crime is St Theresa'. (And he need not conceive the intercession on the model of communication between living organisms by making sounds: words like 'intercede' are used to indicate that the dead friend is responsible not alone but in union with God.) This way of thinking may involve other problems, but I do not think it founders on difficulties about identity.

3

I now return to the serious difficulties in the idea of a life after death. These are well stated by Hume:[6]

> When any two objects are so closely connected that all alterations which we have seen in the one are attended with proportional alterations in the other; we ought to conclude, by all rules of analogy, that when there are still greater alterations produced in the former, and it is totally dissolved, there follows a total dissolution of the latter. Sleep, a very small effect on the body, is attended

with a temporary extinction, at least a great confusion, in the soul. The weakness of the body and that of the mind in infancy are exactly proportioned; their vigour in manhood, their sympathetic disorder in sickness, their common gradual decay in old age. The step further seem unavoidable; their common dissolution in death. The last symptoms which the mind discovers are disorder, weakness, insensibility and stupidity; the forerunners of its annihilation. The further progress of the same causes increasing, the same effects totally extinguish it.

This argument cannot hope to decide the issue at a single blow. Suppose I am a first-class typist: it would be wrong to think I have lost my expertise just because my type-writer gradually wears out, and the documents I type become increasingly uneven and hard to read. Neither is it clear that my skill is impaired if my fingers become gouty or arthritic with the same result. It is possible to see senile dementia as a wholesale extension of this case. Those who have had a friend become demented can have the sense that although the shutters open, so to speak, more and more rarely, when they do their friend can still be glimpsed intact behind them.

There is a further weakness to the Humean argument. Hume asks us, in effect, how we can have thoughts and desires without a body. I do not think we can be forced to reply 'We can't' until we have been provided with a convincing account of how we can have them with a body. No amount of detail about our cerebral hardware will answer this question because neurons, brain circuits and so forth can explain only how one thing causes another, and what we need to be shown is how a purely causal story can capture what we might describe as the peculiar thinkiness of thought.

The problem here is well known to philosophers of mind. We are tempted to conceive thinking as the appearing of pictures or the coming into being of structures of some kind. But pictures, structures and their coming into being are objects of awareness, and what we wish to understand is being aware. We exercise thought in using things intelligently; so it seems that we should have ideas both of the things we use and of our using of them; but if someone does not know how to use an instrument we do not give him a further instrument to use it with, and it is vain to seek an idea of using which will be like our ideas of things we use.

Until these problems in the philosophy of mind are solved, the Humean argument cannot go through. We should admit, however, that it is extremely threatening. I think we should admit, in fact, that in the ordinary course of nature it would be quite impossible for us to continue to exist after death and when our bodies have been destroyed. If, despite that, we can survive, that must be through some altogether extraordinary action by God. Rather than pin his hopes on a dualistic account of man which makes the soul belong all along to the supernatural order, the Christian will be well advised to connect the doctrine of personal immortality quite closely with that of the Incarnation.

We come into being as material objects, members of the animal kingdom. If we are to exist after our bodies have perished, it follows that we must become separate from them; with, a Christian will insist, God's aid, we must separate ourselves from them. It is not too hard to see how we might make a start.

As persons we are the beneficiaries of our behaviour. Action for first-level reasons is beneficial to us as persons with bodies. It is only because we have bodies that we experience pleasant and painful sensations; it is only because we have bodies that we are causal agents, and can be benefited by enhancements of our causal powers. But the benefit to us of second-level action is independent of our having bodies. It is fairly obvious that I am not benefited as a material object or as a causal agent by your experiencing pleasant sensations or having your car repaired; but the point is even clearer in more complicated cases. If my sister is quarrelling with her husband I act not just in order that she may stay with him and do what is useful to him, but in order that she may stay voluntarily and do what is useful out of affection. But the difference between doing something voluntarily, and doing the same thing but not voluntarily, is not itself a physical difference. There may be physical differences in the two cases, but they are not relevant to the explanation of my action. Since there is no physical feature which differentiates what I am aiming at from what I am not, my objective cannot benefit me as a material object. Its benefit to me is independent of my having a body.

In second-level action, then, we benefit ourselves as persons without benefiting ourselves as causal agents. Hence we may be said to separate ourselves as persons from ourselves as causal agents. The same thing may be said on a slightly different ground. In second-level action I make another person's reasons and purposes my own. I therein identify myself with him as a purposive agent. But I remain separate from him as a causal agent. So again I separate myself as a person from myself as a body.

In third-level action we do not have a separate causal agent in the way we have in second-level action. The purposive causal action we desire is our own. Nevertheless we still separate ourselves as persons from ourselves as causal agents. For the benefit to us of third-level action is self-awareness and understanding of our behaviour, which is something distinct from the first- or second-level purpose we approve and act deliberately to achieve. In third-level action, moreover, there is a new factor. We have creative responsibility for ourselves as persons, whereas we do not have creative responsibility for ourselves as causal agents. I fix my nature as a person by my choice. If I want to change my nature as a causal agent I must do physical exercises or apply myself to acquiring new forms of know-how – and even then I shall not change my nature very much. A third-level agent, then, not only separates himself as a person from himself as a body, but acquires some responsibility for his existence as a person.

These considerations take us only a certain way. A philosophical judgement on whether we can exist without bodies must rest on a theory of how we exist as persons with bodies. I have suggested that physicalist accounts shed no light on this at all, and that existence as a person should be analysed in the first instance as acting (and refraining from acting) for reasons and purposes. Christians explain our acting in this way by saying that God is acting in us. They also say we can become aware of this. We can know that God wants us to act for certain first- second- and third-level reasons, and accept existence as persons from him. This acceptance is not like accepting medical treatment; it is not a matter of letting existence trickle into us like a saline drip. Rather, it is third-level action to please God. Once our existence as the sort of conscious agents he wants us to be is our own purpose we are completely identified with God acting in us.

I suggest that at this stage our relationship to our bodies changes from the Aristotelian to the Platonic. We still rely on our sense-organs for information about the world and on our limbs for action in it; but as the persons we have become, we may be said to act through our bodies. We have made ourselves separate from them as God is separate from them. If God, then, is capable of separate existence, so should we be.

The difficulty is to see what a separate existence for us could consist in. Sceptics who do not want to seem to have too easy a task, or who want to give believers a run for their money, commonly suppose it would be like a dream: it would consist in experiences just like our ordinary experiences of seeing and hearing things, except that they would not, of course, depend on physiological processes. I doubt if an existence like this is even a logical possibility. Although the concept of a non-physical sense-experience has played a large part in philosophy since the time of Descartes, it may well be incoherent. Even if a life of the kind imagined is possible it is not what Christians either want or look forward to; it would be exceedingly boring and futile.

Christians sometimes describe life after death as consisting in a blissful vision of God. But there are difficulties here too. The vision must be conceived as engaging our cognitive and desiderative faculties: we must conceive it as a kind of mental activity, and on the model of our present awareness of persons and things. In the first place – and this is probably the greatest difficulty in the whole idea of a life after death – thinking and wanting have been explained as aspects of what, in another aspect, is physical causal action: we believe things and desire things in acting for reasons and purposes. *Ex hypothesi* a bodiless person cannot act causally; how, then, can a bodiless person have mental activity?

Secondly, the people and things we are aware of now are perceptible whereas God is non-material. How can we be aware of him? We can, of course, form mental images of gods in human form, but even if bodiless persons could have mental imagery, that would not be direct contemplation of an atemporal creator.

At present our knowledge of God is not, in fact, primarily knowledge of him as creator of the physical universe; rather, we know him as the person who wants us to act for certain reasons. These reasons relate chiefly to other human beings. We are to please God by acting to benefit them, and sometimes by acting to be the persons they want us to be. (In particular, as will be seen later, we should try to accommodate ourselves to the wishes of our spouses, parents and children.) The vision of God after death ought not to be unrelated to this present conception of him. Indeed, it ought not to be separate from a vision of other human beings; we should see God in them even if we also see him apart from them.

The difficulties, then, are that our cognitive powers seem to be ordered only to a vision of human beings, and do not seem to be exercisable independently of corporal action. I suggest that the beginning of an answer might be as follows. Here and now I can act not only to be the person God wants me to be, but in order that you may be the person he wants you to be. I can speak to you or act towards you directly with this end in view. But I can also pray for you. What is this praying supposed to achieve? I am hardly asking God to love you more than he would otherwise or to do things for you he would not otherwise do. If in acting to be the person he wants me to be I identify myself with him acting in me, is it impossible that in praying for you I identify myself with him acting in you? I suggest that part of the idea of praying for others is that we can thereby cooperate with God in animating those others.

But what use is that? Surely God by himself is sufficient; what can we add? Nothing if human beings are completely separate atoms. But if the human race is, at least in principle, a kind of unity, then the life of one part should intermingle with that of others.

If when we are alive we can act with God in other people it becomes possible to suggest we could do the same when dead. In point of fact Christians pray to the dead to help them to love God. As I said a moment ago, though we speak of dead people as interceding with God the intercession cannot be conceived as similar to pleading with an ordinary human being, since that involves physical action. The best view to take is that the dead can act with God in us. We sometimes try to be the people our ancestors or dead friends would like us to be; in these endeavours we think of the dead as actually existing, and our thought will gain in coherence if we believe that they can help us to become or remain as they would wish. If living and dead both exist through some kind of sharing in God's existence, and if God gives us existence not just as individuals but as members of a collectivity, the dead and the living should not be, so to speak, insulated from one another.

This line of speculation is finely spun, and by itself we might be reluctant to trust to it. Christians, however, can support it with at least three further considerations. First, they do not have to oscillate between thinking of God as an atemporal creator and thinking of him as glimpsable through or behind human beings. God is supposed to have become incarnate in Christ. Thereby he comes within our powers of apprehension and it is not unintelligible to speak of seeing him face to face.

Secondly, the process of separating ourselves from our bodies does not have to take place in a wholly private and unobservable fashion. It does not have to be all a business of purely mental acts – if, indeed, such acts are possible for us. Christians may hold that Christ has arranged for the process to engage our whole nature as material objects and social organisms by instituting a visible society, the Church, and bodily acts, the Sacraments. Equipped with these institutions Christians can think, not in the abstract terms I have been employing, but in terms of being adopted as children of God and receiving the divine Spirit.

Above all, whether death is the end is not, for orthodox believers, an open question: that there is a life after death is proved by the resurrection of Christ. And Christ is not just a random sample of the human race who happens to have been seen surviving death. He is our friend and leader. Christians do not have to think of death as a leap into unexplored darkness: Christ is there, as many pictures show, ready to catch us and lift us up.

In Christian thinking the doctrine of the immortality of the soul is not separate from the doctrines of the Incarnation and the Redemption. I shall be discussing these in the next two chapters. Before ending this chapter, however, I should like to say something about the doctrine of the resurrection of the body.

4

That there will be a resurrection of the body, that at the end of the present order of things the virtuous at least will again have bodies, has been a central belief of Christians from the earliest times. It comes into the oldest professions of faith. But why should there be this bodily resurrection if a man does not depend on his body for his identity, and if, as Christians believe, existence without a body is possible for us?[7] Two reasons suggest themselves.

First, we start our existence as material objects. While we are alive we have the limitations which have been mentioned earlier: we are aware of reasons for action only if our sense-organs and brains are affected in a corresponding manner; we are morally responsible only for changes which we effect, or could prevent, as causal agents; and our characters and technical expertise are built up over time. Even if we do not have to stay subject to these limitations to preserve our personal identity, a capacity for causal action, and perhaps also a capacity for pleasurable sense-experience, belong to our nature. To be without them is to have lost something. For our condition to be perfect they would have to be restored; there would have to be some scope for productive or artistic activity and aesthetic satisfaction.

Secondly, I have suggested that even a bodiless existence for men would have to involve knowledge of other men. Our dependence on one another as conscious, purposive agents is surely an extension and development of our dependence on one another as living organisms, as animals that mate together and rear their young. Even if God makes it possible for dead persons without bodies to know about living men and help them, that social existence which belongs to our nature seems to call for bodies. We can reasonably wish that in a future life we should be able to enjoy each other's company as causal agents.

In the light of this, how should the restoration of our bodies be conceived? We need not suppose that the body a person gets back will consist of the same particles as the body he now has. The body he has now does not consist of the same particles as the body he had ten years ago. Bodies derive their identity not from the particles of which they are composed but from the persons whose bodies they are. Paul in 1 *Cor.* 15 clearly understands a risen body as not consisting even of the same kind of materials as the bodies we have now.

Perhaps our speculations on this topic should be guided by the Gospel accounts of the risen Christ. Among the points we may take from the Gospels are these. First, Christ is able to act causally: he produces sounds, he can be seen and felt, he cooks and eats. If, of course, he had not been able to act causally he could not have been said to have a body at all, since the notion of a body is precisely the notion of a causal agent.

Secondly, it is only to a limited extent that other things appear able to act on Christ. He is not excluded by locked doors, or pained or impeded by wounds. If it is correct to say that he saw and heard the disciples, they must have affected his sense-organs, but perhaps a person with a risen body is affected by causal action only insofar as he wants to be.

Next, the appearances of Christ are separated by intervals of time and space. It is not implied that he existed as a material object during intervening times or at intervening places. I expressed doubt earlier about whether it is necessary in general for our existence to be spatio-temporally continuous. Perhaps a person with a risen body exists only at times and places at which he wants to exist. Some Christians have speculated that if Christ has recovered his body he must now be bodily located somewhere in the universe. I think it neither convenient nor necessary to suppose this.

To these points we may add that New Testament writers conceive the resurrection of the dead not as an isolated phenomenon but as part of a renewal of the whole universe. There will be 'new heavens and a new earth' (2 *Pet.* 3.13, *cf. Rom.* 8. 18–23, *Rev.* 21.1). If these are to last for ever, like the risen human bodies they must be immune to destructive action and to some extent independent of time. It is possible to make a further conjecture. If risen persons are affected only so far as they choose to be affected and exist only when and where they choose, they have some responsibility for their existence not only as persons but as bodies; perhaps they could have a similar responsibility for the whole of the reconstituted universe.

That would be possible without chaos, of course, only if they cooperate, only if they form a kind of society for the management of the universe. Christians believe, however, that those who are redeemed do form a political society with Christ at the head, and Paul represents the government of the universe as being transferred to Christ. As the Son of God who always existed he shared in the original creation of the universe (*Col.* 1.15–16); but as the man who has died and risen he receives the universe from God the Father (*Phil.* 2.9–11); the ultimate plan being that 'all things, both in the heavens and on earth, should be placed under the headship of Christ' (*Eph.* 1.10).

CHAPTER EIGHT
The Incarnation

I

On the one hand we tend to destroy ourselves as persons by crime and hatred; on the other it is not impossible for us to transcend the limitations of physical, time-bound existence and achieve eternal happiness. Unless we accept these points the traditional Christian doctrine of salvation is nonsense; but it does not follow that as soon as we accept them it becomes plausible.

Many thinkers today seem to have real difficulty in taking seriously the idea that God should become man. The sources of the difficulty are seldom spelt out and the sceptics may not themselves understand what they are, but they must be either a feeling that God would not want to become a man or a feeling that he would not be able to. If we think that God would not want to be incarnated that must be because we think that human beings are low class, and the author of the universe is too grand to become one. But there are no rational grounds for holding that God must be proud (or afraid of what the angels might think of him), and if we were made by him in his image it is uncomplimentary to think of ourselves as cheap and nasty products. Plato complained that the Homeric poems give an unedifying picture of the divine nature, but at least their theology is not snobbish. If we think God *could* not have become incarnated we must imagine there is some impassable ontological gulf between him and us. One possibility is that we are mere creatures of his imagination, and he can no more become a man than a novelist can become a character in one of his own stories. This picture of the universe as not really real, however, belongs more to Oriental than to Judaeo-Christian thought. In our society a commoner source of the feeling that God could not have become incarnate is probably a feeling that God himself is not really real. If God exists and wants us to know something, what more natural than to assume a form in which he can tell us?

Maurice Wiles believes that God exists but says it is 'extremely difficult (I am tempted to say impossible but that would be to prejudge the issue) to ascribe absolute authority to any particular occasion or any particular set of experiences within the world.'[1] By 'absolute authority' I take him to mean permanent and unsurpassable importance. If Christ were an incarnation of God his life would be a particular historical episode with this kind of importance; so Christ cannot have been God incarnate.

Why cannot any single historical episode have 'absolute authority'? Wiles' own thinking is hard to follow. He professes a doctrine he calls 'historical relativism' according to which we can never (presumably outside of pure mathematics) attain to absolute truth but our cognitive powers are always at the mercy of pressures and preconceptions existing at the time at which we live. Applying this doctrine we might hold either (i) we are at the moment subject to pressures which do not allow us to believe that Christ's life has absolute authority, or (ii) the authors of the New Testament were subject to pressures which make them undependable witnesses. These are both sceptical theses of a kind philosophers have come to mistrust and the first, if generalised, leads to a complete surrender of intellectual responsibility; but neither establishes that there could not be an episode of permanent and unsurpassable importance.

I think there are indeed some constraints on how far a single episode can have 'absolute authority' for us. In the first place, a single, momentary action cannot have decisive moral, as distinct from physical, significance. A single movement can detonate a bomb with catastrophic results, but a person's character is not formed by a single act. It develops over a stretch of time in which success can be spoilt and mistakes retrieved. (This may be connected with the fact that there is a good deal of duplication in our physical make-up: the functions of one organ or one part of the brain can be taken over by another; we are enduring, not momentary organisms.) Secondly it seems unjust or unreasonable that our destiny as persons should be completely settled by something in which we can take no part whatever – something inaccessibly removed from us in time and space.

These considerations, however, are accommodated by the traditional teaching. The life of Christ is not a single action, much less something instantaneous. Indeed, as I suggested earlier, it can be viewed as the culmination of a historical process going back into the early history of the Jews and forward into the present. Neither is Christ's redemptive action totally remote from us or (according to the majority of Christians) independent of us. We are supposed to have access to it through the Church and the sacraments, and we should respond to it in third-level action.

The importance Christians attribute to the life of Christ does not make everything else, before or since, irrelevant to our destiny; but that does not stop it from being permanent and unsurpassable. One can always say, of course, that no human action or sequence of acts can ever be of permanent importance: it can make a difference for a time, but in a million, a thousand or even a hundred years its effects will have become negligible. That, however, is a line of talk Christians should resist. One way in which Christianity gives meaning to life is through the hope that our actions can have permanent significance; and Christ is supposed to have shown that human nature can accomplish more than we should otherwise have hoped.

I do not think, then, that there are good philosophical grounds for rejecting the traditional idea of a decisive divine intervention. Neither do I see any philosophical, as distinct from historical, objections to the traditional account of how that intervention occurred. Some early Christians asked why it was delayed so long. The Fall of Man, or the first sins, may have occurred millions of years before Christ's birth. The question is idle because we know nothing whatever of the early history of mankind. The discovery of a single bone here or a single tool there which might date back fifty thousand or two million years is completely uninformative about the nature and institutions of the men or pre-men of the time. Perhaps God did intervene, and put into operation a system which worked splendidly for a long time. But another possibility is that men were offered chances they did not take.

Genesis represents Abraham as contributing to the redemptive plan. He is a tribal leader and an individual of considerable personal stature. God approaches him after he has achieved a form of monotheism and has given the best land to his brother. A further important step is taken when he is willing to offer his son as a human sacrifice. That is no longer friendly second-level action but third-level action directed towards God. Only after this step does God make the promises which, on the traditional view, he fulfils by offering his own son on behalf of mankind. The suggestion is that the redemptive plan required the cooperation of individuals and a society, and that is reasonable. Someone might ask, indeed: 'If with God all things are possible, could he not have enabled us to share in his eternal life simply by working within each of us?' But the transformation we require is not like that of a cake mixture when it is baked into a cake: it could not be affected by causal action. Even the transformation of a child into an adult has to be partly the work of the child. That separation from our bodies which I tried to describe above depends on loving and adoring action by us.

Many scholars say that the *Genesis* accounts of Abraham and Moses are legends without historical basis. I have said that I do not feel obliged to agree, but in any case there are plenty of individuals of undisputed historical status who play modest but genuine parts in the traditional story of the redemption. Christ was born at a place and time of great historical significance. Palestine lies in the middle of a ring of pre-Christian civilisations: to the south, Egypt, to the north-east, Babylon and Persia, to the north-west, Greece and Rome. The reigns of Augustus and Tiberius mark a high point in Greco-Roman civilisation: a period of peace and justice in which communications were good and safe and in which there were high standards of moral conduct and intellectual discipline. So far as we know, there had never before been such an opportunity for a revelation to the whole human race and a decisive redemptive act. The monotheistic society into which Christ was born was preserved and developed by many generations of Jews; the favourable attendant circumstances existed not by chance but thanks to conscientious administrators, jurists and philosophers in other nations.

Of individuals involved in the redemption the most important, after Christ himself, will have been his parents. He must have obtained his conceptions of himself as a human being chiefly from them; and in general we become the persons those closest to us seem to think we are. According to Luke, Jesus' mother Mary played a further part. An angel said to her:

> You have found favour with God. You will conceive, and bear a son, and call him Jesus. He will be great; he will be called the son of the Most High; and the Lord God will give him the throne of his father David. He will be king of the House of Jacob for ever, and there will be no end to his rule. (1.31–3.)

Mary replied: 'I am the slave-girl of God. Let it happen to me as you say.' She accepts the working of God in her, we might say, as an individual but for the benefit of the whole Jewish people. Matthew further tells us that Joseph endorsed the arrangement and he and Mary thereafter acted in it as a united married couple.

We have seen that the modern orthodoxy is that Christ's followers either never enquired, or having ascertained forgot, about his parentage and childhood; and the opening chapters of Matthew and Luke are fictions to fill the gap in late first-century knowledge. I find this incredible, especially of so pedigree-minded a people as the Jews, and I shall say briefly why I find the chief objections to these chapters unconvincing.[2]

One difficulty concerns Luke's dating of the birth of Christ. He gives three indications: a decree of Augustus that the 'whole world' should be registered (*apographē*), Quirinius' holding a command (*hēgemoneuōn*) in Syria, and Herod's being King in Judaea. These indications cannot be made to coincide. Josephus reports a tax assessment (*apotimēsis*) made by Quirinius as a governor (*dikaiodotēs*) of Syria (*Antiquities of the Jews* XVIII 1ff.), but this was in AD 6, and Herod the Great died in BC 4 before Quirinius became governor of Syria. Moreover in the time of Herod Palestine was not technically (though it was in fact) part of the Roman empire; so Jews should not have been liable for tax assessment.

A historian writing in AD 60 would have had great difficulty in establishing a firm date for Jesus' birth even if he had access to Jesus' family: there were no registers of births, years were not popularly distinguished by agreed dates, and Jesus' family was not politically important. Luke could have been mistaken about the king; Herods abounded in Palestine at the time, and Jesus could have been born under a Herod other than Herod the Great. Alternatively (and more probably) the registration in Luke could be different from the assessment in Josephus. In his autobiography Augustus claims to have taken three censuses of the empire (*Res Gestae* 8) none of which coincides with Josephus' assessment. Luke's registration could be a follow-up of the second, in 8 BC; and so long as Palestine was effectively under his control Augustus could have collected population statistics from it whatever its precise constitutional status.

A second objection is that the narratives of Matthew and Luke do not agree well with one another. Matthew concentrates on Joseph and Bethlehem, Luke on Mary and Nazareth. If Matthew had said that Jesus was born in Bethlehem and Luke that he was born in Nazareth there would have been a serious discrepancy. In fact both agree he was born in Bethlehem, and that they supply different details no more discredits them here than when they are relating later events in Jesus' life.

A particularly feeble objection is that if Jesus and John the Baptist had been cousins as Luke says, John would not have failed to recognise Jesus at his baptism. Even today people do not know all their second cousins by sight.

There is not the same problem about the Crucifixion as about the Annunciation or the sacrifice of Isaac: nobody denies that it happened. But it gives rise to a question of a different kind. Christ died in a most agonising and shameful way. Crucifixion is not a pretty death, and Christ on the cross cannot have been the clean and decently-draped figure crucifixes present to the pious. Was this necessary? Could we not have been saved without this blood and horror?

According to Luke, Christ began his mission by going into the synagogue of his home town and reading the optimistic text about the Messiah in *Isaiah* 61.1–2; then:

> Shutting the book, he gave it to the attendant and sat down. The eyes of all in the synagogue were fixed on him. He began to speak to them and said: 'Today this text is fulfilled.' (4.20–1.)

I see no ineluctable reason why the Jews and their religious leaders should not have believed this; why they should not have recognised Jesus as the Messiah and even as the Son of God. Neither, since he had no political ambitions, was there bound to be an early clash with the Roman authorities. Pilate, at least, did not consider him dangerous, and the emperor of the time is reported to have been hostile and caustic towards people who try to deify him or to institute prosecutions for not treating members of the imperial family as divine. There has been no better damper on religious persecution than Tiberius' epigram: 'Deorum iniuriae dis curae'.

I said earlier that if we are to take seriously the idea that God can be made to suffer by men, his sufferings must be horrific. The particular manifestations of that suffering, however, which the Evangelists show us in Gethsemane and on Calvary appear to be caused by the response to Christ of his contemporaries. Gratuitously, but as a courageous leader would wish to, Christ takes us at our worst.

2

> God so loved the world that he gave his only-begotten son in order that everyone who believes in him, instead of being lost, may have eternal life. (*Jn.*3.16.)

If we do not reject this doctrine either on philosophical or on historical grounds we have the task of understanding it. What does it mean to say that Christ was the son of God?

One view is that he was a human being whom God adopted as his son and made divine.[3] Some scholars see this view in the opening chapters of Matthew and Luke. Others, while disowning the idea of adoption, say Matthew and Luke represent Christ not as a pre-existent divine person but merely as somehow 'marked off' (a word with this sense is used at *Rom.* 1.3) as divine at conception. These scholars put much weight on the reply of the angel when Mary asks how she can conceive a son 'when I know not man'. The angel says

> The Holy Spirit will come upon you and the power of the Most High will overshadow you. That is why the holy one that is generated will be called 'Son of the Most High'. (*Lk.* 1.35.)

Luke's use of the (rather weak) connecting particle *dio* which I have translated 'that is why' is said to imply that Christ is Son of God only because he is miraculously conceived and not because he is an incarnation of a divine person that already exists. None of the Fathers of the Church detected these implications in the passage; that required the ingenuity of modern scholarship; and exactly how this marking off differs from adoption I find unclear.

To understand Christ's relationship as divine Son to God the Father I think we should look first at his own reported teaching. Among the points he makes are these:

(1) The Father and the Son have special knowledge of each other: No one knows the Son except the Father, nor does anyone know the Father except the Son and those to whom the Son chooses to reveal him. (*Mt.* 11.27, *cf. Jn.* 6.46.)
(2) The Father loves the Son. (*Jn.* 5.20, *cf.* 17.23, 26.)
(3) The Son existed before the creation of the universe: 'The glory I had with you before the universe existed.' (*Jn.* 17.5, 24.).
(4) The Son is in some ways subordinate to the Father: 'The Father is greater than I.' (*Jn.* 14.28.) The Father, but not

the Son, knows the date of the day of judgement (*Mt.* 24.36; commentators, however, traditionally take Christ to be speaking here as man, not as God). The Son does the will of the Father (*Mt.* 26.39), and came into the world 'not from myself, but he sent me' (*Jn.* 8.42); nor can he do anything 'from himself' (*Jn.* 5.19, 30).

(5) The Son derives power and authority from the Father: As the Father has life under his control, so he has given it to the Son to have life under his control. (*Jn.* 5.26.)

The Father has given the Son 'power over all flesh' (*Jn.* 17.2), and the Son will judge the world (*Mt.* 25.31ff., *Jn.* 5.22).

(6) Nevertheless: 'The Father and I are one.' (*Jn.* 10.30.) 'The Father is in me and I am in the Father.' (*Jn.* 10.38, 14.10.)

To this reported teaching of Christ himself we may add the point emphasised in several New Testament writings that the universe was created through the Son:

> In him were created all things in Heaven and earth ... All things were created through him and towards him. (*Col.* 1.16.) Through him God made the universe (*aiōnas*). (*Heb.* 1.2.) In the beginning was the *Logos*; the Logos was in relation to God; and God was the Logos ... All things came to be through him, and separately from him there came to be none of the things which came to be. (*Jn.* 1.1–3.)

These passages plainly imply that the Son existed before or independently of the conception and birth of Christ; but how can we conceive the relationship of such a person to the God of bare monotheism? The terms 'father' and 'son' can apply literally only to living organisms. We find two slightly different, though closely related traditions in Christian thought.

In 1 *Cor.* 1.24 Paul calls Christ 'the wisdom of God'. The phrase is not accidental. From perhaps the fifth century BC onwards it became common for Jewish writers to personify God's wisdom. They did not mean to postulate a genuine person distinct from God, but their language had an aptitude to be applied to Christ. A particularly striking passage is *Wisdom* 7.22-31:

> Within her [wisdom] is a spirit intelligent, holy, only-begotten, manifold, subtle, mobile, bright, unsullied, clear, invulnerable, good-loving, sharp, irresistible, beneficient, loving to man ... She is a breath of the power of God, pure emanation of the glory of the almighty; hence nothing defiled can infect her. She is a flashing out of the eternal light, unspotted mirror of God's activity, image of his goodness. Although she is alone she can do all things; remaining within herself she makes all things new.

This description seems to be applied to Christ in *Heb.* 1.2-3: 'He is the flashing out of God's glory and the representation of his substance.' There may be an echo of it in *Col.* 1.15, 'the image of the unseen God'. Moreover Christ himself may have wished to remind his hearers of descriptions of the divine wisdom when he says 'I am the bread of life' (*Jn.* 6.35, *cf.* 53-4): in *Proverbs* wisdom summons people to a feast and says 'Come and eat my bread'. A speech put into the mouth of wisdom in *Prov.* 8.22-31 will have been familiar to the writers who say that all things were made through the Son:

> The Lord possessed me at the beginning of his way, before his works of old. I was set up from everlasting, from the beginning, or ever the earth was ... When he prepared the heavens I was there with him ... When he appointed the foundations of the earth then I was by him as one brought up with him [or, better, as a master craftsman], and I was daily his delight, rejoicing always before him.

The other tradition appears in John, who calls the Son the '*logos*': the 'word' or, more literally, the 'linguistic act'. John seems less to be proposing an alternative idea than expressing the same idea in different terms. *Ecclesiasticus* (Ben Sira) 24.3 makes the Divine Wisdom say 'I came out from the mouth of the Most High, and covered the earth like a cloud'. It is natural, of course, to think of wisdom as being expressed or present in speech. When Ben Sira says 'In the *logoi* of the Lord are his works' (42.15; meaning they are accomplished by his word) or the author of *Wisdom* speaks of God as making 'all things in your *logos*' (9.1) they will not have thought they were correcting *Prov.* 8.22–30.

John's use of '*logos*' can be explained by this tradition, but today we may connect the divine Son with speech in other ways. First, when a human being exercises a skill he not only does what is effective but does this knowing it is effective and for reasons which render it effective. No doubt when a bird builds a nest it proceeds in accordance with a kind of architectural principle and does what is right not by chance, but in a way, because it is right. We do not think, however, that the bird understands why its movements result in a satisfactory nest or that it formulates the principles on which it proceeds (though some kind of formulation may be transmitted in its genes). The intelligent craftsman, in contrast, does what is correct not only non-accidentally but consciously; he can formulate both the general principles of his craft and the particular circumstances which are the technical reasons for his technical decisions. Insofar as he understands why his movements are effective and acts consciously, he depends on language and therefore acts, in a way, through speech. We may suppose that when God acts creatively his action is conscious. If he is not conscious in the way we are, at least his activity should be more like ours than like a bird's, and he surely knows the causal principles in accordance with which he decides changes shall take place. He too, then, must act in a way through speech. But there is the difference that the human craftsman formulates causal principles which hold independently of his formulating them; it is contrary to the cook's will that if the hollandaise sauce gets too hot the egg becomes lumpy; whereas God is the source of causal principles, and they hold because he formulates them. Even, then, in purely physical nature his activity depends on something analogous to speech.

Secondly, when God animates a living thing he makes its surroundings known to it. Making something known to a purposive agent is a kind of speech. In the case of sub-rational creatures we saw that this speech was to be identified with the organism's purposive movements. But if God is to create us not merely as living things but as beings conscious of the persons he wants us to be, this calls for an even more linguistic act: on the one hand, perhaps, a speech in human words from human lips, on the other, a response by us of doing what that speaker says.

These are reflections which may specially appeal to the philosophically-minded Christian today, alert to the role in life of speech-acts. For philosophically-minded Christians of the first two or three centuries, *logos* had other associations. It was used in a variety of ways by contemporary Greek philosophers, and its application to the Son of God accompanied and facilitated that immigration of Greek ideas into Christian thought which had such an influence on theology in the patristic period. To take one notable example, the Second Hypostasis or Substance in Plotinus' trinity of divine Hypostases was the Logos.

New Testament writers, then, identify Christ with the wisdom or creative speech of God. This gives rise to an obvious problem. It is easy to see – we have just seen – how a writer can personify these things. But wisdom is a kind of attribute and speech a kind of act: how can an attribute or an activity literally be a person? Since there is no doctrine that there are two Persons in God separate from the doctrines that there are three, before going further into beliefs about the Son, we should see what Christians believe about the third member of the Trinity, the Holy Spirit.

3

Christian belief concerning the Holy Spirit was initially uncertain. Some writers, like Irenaeus, identify the Spirit, not the Son, with God's Wisdom. In the original Nicene creed (325) we find only the laconic words 'We believe in the Holy Spirit'. Even in 380 Gregory of Nazianzum could say:

Of our wise men, some take the Spirit to be a kind of divine action, some a creature, some God, and some do not know which he is. (*PG* 36.137.)

The word 'spirit' (Greek *pneuma*, Hebrew *ruah*) literally means 'breath'. In the Old Testament the breath of God is spoken of as a life-giving force (*Ps.* 104.27–30, *cf. Gen.* 2.7); it inspires the craftsman Bezalel to make the furnishings for the Sanctuary in *Exod.* 31.3; it brings moral regeneration to sinners (*Ps.* 51.10–11); it will be given preeminently to the Messiah (*Is.* 11.2, 42.1). But Old Testament writers do not personify it. New Testament writers, in contrast, confidently represent the Spirit as a person who speaks (*Ac.* 13.2), issues decrees along with Church leaders (*Ac.* 15.28), and helps individuals with their prayers (*Rom.* 8.26).

No less remarkable, the Spirit is grouped with the Father and Son in formulations of the greatest antiquity. *Mt.* 28.19 reports that Christ instructed the apostles to baptise 'in the name of the Father, the Son and the Holy Spirit'. 2. Cor. ends (13.13): 'May the grace of the Lord Jesus Christ, the love of God and the sharing in (koinonia) of the Holy Spirit be with you all.' *Hb.* 9.14 formulates Christ's redemptive offering: 'Christ, who through the eternal Spirit offered himself to God'; so too 1 *Pet.* 1.1–2.

How is this development to be explained? Why did the early Christians encumber their theology with a third person? In the long speech which John puts into Christ's mouth at the Last Supper (but which may include teaching from other occasions), Christ refers to what John calls a 'paraclete', a word for a person called in for some purpose, usually to present a case in court (our 'advocate' has the same etymology).

> I will ask the Father, and he will give you another paraclete, to be with you for ever, the Spirit of Truth (14.16).

> The Paraclete, the Holy Spirit, which the Father will send in my name, will teach you all things and call to your minds all I have said to you (14.26).

It is to your advantage that I should go away. If I do not, the Paraclete will not come to you, but if I go I shall send him to you (16.7).

Christ seems here to be speaking of a person distinct from himself and the Father, but identical with the Spirit of God. *Acts* 2.1–4 records the coming of the Spirit of God to the apostles at Pentecost. I think we can understand the Christian view of the Spirit only if we suppose that from the beginning the apostles identified this Spirit which came at Pentecost with the Paraclete promised by Christ.

Christian thought about the Trinity developed between two constraints: we must neither 'divide the essence' nor 'confuse the persons'. We should be dividing the divine essence if we thought that the Father, Son and Spirit are three distinct gods. To avoid this tritheism we must deny that they can exist independently of one another in the way which a human father and son can. On the other hand we confound the persons if we think that the Father, Son and Spirit are merely three aspects of a single God.[4] We must not say, for instance, that the name 'Father' applies to God in his role of creator, 'Son' in his role of redeemer, and 'Spirit' in his role as guide of the Church; still less that these words signify different phases in God's existence, as 'lamb', 'gimmer' and 'ewe' signify different phases in the life of a sheep. If we say this, we no longer have distinct persons. These constraints apply to the Father and the Son, even if we leave the Spirit out of account. They must be neither separate gods nor the same person in two aspects, say as unknown and as revealed.

Western Christians have been much influenced by the work *On the Trinity* completed by Augustine in 416. Augustine proposes as a model for the Trinity a mind which knows and loves itself perfectly: Father, Son and Spirit are related as would be the mind, its knowledge and its love (IX. 3–8, *PL* 42. 962–5). There are two objections to this account. A theologian might object that the Bible does not connect the Spirit specially with love. The Spirit gives life or animates; if these are in fact the workings of love, the point is unrecognised either in the

New Testament or in early professions of faith. A philosophical objection is that the Father, Son and Spirit are supposed to be persons, whereas knowledge and love are attributes, states or activities of persons.

This second objection Augustine tries to meet by saying that knowledge and love are not attributes or properties in the same way as colour. The greenness of a leaf is the greenness only of that leaf; but Socrates' knowledge may be knowledge of things other than Socrates. This is an unconvincing defence. Augustine seems to be confusing two different kinds of genitive, the possessive and the objective. Love and knowledge have objects as well as possessors, whereas greenness does not, but that does not make them any the less properties or attributes. Augustine goes on to compare 'knowledge' and 'love' to words like 'friend' and 'head'. 'Friend' is a relative term – a friend must be the friend *of* someone – but a friend is also a person who can exist separately from people he is a friend of. The application of this analogy would be that 'knowledge' is a relative term in that knowledge must always be someone's knowledge; yet God's knowledge is also a person who can exist separately from the Father. The analogy seems to be false, since we think that in general knowledge *cannot* exist apart from the knower in the way friends can exist apart from one another, and in any case if the persons of the Trinity were analogous to friends they would be distinct gods. As for the comparison with heads and things which have heads, Augustine himself sees the difficulties in making the Son and the Spirit stand either to the Father or to the one God as parts to a whole.

Aquinas follows Augustine in identifying the Spirit with God's love, but defends a slightly different account of the Trinity in the *Summa Theologiae* (I. 28–30). Since God knows and loves, there are real relations between him and his knowledge and love. His relationship to his knowledge is like that of a father to a son, so there are the relationships of fatherhood and sonhood; his relationship to his love is like that of a breather to his breath, so there are the relationships of spiration and procession. Now if one thing A stands in a real relationship to another B, this relationship is a positive reality in A. If A is a material object, this reality will be something different from *A*'s essential nature and, so to speak, adventitious. But there is nothing adventitious in God. Neither has God any component parts: he is absolutely simple. Anything in God must be identical with his essential nature. All this Aquinas has argued before he starts discussing the Trinity; he has argued, for instance, that God is identical with his wisdom, his justice and so forth. The fatherhood in God, it follows, is not a mere adventitious property of God, but God himself, and so is the sonhood. Aquinas suggests, finally, the Father just is this divine fatherhood, and the Son and Spirit are the divine sonhood and divine procession.

This account is even harder to accept than Augustine's. The part which concerns the Spirit is obscure, and spiration and procession sound more like processes than relationships. Fatherhood and sonhood are relationships, right enough, but Aquinas' exposition depends heavily on two metaphysical doctrines which a modern philosopher has to consider extremely dubious: the doctrine that the relationship in which one thing stands to another is, as Aquinas puts it, 'inherent in' the first, and that God is identical with all the things which, if he were a creature, we should say inhere in him. Aquinas runs, with his personified, subsistent relationships, into all the same difficulties as Augustine, and into others besides. (I may add that the question whether God's wisdom, justice, etc., are attributes inhering in him or are identical with him seem to me improper. It rests on the assumption that words like 'wise' and 'just' signify properties in the same way as words like 'red' and 'spherical', the only difference being that the one lot of properties are mental and the other physical. As I have indicated earlier, this seems to me a completely wrong approach to our notion of the mind.)

Tertullian, the author of the earliest work on the Trinity that has come down to us (*Against Praxeas*, *PL* 2. 154ff.) was less philosophically ambitious than either Augustine or Aquinas. He compares the Persons of the Trinity with a spring, a river and a stream taken from the river or, his preferred analogy (sections 8, 13, 17), with the Sun, a ray and the tip of the ray. The Greek Fathers proceed similarly, Gregory of Nyssa says:

> If someone were to see a flame distributed between three lamps (and we may suppose that the cause of this is the first flame which reached the third through being transmitted by the second) [it would be wrong to say] that heat abounds in the first, is reduced in the second ... and in the third is not fire at all. (*On the Trinity* 6, *PG* 45.1308).

He takes his stand on the doctrine:

> Every action which goes from God to creation and which can be described according to a variety of conceptions originates out of the Father, proceeds though the Son and is completed in the Holy Spirit. (*Not Three Gods. PG* 45.125.)

There are not three gods but only one because the Father, Son and Spirit do not act separately but together, and together in this complementary way.

So far as it goes, this account is unobjectionable. The Father, Son and Spirit are persons because they act. That they act in distinct and complementary ways not only makes them distinct but prevents them from being coordinate, separable sources of action. It might be prudent to leave the matter at that, but I shall venture a few further remarks.

A trio of friends would not do as a model for the Trinity not only because it is tritheistic but because the relationship between the Father and the Son, at least, appears from Christ's teaching to be essential to them in a way in which relationships between human beings are not essential. A man becomes a father through causal action he need not engage in. Abraham need not have been the father of anyone. Saul Kripke in *Naming and Necessity* (Oxford 1980, pp. 112–13) suggests it was essential for Isaac to be Abraham's son: the same individual could not have had different parents. But however that may be, Isaac was not only a son but also a father, and Abraham was not only a father but also a son. The fatherhood of the Father, in contrast, and the sonhood of the Son are not, for the Christian, extraneous to them. The Son could not also be a Divine Father, though he might, perhaps, have been a human father, and the Father could not also be a Divine Son. But if the relationships between Father and Son – and the same, presumably, goes for the Spirit – are in this way essential to them, they cannot be of the same ontological kind. I call things 'ontologically' similar if they are all material objects, or all shapes, or all games. It is an advantage of Augustine's account that the Son and the Spirit are ontologically different from the Father, even if not from each other.

But if Father, Son and Spirit are all persons, must they not be ontologically similar? Do not all persons belong to the same ontological kind? The word 'person' comes from a word for the sort of mask actors wore on the ancient stage. It is not used of the Trinity in the New Testament and is avoided by early Greek theologians; they prefer a word meaning 'subsistence' or 'thing which exists of its own right'. It is with great circumspection, then, as later theologians have stressed, that we should call the Father, Son and Spirit 'persons'. The word does not by itself commit Christians to making them ontologically similar, or even to holding that they are all persons in the way in which men are persons. Father, Son and Spirit could be persons in different ways.

I argued that, on the one hand, a man's notion of himself is derived from other human beings, generally his parents, but on the other it is quasi-creative, determining his actual nature as a purposive agent. The sort of person I think I am I decided to be and do in fact become. It is possible, then to distinguish between a man as a person who is responsible for himself, and as the person for whom, in this way, he is responsible. I suggest that the Christian theologian might use this as a model for the distinction between the Father and the Son. God does not, of course, derive his notion of himself from anyone else. Whereas a man gradually acquires an idea of himself, God must be supposed to have had an idea of himself all along. Equally God did not become the person he wanted to be, but was that person all along. Nevertheless, like a conscious man he is creatively responsible for the person he is. The relation of God as person who decides what he shall be to God as the person he decides to be is therefore comparable to that of a father to a son he has begotten from all eternity.

This model, it will be seen, makes the Son analogous to the person a man decides to be, not to the man's idea of that person. Does this fail to do justice to the doctrine that the Son is the divine Wisdom, the Word through which God acts? When a human being forms an idea of himself as a person, he conceives himself as an agent with knowledge, an agent who acts for certain reasons and who possesses certain skills. God would conceive himself as, and decide to be, not an intelligent agent in a world which is already there, but a world-creator. He decides to be a person who creates a world for certain purposes, for the benefit of certain living things. It is through this person, and this person's ideas, that the Father acts. It is unfruitful to press the question whether the Son *is* God's wisdom or merely *has* it. Wisdom is not well conceived as a possession even when it is human wisdom. But the Son will be the locus of divine wisdom if he is the person God chooses to be, and that person is a creator whose ideas do not conform to reality, but to whose ideas reality conforms.

Besides forming an idea of himself as a person, a man can identify himself as a person with other human beings and act in order that they may act. I suggested that this gives us a model for God's creation of us as purposive agents: he identifies himself with us and acts in order that we may act. He differs from a merely human friend in that he acts within us, and it is his action that animates us. Now the Judaeo-Christian doctrine is that it is the Spirit of God that animates living things. It looks, then, as if the Spirit is God acting within us, the self that God identifies with the creatures he loves. As we can distinguish between the person who forms a concept of himself and the self he decides to be, so we can distinguish between the person who identifies himself with others and the self he so identifies. This latter distinction I propose as a model for the distinction between the Father and the Spirit.

It is sometimes said that whereas Latin Christians make the

Spirit proceed from both Father and Son, the Greeks make him proceed from the Father alone. That is an oversimplification. The Greeks make the Spirit proceed from the Father through the Son, as Gregory of Nyssa's image of the flame illustrates. The Greek Fathers were aware that in the New Testament the Spirit is often (e.g. *Gal.* 4.6) spoken of as the Spirit of the Son, and speak of him as 'from God' and 'of Christ'. The famous dispute between East and West about 'the procession of the Holy Ghost' was more political then theological.

On the present showing, each of the persons of the Trinity corresponds to a different notion we have of a person or self. A self is one who forms an idea of himself and identifies himself with others; a self is what one makes of oneself; and a self is what one identifies with others. The Father who, in the Christian tradition, is the unoriginated origin, the one who knows and loves, is a person in the first way; the Son, an agent who acts for the benefit of creatures in accordance with the Father's will or decision, is a person in the second; the Spirit, who is God's gift of himself to men, is a person in the third. But although all these notions of a person fall within our grasp, it is perhaps only the Son who is a person in the same way as a human being. The notion of a person which we apply to men is not primarily that of an origin, still less of something given or identified; it is the notion we have of ourselves as the conscious, purposive agents we decide to be; and this is the notion which applies to the Son.

Theologians sometimes maintain that the notion of a person is too narrow and anthropomorphic to apply to God. If our notion of a person applies primarily only to the Son, there will be some basis for this view. God will, so to speak, exceed our concept of a person. The notion of the Father as unoriginated origin will be logically prior to that of a person. On the other hand the Christian must deny that thinking of God as a person is anthropomorphising God. The concept does apply directly to the Son; and since men are supposed to be made in the image of God, thinking of them as persons is theomorphising them. Moreover it will not be improper, on the view I have been sketching, to apply the notion of a person either to the one God or to the Father. For on that view a person is what the Father has decided to be; the logical category of person, we might say, is the category to which he has chosen to belong. In any case, of course, the Christian must take account of the fact that Christ invariably speaks of the Father as a person in our sense. The most that can be maintained is what orthodox theologians would wish to maintain,[5] that the Son is the only member of the Trinity for whom becoming a man was a logical possibility.

A man conceives himself as he thinks someone else conceives him, and in accepting this concept he wants to please that other person. We must suppose that God conceives himself as he himself chooses, and fulfils this conception to please himself. Presumably it was from all eternity part of God's conception of himself that he should create a physical world for the benefit of living things in it – though the world itself, I have argued, has existed for only a finite time. Was it also part of God's concept of himself from all eternity that he should become incarnate, and even that he should suffer for men? Whichever way we answer we are in danger of making God's knowledge temporal. If we say 'yes' we suggest that God knew how men would act before they acted; if we say 'no' we suggest that the decision to become incarnate came later than the decision to create the universe. The Christian does best, I think, to reply by insisting that God's thoughts do not stand in temporal relations. In one way he decided to create the world a finite time ago and to become incarnate two thousand years ago; but in another both decisions were part of his eternal nature.

4

'The Word', according to *Jn.* 1.14, 'became flesh'. How are we to understand this? Water becomes ice; wood, when put on the fire, turns to ashes. This kind of becoming is possible only for quantities of material, and for them it is a passing away or a ceasing to be. The Word cannot have become flesh in this way. Neither can he be supposed to have become a human being in the sort of way in which a caterpillar becomes a butterfly. It is significant that early Christian formulations do not speak of his becoming a man, and in place of saying he became flesh they often say 'He took flesh from the Virgin Mary'.

A man is morally responsible only for changes he directly or indirectly causes, and is aware only of circumstances which directly or indirectly affect his sense-organs. In general, as we have seen, God is not a causal agent, and is aware of what happens in the universe because he is responsible for its happening. The Son took flesh from the Virgin Mary in that he took moral responsibility for the causal action, or some of it, of the material object which developed in Mary's womb. This was action for reasons correlated with states of that object's brain and sense-organs. Such a taking of flesh or becoming flesh was the conception or coming into existence of a human being who had not previously existed. The Son of God did not become this human being – it does not, in fact, make sense to talk of becoming a particular individual – but that does not prevent us from saying that *qua* conscious, purposive agent, this human being *was* the Son.

'He emptied himself', says Paul (*Ph*. 2.6–7), 'and took the form of a servant.' Insofar as the Son limited himself to causal action with the limbs taken from Mary, he was certainly emptying himself. Christians, however, deny that the Son's incarnation involved any reduction either in his divinity or in his power. The orthodox doctrine, as formulated, for instance, in the Chalcedonian Definition quoted in Chapter One, is that Christ was a single person with two natures, a divine nature and a human one. According to Greek formulations these natures are united in one person (*prosopon*) or *hypostasis*. Latin formulations sometimes speak of a hypostatic union or substantial unit, but these phrases, at least for the modern reader, are more likely to obscure than to clarify the doctrine. As Descartes said in a different context, nobody knows what 'substantial unity' means; it suggests, however, a mixture of two substances (like tea and sugar, for example) and that is not what is intended. The Greek formulations mean simply that the Son of God and the son of Mary are one and the same person; '*hypostasis*' in this context signifies the individual to which (as Aquinas puts it in *Summa Theologiae* III.2.3) 'are attributed operations and properties'.

The doctrine that Christ is a single person with two natures is rejected, of course, by those modern theologians who deny that he was anything more than human. They, as we saw, are influenced by the belief that Gospels are not historically reliable. The doctrine has been found difficult, however, by theologians of the past who show no suspicions about the Gospel narratives. Gregory of Nyssa says that we know the fact that Christ was both divine and human from the recorded miracles, but 'we are not capable of discerning how the divine and human elements are mixed up together' (*Great Catechism*, xi). At first, indeed, it might seem that there is no problem. The same person can be a general and a motorist. *Qua* general he is empowered to command thousands of soldiers; *qua* motorist he has to do what he is told by common policemen and traffic wardens. Why, then, should not Christ be *qua* God, all powerful, and *qua* man capable of acting only with the limbs of a single human body? The parallel, however, is only superficial. The powers of a general are conferred by human agreements; those of God are not. Being God is not, so to speak, an institutional position.

To say that the Son of God and the son of Mary are the same person is to say that they are the same conscious, purposive agent, the same beneficiary of the causal action of Christ's limbs. In Chapter Six I explained the notion of a soul as that of a conscious, purposive agent. Is the traditional doctrine, then, that Christ was identical with the Son of God in soul, though not in body? Those who are more familiar with the Fathers of the Church than with contemporary philosophers may feel very uneasy about such an interpretation. Despite some temptation (see Denzinger 76, Gregory of Nyssa, *Great Catechism*, xi) to compare the relationship of the divine and the human in Christ to that of soul and body, the Fathers eventually come down against the suggestion that the Son of God was Christ's soul. Christ, they declare emphatically, had a human soul. But what motivated them in this was the need to insist that Christ was truly a human being. To be a human being, they reasoned, he required not just a human body but a human soul. The modern Christian will agree that Christ has to be a human being. But he will be a human being if, as I say, he acts with human limbs and because of circumstances which affect human sense-organs. We do not have to ascribe to him a non-physical component called 'a human soul', and my own opinion is that the concept of such a component, whether of Christ or of any other human being, is incoherent.

Besides saying that Christ had a human soul the Fathers (particularly those of the Third Council of Constantinople) say he had a human will. The reason for saying this is the same: to understand how he redeemed us we must suppose that it was as a human agent that he chose to be the sort of person God wanted, and as a human agent that he did the acts which qualified him for, or entitled him to, a share in the divine life. Human beings certainly act for reasons and purposes but as I said earlier, the notion of a special faculty of will is absent from classical Greek philosophy and is now suspect. I think, therefore, that the teaching of Constantinople III is adequately expressed today by saying simply that Christ was a human purposive agent; and that is not something anyone today will have difficulty in accepting.

As a human agent he must have had knowledge acquired through the senses and a human capacity for understanding. If he was also a divine person, did he also have superhuman knowledge and understanding? Theologians have given much attention to this question. In the past it was common to say that as God, Christ had divine omniscience. Modern theologians mostly prefer to say that Christ did not even know he was divine until his teaching career began; his understanding of his own nature and of the nature of his mission gradually deepened throughout his public life.[6]

Both views are open to objection. I have already indicated a difficulty for the second view. If Christ did not know all along that he was divine, he could never have had good reason for coming to believe he was. If he did not already know what God wanted him to do, he could never have had good reason to accept any apparent revelation as genuine.

An obvious difficulty about supposing that Christ as God knew everything, but as man knew only what he could have learned through his senses, is that this sounds like a contradiction: the same person both knows and does not know the same things. We could say Christ's divine knowledge was repressed in a Freudian sort of way, but that is a fairly desperate move. There is also some awkwardness in speaking, as conservative theologians have been inclined to speak, of Christ as having a divine will and a divine intellect in addition to a human will and intellect. When the Greek Fathers say that Christ has two wills, what they want to emphasise is that he has a human will. That he has a divine will, they think, follows automatically if God has a will and Christ is divine. But whereas a Christian who talks about faculties of intellect and will can reasonably say God has these faculties, it sounds a little tritheistic to say each Person has his own intellect and will. Rather than 'The Son has an intellect' a monotheist might favour the locution 'The Son *is* the Divine Intellect'.

I favour, then, a middle view. Christ knew all along that he was divine (though this knowledge may have had no application in his infancy); knew all along that the Father wanted to give men, through himself, a share in the divine life; knew, in fact, all he needed to know to accomplish his mission: but no more. This view is simple and economical. Christ has no knowledge he does not need to accomplish his mission. The knowledge he does need for this purpose is sufficient to ensure that he is the Son. Yet it is not such as to do violence to his nature as a human being. For though no mere human being could have been the first person to possess it, he can impart it to us and we can have it through believing him.

The opinion that Christ had more knowledge than this might seem to be supported by passages in the Gospels like *Jn*. 1.48, 4.18 which represent him as knowing things about people which, if he had been an ordinary human being, he could not have known. This miraculous knowledge, however, should be viewed as of a piece with his other miraculous powers. Some Gospel accounts represent him as achieving miraculous cures by his own power, others represent the miracles as done by the

Father at his request, and both ideas have had theological support (*cf.* Denzinger 260). If the universe was created by the Father through the Son, presumably the same goes for the quelling of the storm, the raising of Lazarus, and the conversion of the woman of Samaria.

On the view that Jesus came to know or believe that he was divine at some late stage in his career, there is no philosophical problem about how he could have come to believe this or what it would have been to know it. His coming to think or know that he was divine would be like someone's coming to realise that he is the most able politician in public life, or that he is passionately loved by some other person, or that he is some other person's long lost child. The only difficulty is the common sense one that coming to think in this way that you are divine sounds crazy. But on the modified traditional view that I am advocating there are at least two philosophical difficulties.

First, if Christ did not come to believe but knew all along that he was God, how should we conceive this knowing? Not on the model of knowing that one is the child of a particular pair of human parents: that is a piece of causal information that one learns by hearsay or personal detective work. The model for Christ's knowledge that he was the Divine Son must be an ordinary person's grasp of his personal identity as a purposive agent, his knowledge that he is the person who now has or formerly had certain beliefs and desires, and who is responsible for certain actions. This kind of knowledge is not infallible: I can misremember and think I did or thought something when I did not. Such mistakes, however, are rare, and they are not in general due to careless investigation, since our knowledge of our identity as persons is not based on investigation; it is immediate or direct.

In general I know that I am the person who did or thought something because I know why I did or thought it. I grasp my identity in understanding my past and present behaviour. If Christ knew that he was God I suggest that this knowledge could have been quite simple: all he needed was to understand for what reason or purpose he was incarnate. If he knew that his purpose was to give all men through himself a share in the divine life he knew he was God, since this is a purpose only God could have. In general, purposes depend on reasons. If it is my purpose to go to London I must be aware of something which makes getting there desirable or necessary. But for Christ to have the purpose of uniting all men to God nothing empirical needed to be known or believed. It was necessary, no doubt, to know that God existed. Did Christ also need to know that men existed and were not, as yet, sharing in the divine life? Such knowledge would, of course, have been available to him from his infancy onwards but it is doubtful how far he required it. For redemption is a continuation of creation, and a creator does not have to know (whether by observation or otherwise) that there are not as yet creatures of a certain sort in order to create them.

These considerations help to reduce the second difficulty. We think that if a human being is in possession of a piece of knowledge which he can call to mind on occasion, there must be some corresponding physical structure somewhere in his brain. If Christ knew from the start that he was God must there (perhaps from conception) have been a corresponding modification of his brain or his genes? All that is essential for believing that something is the case is having that thing function as a reason. Where an agent's reason is a matter of empirical fact (as reasons in the strict sense for human action perhaps always are) it is part of being a living organism to have a corresponding physical modification; to act for such a reason without a corresponding brain state would not, as far as I can see, be logically impossible, but it might fairly be described as miraculous. If, however, what I have just said about Christ's knowledge of his divine nature is correct, it would not depend on knowledge of any particular empirical facts. Christ might have to know empirical facts to activate his knowledge of his divine nature. For this knowledge might be activated only when he acted in order to unite men with God, and such action – teaching or even prayer – would require perceptual knowledge of his surroundings. But what makes this action knowledge of his divine nature is its being for the divine purposes of existing among men and uniting them with God. If our ordinary behaviour can be for some personal purpose without there being any special state of the brain which makes it be for this purpose, Christ's action could be for a divine purpose without there being any singularity in his cerebral hardware.

The union in Christ of the two natures may seem to do less violence to both if we accept that human beings were made in the first place in order that they might share in the divine nature; if, also, they were made in the divine image, we need not exaggerate the difference between the person God wants to be and the persons he wants us to be.

Isaiah 11.2 prophesies the coming of a saviour in whom the Spirit of God rests. The creed, following *Mt.* 1.18 and *Lk.* 1.35 says that Christ was conceived through the Spirit, and the Spirit also appears (*Mt.* 3.16) at his baptism. Should we connect the union of the divine and the human in Christ in any special way with the Spirit?

I suggested that it is in the person of the Spirit that God acts in us. If Christ knew better than other human beings what God wanted him to do and be, the Spirit will have been able to act in him more completely than in anyone else. But perhaps the Spirit's action in him should differ in kind and not just in degree of completeness. We act at the third level in order to exist as persons of a certain kind. Insofar as Christ was divine he existed independently of any flesh taken from Mary; his action, then, was not in order that he might exist but in order that he might be incarnate, and if he acted because the Spirit acted in him, the action of the Spirit was in order that he might be incarnate.

New Testament writers speak of the Spirit sometimes as the Spirit of God, sometimes as the Spirit of Christ. The Spirit is of God in that it proceeds from God; is it of Christ only in that it acts in him? If it is through the action of the Spirit that the Son is incarnate, and if, as we shall see to be Christian belief, it is through some kind of union with Christ that we are to share in the divine nature, our sharing in that nature must be a sharing in the Spirit's action in Christ. If we are to become divine, it will be through the Son's becoming incarnate in us too.

CHAPTER NINE
The Redemption

I

We are now ready to consider the question: how have we been saved? How has Christ cancelled the effects of sin and made us capable of eternal life? Anyone who expects a single straightforward answer is unacquainted with the history of Christian thought. Different writers exhibit differences in emphasis and even in substance. Some emphasise the Incarnation itself, God's taking human nature; some the final victory of the Resurrection; in the past, Western theologians have concentrated on Christ's passion and death; their successors today prefer his teaching and life. Of accounts which have been proposed some today seem unacceptable, but others may be accepted as complementary.

Gregory of Nyssa is representative of many of the Fathers when he reasons that men had sold themselves to the Devil in the way in which, in his time, men used to sell themselves to other human beings for money. That being so, it would have been unjust on God's part to deliver us by force: he had to buy us back on the Devil's terms. (*Great Catechism*, 22, PG 45.60–1.) The Latin word *redemption* (literally 'buying back') is in fact the regular word for just this sort of ransoming, and so is the Greek *lutron* or *antilutron*; and Christ says explicitly (in words echoed by Paul at I *Tim*. 2.6) that he has come to give himself 'as a *lutron* for many' (*Mt*. 20.28). The Devil, Gregory proceeds, thought that Christ, with his miraculous powers, virgin birth and so on, was more valuable than the rest of mankind put together, and was therefore willing to accept him as a ransom. So the Incarnation occured:

In order that, as happens with greedy fish, the hook of the Deity might be swallowed along with the bait of flesh; and life thus taking up its abode with death, and light appearing in darkness, the light and life would make their opposites disappear. (*Op. cit.* 23–4, PG 45.61.)

On this view, by concealing Christ's divine nature in flesh, God tricks the Devil. Theologians in the past have thought such trickery immoral, but Gregory defends it (ch. 26) and the standards of the 1980s may incline us to accept the defence. But there is a further objection, forcefully expressed by Anselm (*Cur Deus Homo?* 1.7). The Devil does not have justice on his side in treating us as he does. There is a difference between a free man who legally buys a slave and a slave who incites a fellow slave to rebel. The second has no rights. Anselm therefore proposes an alternative account.

Why, he asks (in words which anticipate a famous passage in Hume), did God not save us simply by saying we were forgiven?

If he could not save sinners otherwise than by condemning the just, where was his omnipotence? If he could, but would not, how shall we defend his wisdom and justice? (1.8.)

He replies:

Since the only right way to deal with sin for which there has been no satisfaction is to punish, if it is not punished it will be forgiven without being properly dealt with (*inordinate*). (I.12.)

Human beings cannot make satisfaction, since all that they can do – fast, toil etc., – is owed to God in any case.

No one except God *can* make satisfaction ... No one except a man *should* make it; otherwise men cannot make amends ... So it must be made by one who is both man and God (*necesse est ut eam faciat Deus homo*). (II.6.)

A sinless redeemer can give up his life to God, since this is not owed as a debt. His life can atone for all sins because destroying it would be a greater sin than all the rest put together. And:

> He who of his own accord gives God so great a gift ought not to go without reward.

Anselm's theory is sometimes called that of 'substitutional penal expiation'. It is partly anticipated by Athanasius (*PG* 25. 112–13), and it may be supported by the words of *Isaiah* 53.6: 'All we like sheep have gone astray, we have turned every one to his own way; and the Lord hath laid on him the iniquity of us all'. Many readers today, however, may feel the same difficulty as Paine:

> If I owe a person money and cannot pay him, ... another person can take the debt upon himself and pay it for me; but if I have committed a crime ... the case is changed; moral justice cannot take the innocent for the guilty, even if the innocent should offer itself.[1]

At the Last Supper Christ says: 'This is my blood, the blood of the Covenant, which is to be poured out for many for the removal of sins' (*Mt.* 26.28). The reference to a covenant will be discussed below, but in saying that his blood will be poured out for the 'removal' of sins (the word used here, *aphesis*, signifies not forgiveness so much as getting rid of or getting loose from), Christ suggests that his imminent death is a sacrifice to atone for sins. This idea is developed in *Hebrews*. Christ is there represented as a high priest offering himself as a sacrifice for sin, and thereby 'perfecting for ever those whom he is sanctifying' (*Hb.* 10.15).

To sacrifice something is to set it apart, to make it over to a god. The idea does not become invalid once it is recognised that gods do not need the things thus set apart. Small children sometimes give presents to their parents. The presents are bought with money originally provided by the parents, and they are often things the parents do not need; nevertheless the institution helps to foster good relations between children and parents. When an offering is made to a god, instead of or besides showing devotion the offerer may wish to express the idea that the thing offered was originally given by, and still belongs to, the god. Where a number of individuals form a society, it is natural that one of them should make offerings on behalf of the whole society. It is clear that such offerings could be part of the development of relations with the god as well as a vivid way of expressing sorrow for sin and the wish to amend. But although the Thirty Nine Articles represent Christ's death as a sacrifice which suffices by itself to obliterate 'all the sins of the whole world, both original and actual' (Article xxxi), we have seen that modern Anglicans doubt whether any single historical act could have this significance. Besides, Christ did not look as if he was sacrificing himself, and he was not appointed by the human race to act on their behalf. The sacrificial aspect of his death becomes more significant, I think, if we believe that it is perpetuated in the Eucharist and that the faithful can participate in it.

2

Modern theologians are inclined to say that Christ saves us by revealing to us how to save ourselves. This view is popular today because the narratives of Christ's passion and death are thought untrustworthy and the ideas of substitutional satisfaction and sacrifice for sin are out of fashion. But the view has been held from the earliest times and seems perfectly sound.

The revelation is partly by direct instruction. We get rid of our sins by repentance or change of heart, *metanoia* (*Mt.* 4.17), by prayer, and by forgiving those who have injured us (*Mt.* 6.11–15). We make ourselves fit to share in eternal life by following a code of behaviour which is spelt out in some detail in the Sermon on the Mount elsewhere. If we are to respond to God's love, we must know that he has a kind of personal love for us; if we are to accept the gift of eternal life, we must know it is being offered. Christ tells us these things in so many words in *Mt.* 6.25–34, 7.7–11, 25. 31–46, etc.

But he also makes the information available in other ways. It is a new idea that all revelation is non-propositional, but an old idea that some is. According to Athanasius, one reason for the Incarnation is that the created universe is not sufficient to give men knowledge of God who is uncreated and incorporeal. Hence God

> makes men sharers in his own image, our Lord Jesus Christ ... in order that, contemplating the image, I mean the Word of the Father, they may have cognition through him of the Father, and knowing their maker live a happy and truly blessed life. (*The Incarnation of the Word*, 11; *PG* 25. 116.)

God's love for men is to be gathered from Christ's curing of diseases, his giving of food and wine, and above all his death. But it is not only the nature of God that Christ reveals in this way; he also reveals the sort of person God wants us to be. His life is a model, and not just an ethical one. It is from him that we derive our present concept of a person as a conscious agent. This notion is foreshadowed in pre-Christian thinking, but unclearly. It is sometimes said that the ancient world had no concept of self-consciousness, no concept of a person and someone who is self-aware, at all.[2] That seems to me an exaggeration. But the ancients had to derive their ideas of a person from human educators; Christ offers us a superhuman conception of a person, and thereby enables us to become superhuman persons.

But the knowledge of God and of the persons he wants us to be must be expressed in action, and this is possible only if God acts in us. Before the coming of Christ God must be supposed to have acted in individuals, but they were not, on the whole, aware of this, and did not consciously make the Spirit welcome. The nearest we come to consciousness of its action is in the Prophets. Jeremiah says that God chose him to be a prophet, that he himself did not know what to say, but that God put words into his mouth (*Jer.* 1.4–9). This, however, is viewed as something exceptional, affecting only certain individuals in certain roles; it is a long step from this to the idea which we find in Paul of everyone living constantly with Christ's life. Christ is not only conscious of the presence of God in himself; he himself is a divine person present and active in human society.

This is a new kind of divine presence. The Jewish people was a society with which God had relations, but the God of Abraham was not a member of that society; he stood apart from it. Can the notion of God's action in an individual really be extended to a society? I think it can. God acts in an individual in that certain changes in that individual take place for God's purposes, in order that the individual may exist as a person. The individual may recognise that God is acting within him, and identify himself with God. Christ may be seen as acting within the society of Abraham's descendants for a divine purpose, in order that it may exist as a society in which the members share in the divine life. Christians can identify themselves with this action of his.

Not only is Christ's action in the community analogous to God's in the individual; up to a point it supersedes it. When human beings become conscious of the action of God in them, it is not altogether satisfactory to have that action hidden in the invisible depths of individual psyche, and known only to faith or theological speculation. We could wish God as an agent in us to be known more directly. Moreover we do not live as solitary atoms but in society, the behaviour to which we are inspired is primarily social, and once God's action in us is recognised and welcomed, we should wish to have it somehow socialised. Christ's action however, as a priest of the human community or as head of the Church need not be seen as simply replacing the action of God in the individual: that action continues but Christ mediates it. The individual welcomes God into himself by welcoming Christ into the community. Nor is there any confusion of roles among members of the Trinity. In Christian theology God's action in the individual remains that of the Spirit even when mediated by Christ, and Christ is able to act as priest and head of the community only because (as was said in Chapter Eight) he is filled with the Spirit more completely than other individuals.

3

As so far explained, our salvation consists in the Son's Incarnation and Christ's teaching and life as much as, or more than, in Christ's suffering and death. To understand the significance of these latter events we must try to see why they occurred. Why did Christ die? His death was not, surely, an act of suicide; neither is the suffering of anyone, let alone an innocent person, in itself pleasing to God.

The first answer is that Christ died because his contemporaries disliked his teaching, and he refused to give it up and retire into private life:

> To this I was born, to this I came into the world, to bear witness to the truth. (*Jn.* 18.37.)

It is not unusual for people to suffer for their ideas, and dying for them is a heroic act and an inspiring example. But while this account of Christ's death is surely correct, it raises further questions. What exactly was the teaching, and why did it arouse hostility?

John 11.47–53 contains an account of a debate among the Jewish leaders which terminated in a decision to bring about Christ's death:

> What are we doing, with this man working so many signs? If we let him go on like this, everyone will believe in him; and the Romans will come and make away with our Holy Place and our nation.

John is well informed about the chief priests and I think we should accept that this was said and even, up to a point believed. But it is surely a piece of self-deception, masking other considerations. For why, even if everyone did believe Christ, should the Romans object? His teaching was not political or antisocial. Pilate judged him harmless. In the period covered by *Acts* the Romans appear quite indifferent to the spread of Christianity; opposition comes only from the Jews.

The synoptic gospels make it plain that Christ was condemned for claiming to be divine. Such a claim could be regarded as blasphemous; were the Jews, then, motivated by a straightforward horror of blasphemy? If we can judge by two famous and provocative parables, that was not the opinion of Christ himself. In the parable of the Banquet (*Mt.* 22. 1–14 *cf. Prov.* 9.1–6) the guests do not fail to receive or understand the invitation; they maltreat or kill the servants bringing the invitations, and prefer what they have to the benefits offered. The parable of the Wicked Husbandmen (*Mt.* 21.32–43, *cf. Is.* 5.1–2) implicitly accuses the Jewish leaders of intending to usurp the position of God and run Church and State (in Israel never distinguished) as they thought fit: 'This is the heir, come on, let us kill him and take over his inheritance.' These words suggest that in his response to the blasphemous-sounding claims of Christ Caiaphas was not himself totally free from blasphemous thoughts of deicide. If the Jewish leaders had acted in completely good faith, Peter would hardly have been justified in saying (*Ac.* 3.14–15): 'It was you who accused the Holy One, the Just One, you who demanded the reprieve of a murderer while you killed the Prince of life.' That the motive of those responsible for Christ's death was not so much love of God as hatred of God, receives some confirmation from the Gospel accounts of the Passion: the organising of the mob to chant, 'Crucify him, crucify him'; the very unJewish declaration, 'We have no king but Caesar'; the mocking of the dying man on the cross.

I said earlier that it is not easy to love God the Father; neither is it easy to hate him. The rejection and hatred of God which are destructive of human personality seem to call for knowledge that God is working in us and wants to benefit us. It is hard to see how anyone could have this hostile attitude towards the Father, but easy to see how people can adopt it towards Christ. He seems to have a power even now to draw to himself the hatred of men; we may see the crucifixion as a focal point to which all human hatred and rejection of God converges.

I suggest that Christ's thus taking on himself our hatred of God was a major part of his redemptive work. In the first place, it makes much more intelligible the forgiveness of sins. Reconciliation of God must come about through his forgiving us, but how is it possible for him to forgive us? Not, surely, by running an invisible pen through an entry in an invisible book in some other world. If I injure you, part of forgiving me is ceasing to feel resentment, and you can do this without my knowing. But God, presumably, does not feel resentment in the first place, and our ceasing to feel it does not benefit the person we are forgiving. To benefit him we must make our forgiveness known to him; we must communicate with him. The Christian view is that we can communicate with the Father only through the Son. Without an incarnation, it is hard to see how God could ever forgive us. But Christ not only could but did forgive. From the beginning of his public life he forgave the sins of persons who applied to him for help, and at his crucifixion he said of those responsible for it, 'Father, let them go free; they do not know what they are doing' (*Lk*. 23.34). (He means, I take it, not that they had no idea whatever of what they were doing, but that they did not have clear understanding.) By drawing our enmity to himself, Christ is able to forgive it, and when he forgives those around him God, the Father speaking through the Son, forgives the whole human race.

Perhaps we can press this point further. Christians believe that God loves human beings and wants us to accept eternal life from him. Critics complain that it is difficult to understand the attribution of desires to a non-temporal, bodiless person, and particularly if the non-fulfilment of a wish must be an object of aversion to the wisher. When someone we love rejects the good we offer and chooses unhappiness instead we are distressed; even a bodiless person, if a bodiless person can be in such a case, should have some reaction. The doctrine of the incarnation provides a reply to this complaint. Christ wanted people to accept a share in eternal life and was distressed by their rejection of his offer in a perfectly normal sense of 'want' and 'distressed'. It may be objected that it was only a handful of people in the first century AD who rejected the offer, whereas their remotest ancestors are supposed to have sinned, and the universe is claimed to have been made from the start for the benefit of sentient and intelligent creatures. Not only, however, did Christ's contemporaries represent their ancestors (as they also represented us); God in his own nature is atemporal. God's suffering in the person of Christ is sufficient to make it true that God had (or has) purposes concerning people living at other times. If it is possible for a single person to be both God and a temporal being, one moment of temporal suffering by that person is enough to disarm philosophical difficulties in attributing purposes to God. It must be remembered that while the doctrine of the Trinity distinguishes the persons of the Father and Son, it does not allow a duplication of purposes between them; God does not have desires separately as creator and as redeemer. If, of course, there is to be a temporal moment of suffering, the appropriate occasion for it is that of the climax of God's action to give us a share in his life; the occasion of his presence among us as a member of our society telling us in lucid ordinary words what we must do to be saved.

I have been exploring the idea that Christ's love and forgiveness were divine in (dreaded word) an ontological way; theologians may be less shocked if I suggest that his last acts were divine in an ethical way too. They transcended ordinary human benevolence and belonged to the sort of person that might be capable of sharing in the divine existence. Acts of forgiveness occurred, no doubt, before Christ's time; Socrates' behaviour towards the gaoler who brought him the hemlock is famous and admirable. But Socrates' death was pleasant and dignified by comparison with Christ's, and Socrates did not have to accept a rejection of the same order as Christ. He was offering the Athenians something of value, but not eternal life in union with God. That Christ as a man continued to love his fellow men in spite of the rejection, because the Father wished it and in order to remove sin: that is the culmination of his lifting our nature to the divine level. It is because of his accepting death on the cross in this way that 'God raised him high, and gave him the name that is above all names' (*Phil.* 2.9). At his death the merging of his divine and human natures is complete.

4

At the Last Supper Christ speaks of his death as ratifying a new covenant. The Greek word *diathēkē* which is translated 'covenant' or 'testament' expresses a notion we find in the opening books of the Bible. In *Genesis* God makes covenants with Noah and Abraham. The idea here is a formal and benign if vague undertaking by God, unconditional in the case of Noah (*Gen.* 6.18), in the case of Abraham conditional of the practice of circumcision (*Gen.* 17.10). The most important covenant in the Old Testament (from which the name 'the Old Testament' is derived) is that between God and the Israelites at Sinai. God here undertakes to make the Israelites a 'kingdom of priests, a consecrated nation' (*Exod.* 19.5–6), and they promise in turn to keep the Ten Commandments (24.3, 7). Moses then has some bullocks killed 'as a communion sacrifice', sprinkles half the blood on the altar, and throws the other half towards the people saying 'Behold the blood of the Covenant which the Lord hath made with you' (24.8). Christ is alluding to this when he calls his own blood the 'blood of the covenant': he means that the blood he sheds on the cross is a ratification of a new covenant. That is how the author of *Hb*. 9.15–21 understands the matter, though he complicates it by trying to exploit the fact that the Greek word is also used for a testament in our sense, that is, a will. The old and important notion is that not of a will but of a pact.

In speaking of a New Covenant Christ is generally (so Fitzmyer) taken to be referring back to *Jeremiah* 31.31–4. Jeremiah says that God will make a new pact with the Jews in place of the old one they have broken. The terms (put into God's mouth) are:

> I will put my law in their inward parts, and write it in their hearts; and will be their God, and they will be my people. And they shall teach no more every man his neighbour, and every man his brother, saying 'Know the Lord': for they shall all know me, from the least of them unto the greatest of them, saith the Lord: for I will forgive their iniquity and I will remember their sin no more.

In 32.39–40 God further promises singleness or steadfastness of heart and speaks of the covenant as everlasting. In 31.29–30 Jeremiah says that the time is coming when people will no longer suffer for the sins of their parents, but each individual will suffer for his own sin. This further idea, however, does not appear in 31.33–4 or 32.39–40, the passages which deal explicitly with the New Covenant, and there is certainly no implication that the New Covenant will be more individualistic than the Old, an arrangement with each person by himself rather than with a whole society.

The authenticity of *Jer.* 31.31–4 has (inevitably) been questioned, and a recent commentator describes the content of the passage as 'a minor and prosaic hope for the future' rather than a prophecy of any covenant ratified by Christ.[3] I think it is doubtful whether Christ was referring to it more than to other passages which look forward to a new order, and on any view Jeremiah leaves it unclear how the new knowledge of God and ability to be faithful to him will come about.

The destiny Christ reveals for us is divine. It is not merely becoming like God but sharing in his existence. To achieve this we must be incorporated into Christ as the branches of a vine are incorporated into the vine, and thereby receive through him the Spirit of God. This gift of the Spirit and union with Christ is the fulfilment of the hopes expressed in the Old Testament, and it is this that Christ's blood attests.

CHAPTER TEN

The Church

I

Christ succeeds in separating human nature *in his person* from the conditions of mortality, and making it capable of sharing in the divine existence. But how does this benefit us? Why, because one human being has entered into divine life, should others do so?

If one man succeeds in climbing a mountain or working out cube roots in his head, we may suppose that others can do the same thing if they try hard enough. Christ has revealed to us how to get to Heaven and set us an example; is it enough to say that we can be saved, or can save ourselves, by following his example and his instructions? Are we simply to act to benefit others because that is to be the persons God wants us to be?

I think Christians should be dissatisfied with this answer. In the first place, it seems to be a Christian belief that Christ has done more for us than give an example and instructions. He has made us more capable than we should otherwise have been of following the example and instructions; and that seems to imply a change in our natures prior to any change we effect ourselves. But then it is a problem how the elevation of human nature in his own person can extend to others. Secondly, Christ is emphatic that it is only through him personally that we can reach eternal life, and to say simply that we reach it through following his teaching is not to do justice to this emphasis. Thirdly, to say that we can get to Heaven by behaving virtuously like Christ sounds polytheistic. That is how, according to Horace (*Odes* III.3) the population of Olympus built up, but the Christian hope of sharing in divine life is surely not a hope of being minor gods along with the Father.

We are to share in the divine existence through, with and in Christ. It is necessary, therefore, to be united with Christ. Up to a point that is like being united in friendship with an ordinary man: we must act to receive benefits from Christ and to be the persons he wants us to be. When, however, he compares his relationship to us with that of a vine to branches, he is making it unlike that of one man to another. A branch which has been cut off a vine and the vine are two separate individuals which can stand to one another in a variety of relationships, but a branch which is still growing and the vine in which it is growing are not separate individuals. Neither is the vine anything over and above its branches. The stump or stock of a vine is a part over and above the shoots or branches, and I think readers have sometimes compared Christ with that. But it seems to me that the image is not meant to represent Christ and the faithful as distinct parts of a whole that embraces them both. That might be suggested by Paul's analogy of the head and the body at *Eph.* 5. 23, though I doubt if it should be. When the analogy of the body appears at I *Cor.* 12.12–30 by 'body' Paul does not mean trunk, as contrasted with head, legs, etc., but body as a whole contrasted on the one hand with head, trunk, etc., and on the other with the person whose body it is. In this image the relation of the faithful to Christ is that of parts to living whole; and the same is surely the intention of the image of the vine.

We may be tempted to say that in the image of the vine, the faithful are the parts and Christ is the *life*. But we shall then find ourselves construing the life as a component, even if one different in kind from the branches. Moreover the life of the vine is a kind of abstraction, whereas Christ should be conceived as something concrete. What is analogous to the life of the vine is not Christ but rather the Spirit uniting the members of his church. The vine is the living thing constituted by the branches. But how can we apply this model?

We must be united with Christ through being united with other living human beings. We can be united with them partly through institutions and partly through non-institutional practices. Before Christ died he founded a church and instituted certain practices. The church is a more or less organized group of people who teach about God and organize the practices. The teaching is directed both to members of the church and to persons outside it. Of the practices the most conspicuous is the Eucharist which Christians repeat at more or less frequent intervals and which is a sign of their union with Christ and of their participation through him in divine life.

The Church and the sacraments, as the more formal practices are called, are the institutional means; we must also act informally to benefit other living human beings not only because Christ tells us to but because, as he plainly states, what we do to them we do to him (*Mt.* 25.35-45). Moreover if his presence in his Church is more than a metaphor we must be ready to believe that what he wants of us is what others want of us, that the persons he wants us to be are the persons they want us to be, and that we have the same responsibilities in relating to them. If participation in the divine life is already a reality, we are already creative of one another as persons.

The Church, the sacraments, human relationships: all Christians agree that these are the means to union with God. I shall now consider each separately, but this procedure is not meant to imply that they are really separable, much less that there is room for competition between institutional and non-institutional religious practices. I shall suggest that on the contrary the sacraments equip us for informal action, and that acquires the value of sacraments.

2

In his teaching, especially as reported by the Synoptics, Christ often speaks of what he calls 'The Kingdom of Heaven'. This appears to be an order of things in which, ultimately, nature will be subject to persons (an idea foreshadowed by some Old Testament passages, for instance *Is.* 25.6-7) and persons to himself. He implies, however, that he is inaugurating it now and that we can enter on a first phase of it now. At the moment it is invisible. But for human beings, adherence to a society could never be a wholly interior business, and for those who wish to belong to the kingdom there is a visible institution.

This is what we call the 'Church'. The English word 'church' translates the Greek *ekklēsia* and the Hebrew *qahal*. *Ekklēsia* comes from a verb meaning 'to call forth'. It is used either for an actual assembly of people who have been called out to a meeting-place, usually for a political purpose, or for a set of persons liable or entitled to be convoked in this way. Such assemblies could be more or less formal and powerful. All full citizens of Athens belonged to the Athenian Assembly, and this was the supreme legislative, judicial and executive body in the Athenian state. The word *qahal* seems to have expressed the same idea. It is applied to the Jews convoked to receive the Law in the desert (*Dt.* 9.10). The Evangelists, writing in Greek, make Christ use *ekklēsia* in his formal speech to Peter:

> You are Peter, (*petros*, literally 'rock'), and on this I shall build my *ekklēsia*. (*Mt.* 16.18)

Paul regularly speaks of the *ekklēsiai* of God in various places, Corinth (I *Cor.* 1.2) Galatia (*Gal.* 1.2), etc. Similarly *Rev.* 1.4. These are visible, organized bodies of Christians. Christ, however, speaks not of *ekklēsiai* in the plural but of a single *ekklēsia*, a single organized collectivity of all Christians.

Organized in what way? That has been a contentious question in the history of Christianity. In *Jn.* 3.4–5 Christ tells Nicodemus that to enter the Kingdom of God it is necessary to be born 'through water and spirit'. He appears to be referring to baptism. He himself was baptised by John the Baptist, and we hear of his followers baptising from the earliest times; *Jn.* 4.2, *Mt.* 28.19, *Ac.* 2.38–41, 8.37–8, 9.18–19. The *Acts* passages make it plain that baptism was the formal procedure for entering the primitive Church.

The Church, then, is the aggregate of baptised persons. Most Christians, however, consider this to be only a minimal conception. Christ choose twelve men from his disciples (*Mk.* 3.13–19). He instructed them separately, if not from other professed disciples, at least from the general public (*Mt.* 13.11). He gave them what seems to have been a standing order to teach (*Mt.* 10), sent them on particular missions (*Mk.* 6.7) and invested them with special powers to forgive sins (*Jn.* 20.23) and to 'bind and loose' (*Mt.* 16.19). The last power is explicitly given only to Peter, and its scope is to some extent a matter for conjecture. One might take it to be a general power to make and abrogate rules; words for binding and loosing, however, are used in a restricted sense in rabbinical writings for excluding and admitting persons to a community and for proscribing or permitting doctrines. Most Christians, though not all, who have reflected on the passages just mentioned and others of similar import, judge them to show that Christ intended his church to have permanent human officials. Perhaps any assembly must have officials of some kind. The first thing an assembly does, usually, is to appoint a chairman. But a chairman can be appointed for just one meeting and need not have any special qualifications. Christ seems to have envisaged a number of men with special qualifications and experience, wielding special powers and authority for indefinite periods. This, at any rate was the understanding of the Twelve. In *Ac.* 1.17 (*cf.* 25) Peter speaks of Judas as a person who had a share in their 'service' (*diakonia*), and they choose by lot another man to take his overseership or episcopate (*episkopē*, 1.20).

The Church, then, is a visible society or collectivity which people join by being baptised and which is hierarchical in the literal sense that it has rulers who are priests. There are two further points about it. First, an essential part of being saved is receiving the Spirit. Individuals receive the Spirit through Baptism and Confirmation – perhaps through all the Sacraments. Christians believe, however, that the Spirit came in a special way to people other than Christ only at Pentecost (*Ac.* 2.1–4). It is this event which seems to be foretold in *Jn.* 14 and 16. The Spirit comes to individuals later through the disciples who were present at Pentecost. New Testament writers speak of the *koinōnia* of the Spirit. The word is sometimes translated 'fellowship' but it means something more like 'sharing in'. The suggestion is that the Spirit belongs primarily to the whole body of the Church, and we receive it through uniting ourselves with that.

The second point reinforces this suggestion. Old Testament

writers regularly describe God as having relations not just with individual Jews but with the Jewish people as a unit. *Is.* 41.8 makes God call Israel his servant. But the most powerful and vivid device is to speak of the people as the bride of God. So Hosea, writing in the eighth century, and many authors after him. The *Song of Songs* has been given an allegorical interpretation as a song of the love of God for his people. (So, for example, Ambrose, *De Mysteriis* 7.) One might expect the Church to inherit the position of being the bride of God, and that is confirmed in the New Testament. Christ speaks of himself as the bridegroom at *Mt.* 9.15; John the Baptist calls him the bridegroom at *Jn.* 3.29; Paul says:

> Men, love your wives just as Christ loved the Church. He handed himself over for it in order to make it holy, purifying it with water and words, in order that the Church he sets beside himself may be glorious and without spot or wrinkle ... 'For this a man will leave father and mother and unite himself to his wife'; this is a great mystery, but I say it applies to Christ and the Church. (*Eph.* 5. 25–32.)

Paul may be thinking here of the Incarnation. In becoming a man the Son left his Father, was joined to the human race, and became one body with it. But we shall see that the union may be seen as consummated in the Eucharist. The doctrine of the Eucharist brings the two points just considered together.

3

A sacrament involves two elements. There is a perceptible, physical element, an action by a human being, and a non-perceptible element, a kind of action by God. In baptism, the perceptible element is pouring water over the baptised person and uttering a verbal formula. The non-perceptible element is a doing away with the baptised person's sins and a spiritual regeneration.

The relationship between these elements is commonly said

to be that of a sign to the thing signified: the pouring of water signifies the obliteration of sin. It does not signify it, however, in the way in which a word signifies something: it does not signify forgiveness of sins in the same way as the phrase 'forgiveness of sins' or the sentence. 'Your sins are forgiven'. Rather it is a sign that the forgiveness is actually taking place. To that extent it is like a high or normal temperature, which is a sign that we are sick or well. But the perceptible act is not a cause or effect of the imperceptible one, and unlike symptoms it is supposed to be infallible: if the water is poured on, the sins cannot but be forgiven.

This may suggest that sacraments are like what are sometimes called 'performative utterances'.[1] The utterances of the words 'I name this ship the *Invincible*' is performative when they are uttered by an authorised person in appropriate circumstances; the ship thereby *is* named the *Invincible*. If I say 'I promise to come' I promise to come. In a similar fashion, if I pour water over an unbaptised infant and say the right words, the infant has its sins forgiven and is regenerated. There is, however, an important difference. Naming a ship and making a promise are what may be called 'institutional' acts. They are performed in societies, in accordance with rules or customs of the societies, rather as serving and trumping are acts performed in games, by complying with rules of the game. Striking the ball in a certain way in certain circumstances constitutes serving, and uttering certain words in certain circumstances constitutes putting oneself under an obligation (enforceable by law or public opinion) to do something. In the case of a sacrament, the non-perceptible act is not institutional. It is supernatural and real. Performing the perceptible act does not constitute performing the imperceptible. The two are not even performed by the same person. The perceptible act is performed by a human being who is called the 'minister' of the Sacrament. (By 'minister' here is meant not a person who is in holy orders, but a person who administers something.) The imperceptible act is performed by God. There is no institutional rule that when the minister performs the one, God performs the other; Christians merely believe that this is what happens.

On the other hand it would be wrong to think that God is completely separate from the minister, and performs the non-perceptible act simply on the occasion of the perceptible, rather as I might with unfailing regularity send you a card on the occasion of your birthday. If that were so, why is there any need for perceptible acts? Why should not God just act directly on the individual soul? It is not as easy as we may at first imagine to form a clear idea of what such action would be; but in any case, if the presence of Christ in the Church is to be more than a metaphor, we must suppose that he is present in those who administer the sacraments, and uses them or acts through them in some way. In what way? Before pursuing that question it will be useful to have a deeper insight into the relation of sign to thing signified, and for this purpose I propose to look at one particular sacrament, the Eucharist. It is this which seems to hold the central place in Christian life.

The institution of the Eucharist is described in *Mt.* 26.26–9, *Mk.* 14.22–5, *Lk.* 22.14–20, and I *Cor.* 11.23–5. These accounts fall into two pairs, Matthew and Mark on the one hand, and Luke and Paul on the other, but the differences are not important. The account in Matthew runs as follows:

> As they were eating, Jesus took bread, and having said the blessing broke it, gave it to his disciples and said: 'Take, eat; this is my body.' And taking a cup, and having returned thanks he gave it to them, saying: 'Drink, all of you, from this; for this is my blood, the blood of the covenant, which is being poured out for many for the remission of sins.'

An account of the celebration of the Eucharist in the mid-second century is given by Justin Martyr in his *First Apology* 65–7:[2]

> On the day called Sunday, all who live in cities or in the country gather together in one place, and the memoirs of the apostles or the writings of the prophets are read, as long as time permits; then, when the reader has ceased, the president verbally instructs and exhorts to the imitation of these good things. Then we all rise and pray. (PG 6.429.)

Having ended the prayers, we salute one another with a kiss. There is then brought to the president of the bretheren bread and a cup of wine mixed with water; and he, taking them, gives praise and glory to the Father of the universe, through the name of the Son and the Holy Spirit, and offers thanks at considerable length for our being counted worthy to receive these things at His hands. And when he has concluded the prayers and thanksgiving all the people present express their assent by saying 'Amen'. This word 'Amen' answers in the Hebrew language to *genoito* ('so be it'). When the president has given thanks, and all the people have expressed their assent, those who are called by us 'deacons' give to each of those present to partake of the bread and wine mixed with water over which the thanksgiving was pronounced, and to those who are absent they carry away a portion. And this food is called among us 'Eucharist', of which no one is allowed to partake but the man who believes that the things we teach are true, and who has been washed with the washing that is for the remission of sins and regeneration, and who is living as Christ has enjoined. For not as common bread and common drink do we receive these; but in like manner as Jesus Christ, our saviour, having been made flesh by the Word of God, had both flesh and blood for our salvation, so likewise have we been taught that the food which is blessed by prayer of his word, and from which our flesh and blood by transmutation are nourished, is the flesh and blood of that Jesus who was made flesh. (PG. 6.428–9.)

What is the significance of this? The meal at which the Eucharist was instituted seems to have been the Jewish Pasch or Passover. The Pasch (for a first century description see Josephus, *Antiquities of the Jews*, III.248–50) was a feast of thanksgiving for liberation from Egypt and for agricultural produce. As its name implies, the Eucharist is also a thanksgiving, but it is not only that.

In instituting the Eucharist, Christ speaks of a covenant: 'the blood of the covenant' in Matthew and Mark, in Luke and Paul 'the new covenant in my blood'. No doubt his death is to be a ratification of this. But his allusion to it at this moment suggests that he saw the Eucharist as a means of implementing it: he planned that the new knowledge of God and ability to be faithful to him (if he has *Jeremiah* 31 in mind) should come to us through receiving it. This suggestion, of course, cannot be said to have very strong scriptural support, and theologians have chiefly sought light on the Eucharist from a chapter in the Gospel of John.

John does not describe the institution of the Eucharist. In *Jn.* 6, however, we are told that after the miraculous multiplication of the loaves and fishes, Christ said: 'Work, then, not for the food which perishes, but for the food that endures to eternal life, which the Son of Man will give you' (6.27). In response to questions he continues:

> It was not Moses who gave you bread from Heaven, it is my Father who gives you bread from Heaven, the true bread; for the bread of God is he who comes down from Heaven and gives life to the world ... I am the bread of life. He who comes to me will not be hungry; he who believes in me will never thirst ... I am the living bread which has come down from heaven. If anyone eats of this bread he will live for ever; and the bread I shall give is my flesh, for the life of the world. (6.32–5, 51.)

When the Jews ask 'How can this man give us his flesh to eat?' Christ does not retract:

> If you do not eat the flesh of the Son of Man and drink his blood, you will not have life in you ... My flesh is true food and my blood is true drink. He who munches my flesh and drinks my blood remains in me and I in him. As the Father sent me, so I live through the Father; and the man who munches me: he in turn will live through me. (6.53–7. The Greek word *trōgein*, 'to munch', has a studied crudity which does not appear in standard translations.)

From Justin's description quoted earlier, and indeed from I *Cor.* 11.27–9, it is clear that from the earliest times Christians believed that they really were eating Christ's flesh and drinking his blood at the Eucharist; they thought they were doing what Christ speaks of in these passages of *Jn.* 6. This goes far beyond offering thanks and ratifying a covenant. Christ's words in John surely imply, and were seen to imply, that it is through this eating and drinking that we are to participate in the divine life. How are we to understand this?

This question has been obscured, it seems to me, by sterile debate about whether, and if so how, the bread and wine turn into the body and blood of Christ. Aquinas in his *Summa Theologiae* (a work taken more seriously by posterity than Aquinas might have wished) reasons that since after the bread and wine have been consecrated Christ is present, and before they have been consecrated he is not, a change has occurred – he has come to be present. This could have come about only in one of two ways: through his moving into the place where the Eucharist is being celebrated, or through the turning into his body of something which is already there, *viz.* the bread and wine; and since we cannot suppose that the first has happened we must suppose that the second has (*Summa Theologiae* III.75.2). In the past critics objected that the notion of one thing's turning into another in this way – the technical term is 'transubstantiation' – is incoherent. That seems to me false: when I eat a pear and it turns into part of me, or when I burn a box and it turns to smoke and ashes, that is not a transformation of an identifiable parcel of matter that remains throughout but a transubstantiation. But there are other difficulties. If at one time Christ is not present and at a later time he is, it follows that there has been a change only in a very broad sense (called by some philosophers, in tribute to Russell who defined it, a Cambridge sense) of 'change'. A philosopher might question whether there must have occurred any change in a stricter sense such as occurs in a man when he comes into a room or in a log when it burns to ashes. But a more damaging question might be raised by a theologian. Suppose the bread and wine *do* turn into the body of Christ: how will receiving Communion benefit us? What we receive goes into our bloodstream and nourishes us, but it is absurd to think that the only benefit to us is that Christ's flesh and blood go into our bloodstream. Aquinas himself seems to think they do not go into our bloodstream; what we are nourished by is the bread and wine (*Summa Theologiae* III.77.6). But if we were nourished by Christ's flesh and blood, this would have to signify something; it would be part of the sign, not the thing signified.[3]

The thing signified is participation in the divine life. For this we have the two images which have already been mentioned. The branch of the vine shares in the life of the vine by being incorporated into it. Sharing in the Eucharist signifies this incorporation:

> The blessing cup we bless, is it not a communion in the blood of Christ? The bread we break, is it not a communion in the body of Christ? Because the bread is one, we who are many are one body; for we all have a share of the one bread. (1 *Cor.* 10. 16-17.)

In the past the Eucharist has sometimes been conceived as primarily a kind of spiritual nourishment. While, however, the Christian must regard it as a source of strength, the idea of nourishment seems to me to apply more to the sign than to the thing signified. The branch is not incorporated into the vine by assimilating nourishment, but rather by receiving sap. The Christian's incorporation into Christ is less like eating than receiving a blood transfusion. Hence the image of Christ as the pelican which, in popular legend, gives its young its own blood. The consumption of the bread and wine signifies the coming, so to speak, of Christ's own blood to circulate in our veins. When, as Justin puts it in the passage quoted, the food which has been consecrated is transmuted into our flesh and blood, our flesh and blood become the flesh and blood of Christ.

The second image is that of the bridegroom. As early as in the story of Adam and Eve, marital intercourse is seen as a way of becoming one flesh. Paul applies this image to the Church in the passage in Ephesians quoted earlier; it is related specifically to the Eucharist by Ambrose in *De Mysteriis* 55-7. Having said that Christ feeds the Church with the Eucharist, Ambrose goes on to explain this by quotations from the *Song of Songs*. Christ says to the Church, 'How beautiful are your breasts, my sister, my spouse. How beautiful they are made by wine, and the smell of your garments is above all perfumes.' The Church, in turn, 'invites the Bridegroom, saying "Let my brother come down to his garden, and eat the fruit of his trees" ... Lastly, delighted with their fertility, the Lord replies: "I have entered into my garden, my sister, my bride; I have gathered my myrrh and my ointments, I have eaten my food with my honey, and drunk with my milk".' Ambrose adds: 'There is no doubt that he himself eats and drinks in us, just as you have read that in us he is in prison.' (PL. 16.425–6.)

How exactly do the bridegroom and the bride become one, and how can this mode of union exist between Christ and the Christian? It is characteristic of good images that they can be taken in a variety of ways, but I shall limit myself to two. First, the parties in sexual intercourse give and receive pleasure. At the basis of the pleasure are pleasant sensations, but one person is not united with another simply in experiencing a pleasant sensation – in itself a sensation is experienced by a person as an individual on his own – and the pleasure of sexual intercourse is not confined to this. More important is the enjoyment of an activity related to these sensations: the activity of causing them in the other person and allowing the other person to cause them in you. Experiencing the sensations is important not only because they are pleasant but because the lover desires to please and is made happy by the beloved's being pleased. It is this activity of mutually giving and receiving pleasure which depends essentially on two persons and makes them one.

Secondly, the bride actually receives the bridegroom into her body. It is common to view this as an asymmetry in marital intercourse; but it could be that we have been led to exaggerate it as part of our general oversimplification of the relationship between men and women. The bridegroom certainly gives the bride an intimate form of physical access to him, and it is not clear that there is a significant difference between what each party permits the other to do.

It is clear that the first of these elements, the pleasurable giving and receiving of pleasure, ought to be involved in union with Christ, though Christian writers sometimes seem to forget the point made by Ambrose, that Christ receives pleasure as well as giving it. The second may for a moment appear more problematic. On reflection, however, we can see an essential place for it. For on the account I was proposing of how we can become capable of supernatural life, we have to recognise, accept and welcome the action of God within us. Of this the eager bride's welcoming of the bridegroom is a vivid image.

Both these elements are signified in the Eucharist. The receiving of pleasure is signified by the pleasure of eating the bread and drinking the wine; and the bride's welcoming of the bridegroom into her body is well signified by the receiving of the consecrated food, since the food is in fact incorporated more completely than the bride can incorporate the bridegroom.

In the Eucharist, then, the Christian is identified with Christ in two ways. He is identified in a social way by being incorporated into the community of Christians as the branch is incorporated into the vine; and he is identified in an individual way, as the bride identifies herself with the bridegroom. I do not say that these are the only ways; the Eucharist has a richness not to be exhausted in half a dozen paragraphs; but the aim is to see if there is *any* way in which we can understand the reality signified in the Eucharist as a participation in divine life.

We can now return to the question why there is a need for a sign. To suppose that God might act directly on the individual soul without any hocus pocus, is to conceive God's elevation of us to his own mode of existence on the model of one physical object's causal action on another. I can raise a stone to the level of my eyes or impart a beautiful shape to a lump of clay, and no cooperation or response is required from the stone or clay. But I have been insisting all along that this cannot serve as a model for our salvation. We must ourselves act, if only to accept the existence offered.

Could we do this by some purely internal act, some act which does not have, or at least which is not intended to have, any public manifestation? In recent years philosophers have become suspicious of the idea that there can be such purely internal acts. No doubt we can say things under our breath, and the Christian can say 'I want to be united with Christ. I want to receive supernatural life through him'. Saying such things is, in fact, private prayer, which is traditionally considered an indispensable part of Christian life. But it is not clear that such acts of saying things can retain validity or even meaning if completely separated from public, social practices. Certainly there is a danger of self-deception: how can we be sure we are responding to God and not dramatising random psychological states? Two things are missing from internal acts taken by themselves. One is the union with other Christians which is essential if we are to take seriously the image of the vine. Perhaps it may be thought that this too can be effected by internal acts: the Christian can shut his eyes and *think* that he and others make up a mystical body. But this only makes more glaring the absence of the second factor, a role for the body.

To rely exclusively on internal acts to ensure the reception of grace is to treat the body as something to be discarded or transcended. But the philosophical truth is that we *are* material bodies, and the Christian view is that the body is not to be cast off but glorified. In an old marriage rite the bridegroom said to the bride: 'With my body I thee worship.' The Christian must worship God with his body. In point of fact he does this even in private prayer; solitude and silence are things we need as living organisms. But once it is admitted that the acts of accepting God and uniting oneself with other Christians must be bodily, the notion of a sacramental sign is almost inevitable. Participation in the divine life involves bodily action (there are no non-bodily human actions) by the Christian. There are actions which take place in the community, which are recognised to have this significance by the community, and which were instituted by Christ; these acts are the sacramental signs.

4

The need for signs might be argued in a different way. If we think of God as acting directly on the individual soul we think of him as an agent like a human being but, so to speak, standing apart from human beings. I said that it is possible to conceive him as acting in this way even when we receive a sacrament, but that such a way of thinking reduces the doctrine of God's presence in the community to a metaphor. If we take that doctrine literally, when we are given a share of divine life in a sacrament we are given it by God in the minister. But if that is so with the sacraments, it becomes a question whether we ever receive divine life from God as an agent separate from the community. Why should we? If Christ is really present in the faithful and can share his life with us in them, why should he do so in some other, more transcendent, way? It is difficult, in fact, to see how Christ *could* communicate his life to us as a person distinct from the faithful. Such communication, if possible, must be extraordinary and unnatural by comparison. The ordinary and natural way of benefiting a human being is as another human being. But if the principal way of receiving divine life is from human beings in whom Christ is present, we need sacraments for these human beings to administer.

This line of argument may seem dubious for various reasons. The ministers of the sacraments are often persons whom, in the ordinary way, we do not much like; and we should hope that we can have access to God without going through them. Quite a lot could be said about this ground for misgiving, but I shall turn instead to a question I raised earlier. Given that Christ is present in the ministers, exactly how does he act through them?

We do not want to say that the man Theophilus Grantley is capable of doing what is signified in the sacrament he administers (doing away with a baby's sins, making himself one with a lady in matrimony or what not); neither do we wish to say that he is somehow possessed by a supernatural being distinct from himself who does these things. If the line of argument I sketched just now implies one or the other of these things, it must be rejected. But there are models which do not carry such implications.

An ordinary individual is not capable of making war or peace, of summoning or dissolving a legislative assembly, or even of punishing a law-breaker. But an individual can do these things if authorised by his society. A minister of a sacrament, we might say, can do the acts signified if he is authorised.

This model is not perfect. A society is not an agent over and above the members; it is simply the members organized in a certain way. The Christian will not want to say that God or

Christ is simply the faithful organized as a church. The acts performed by an authorised member of a society appear to be what philosophers call 'logical constructs' of acts by ordinary individuals: that is, a statement reporting an act of the first sort ('The President made peace') is somehow equivalent to a set of statements reporting acts of the second ('George wrote his name. Henry and John said that if George wrote his name they would stop fighting', etc.). The act signified in a sacrament is not a logical construct of ordinary human acts. A model which avoids these objections to some extent is provided by a master and a slave. If your slave injures me I cannot sue him, but I may be able to bring an action against you, who are certainly an agent over and above your slaves. A slave cannot make a legally recognised contract; but a slave's master can use a slave to make such a contract, and in doing so he uses the slave as an intelligent, purposive agent, not as an inanimate object. Paul (*Rom.* 1.1.; so too 2. *Pet.* 1.1) calls himself 'Christ's slave'; 'slave' today is a dirty word, but there is another model which is similar except in carrying no stigma. Following a lead from Christ himself Christians speak of him as a king. Today a king is thought to derive his authority from society, but in the past a king was conceived rather as the source of all authority within a society, and whatever may be the objections to applying this notion to a purely human king, they do not hold for applying it to God. While, therefore, we should not expect the relation of Christ to those who administer the sacraments to be exactly like any relationship in human society, there are enough partial parallels to allay the fear that the right kind of relationship is impossible.

It is clear that if a person is able to impart divine life to others, he must himself possess it. And if some human beings who possess it are able to impart it, the question arises whether one can possess it without being able to impart it. Divine life in general, and the life of Christ in particular, involves giving life to others; how, then can we receive that life without being able to communicate it?

Most Christians recognise a sacrament of Holy Orders; in this sacrament, what is signified is precisely the recipient's being authorised or empowered to administer sacraments. Receiving this sacrament would seem to be a particularly full way of receiving divine life. The sacrament is administered, however, only to a small minority of the faithful. Should we infer that only this minority, only the clergy or perhaps only the bishops, share in Christ's life to the full? If the Church is the living body of Christ, do they alone constitute the Church?

All Christians agree that this inference is to be resisted. As a kind of block against it, people sometimes say that the plenitude of divine life is received in the Eucharist. But this does not meet the difficulty, which is that sharing in divine life ought to mean sharing in giving it to others.

The solution must lie in the doctrine of the priesthood of all believers. Part of the Sinai covenant was that the Jews should be 'a kingdom of priests'. (*Ex.* 19.6.) *Isaiah* 61.6 speaks of the fulfilment of this promise as still in the future, but for the New Testament writers (I *Pet.* 2.9; *Rev.* 5.10) it has now been accomplished. To be a priest is not in itself to be a minister of sacraments. In the first place it is to be set apart from the community as belonging specially to God. That gives priests a certain immunity: to injure them is sacrilege. Secondly a priest is a person authorised to offer sacrifice. (Greek has two words which are translated 'priest', *hiereus* and *presbuteros*; only the first carries the sense of 'one who sacrifices', but it is that sense which is relevant here.) In Christianity, however, there is only one sacrifice and one person who offers it: Christ offers himself. Hence to be a Christian priest is to share in the priesthood of Christ. Moreover Christ's offering of himself to the Father is not separate from the Eucharist. It was by offering himself that he brought divine life to the human race, and those who receive divine life through the Eucharist do so through participating in his offering. Inasmuch, then as all the faithful join Christ in his worship of the Father, they share in the ministry of the Eucharist.

But is this all? Christian bodies like the Catholic Church which attach a great deal of importance to the sacrament of Orders have difficulty in making the ministry of the unordained faithful in the Eucharist seem very real. According to

Catholic teaching, a layman cannot make the sign which is essential to the sacrament: if he says the words of consecration, it does not count. Catholics hold that the two parties who marry administer the sacrament to one another, but some of the faithful never marry, and nobody gets married very often. It seems that if the notion of the priesthood of all believers is to have any content, the notions of sacerdotal action, administering a sacrament and imparting divine life mut be extended. Let me turn, then to what I called 'uninstitutionalised practices'.

5

Many people who deny that Christ was anything more than a man and who reject his teaching about God and the after-life, nevertheless praise his moral teaching. These people do not always appear too well acquainted with that teaching as it appears in the Gospels. They seem ignorant of many things which Christ did teach, and give him credit for ideas which are common to the whole Jewish tradition. The precept 'Love your neighbour as yourself', for example, goes back at least to *Leviticus* (19.18). Christ's moral teaching, however, is not difficult and can be set out fairly briefly.

Christ abrogates certain Jewish rules, for instance about eating, but he does not do away with what we, along with the Jews and, for the matter, the Greeks and Romans, would consider conventional morality. He takes it for granted and builds on it. In *Mk*. 7.14–23 (*cf. Mt*. 15.19), having denied that what a man eats can make him unclean, he says:

> It is what comes out of a man that makes him unclean. For it is from within, from men's hearts, that evil intentions emerge: fornication, theft, murder, adultery, avarice, malice, deceit, indecency, envy, slander, pride, folly. All these evil things come from within and make a man unclean.

Christ takes it as obvious that these things are evil. Similarly when the Rich Young Man in *Mk*. 10.17–19 asks what he must do to be saved, Christ replies:

You know the commandments: you must not kill, you must not commit adultery, you must not steal, you must not bring false witness, you must not defraud, honour your father and mother.

There is no theoretical problem about how we should live: conventional morality is adequate. The problem is the practical one of how to live up to conventional morality. It may be added that in giving instructions about how we should pray, fast and give alms (*Mt.* 6. 1–6, 16–18) Christ is taking it as uncontroversial that these things are obligatory.

Christ does, however, make additions to traditional teaching. In some domains he calls for a higher standard of behaviour than does conventional morality (*Mt.* 5.17, 20); he requires us to become Christians; he gives certain practical counsels of varying degrees of imperative force; and some of his theological teaching has so clear a practical importance that it must be counted in with his moral teaching. I shall take these four points in order.

First, Christ attaches great importance to our forgiving one another. It comes into his recommended form or prayer: 'Forgive us our trespasses, as we forgive those who trespass against us' (*Mt.* 6.12). In *Mt.* 18.21–35 Peter is told we must forgive people an indefinite number of times, and the point is driven home by a threatening parable. Christ's teaching here is not completely novel. *Ecclesiasticus* 28.1–5 emphasises that we cannot expect God to forgive us if we do not forgive other men. This idea, however, is absent from Greco-Roman ethics, and the prominence Christ gives it suggests that forgiving people may be an important part of coming to share the divine nature.

Christ claims (correctly – see, for instance, *Ecclesiasticus* 12.1–7) to be going beyond the Old Testament when he says 'If anyone hits you on the right cheek, offer him the other as well ... Love your enemies and pray for those who persecute you' (*Mt.* 5.39–44). He also goes beyond Plato, who merely says we ought not to harm our enemies (*Republic* I.335).

In these permissive days Christ's sexual ethics count as strict. Developing the traditional rule against adultery (strictly speaking, against making love to women who belong to the household of someone else), he says: 'If a man looks at a woman lustfully, he has already committed adultery with her in his heart' (*Mt.* 5.28). This seems to be a straightforward application of the idea that our thoughts, as well as our bodily movements, can be morally good or bad. Christ also opposes divorce. In answer to the objection that Mosaic law (*Dt.* 24.1) permits it he says: 'It was because you were so obdurate that Moses allowed you to divorce your wives, but it was not like that from the beginning' (*Mt.* 19.8). Malachi (writing, perhaps in the fifth century) makes God say he hates divorce (2.16). Apparently, however, this was not universally accepted, and Christ's statement that remarriage after divorce was adulterous provoked the comment from his disciples: 'If that is how things are between husband and wife, it is not advisable to marry.' The issue is still sensitive, and there is room for doubt about what Christ actually says in the relevant passages (*Mt.* 5.32, 19.9, *Mk.* 10.11-12, *Lk.* 16.18). Some readers think he is saying that it is adultery to divorce your wife except in the case where she has committed fornication with a third party. My own view is that he says it is adultery to marry someone in the case where you are already married to someone else, but not in the case where you have merely committed fornication with someone else. Where those Christians who wish to get divorced should look for comfort is at Christ's reply to the pessimistic comment I quoted just now: 'It is not everyone who can accept what I have said, but only those to whom it is granted ... Let anyone accept this who can.'

When I say that Christ requires us to become Christians I mean in the first place that he requires us to believe in him. 'If you do not believe that I am He, you will die in your sins' (*Jn.* 8.24, see also *Jn.* 8.31-2). 'No one comes to the Father except through me' (*Jn.* 14.6). These passages are from John, who emphasises this part of Christ's teaching in accordance with the declared purpose of his Gospel: 'These things are written so that you may believe that Jesus is the Christ, the Son of God, and that believing this you may have life through his name' (20.31). It is clear, however, that Christ's insistence that we work out our salvation through him is what above all else brought him into conflict with the Jewish authorities, and the point is quite explicit in the synoptic Gospels. *Mt.* 10.32–7 records Christ as saying:

> If anyone acknowledges me before men I will acknowledge him before my Father in heaven. But the one who denies me before men I will deny before my Father in heaven. Do not suppose that I have come to bring peace to the earth. It is not peace I have come to bring, but a sword. For I have come to set a man against his father, a daughter against her mother ... Anyone who loves father or mother above me is not worthy of me.

In the description of the Last Judgement in *Mt.* 25.31–46 people are praised and blamed not just for their treatment of other men, but for their treatment of Christ in other men.

What else does Christ require besides belief in himself? Baptism: 'Unless a man is born through water and Spirit, he cannot enter the Kingdom of God' (*Jn.* 3.5). Joint prayer: 'Where two or three meet in my name, there I am with them' (*Mt.* 18.20). The Eucharist: 'Do this as a memorial of me' (*Lk.* 22.19, *cf. Jn.* 6.53). And we must attend to the people he sends: 'Whoever welcomes a person I send, welcomes me.' (*Jn.* 13.20, *cf. Mt.* 10.40.)

What I call Christ's moral counsels range from near commands to instructive, sometimes puzzling stories. At the imperative end of the spectrum we have:

> If you bring your gift to the altar and there remember that your brother has something against you, leave your gift before the altar, go off, first be reconciled with your brother, and then come and offer your gift. (*Mt.* 5.23–4.)

Explicitly presented as a counsel of perfection is: 'If you wish to be perfect, go, sell your belongings and give the money to the poor' (*Mt.* 19.21). The parable of the Unjust Steward (*Lk.* 16.1–8) has several suggestions, of which the most obvious is that we should use material advantages in this life to get friends for the next.

Here is a collection of counsels, which I do not claim to be complete, in the order in which they appear in the New Testament:

> Do not back your statements with oaths, but make them plain and straightforward. (*Mt.* 5.33–7.)
>
> Pray, fast and give alms in secret. (*Mt.* 6.1–6, 16–18.)
>
> Do not worry about material prosperity in the future. (*Mt.* 6.25–34.)
>
> When defending your religion, do not plan what to say. (*Mt.* 10.17–20.)
>
> Respect children and take care not to corrupt them. (*Mt.* 18.1–10.)
>
> 'Anyone who wants to be great among you must be your servant' (*Mt.* 20.26.)
>
> Do not give yourselves pretentious titles. (*Mt.* 23.8–12.)
>
> Be vigilant and ready to face divine justice at any time. (*Mt.* 24.42.)
>
> We are under an obligation to use what assets we have to further God's purposes. (*Mt.* 25.14–30.)
>
> Attending quietly to Christ is better than officious activity (Martha and Mary). (*Lk.* 10.38–42.)
>
> Go on praying and do not lose heart. (*Lk.* 11.5–8, 18.1–8.)

The theological doctrine which has the clearest practical importance is that there is a life after death, our happiness in which depends on what we do now. The need to work wholeheartedly for God's gifts is brought out in the parables of the Treasure and the Pearl (*Mt.* 13.44–6); the danger of rejecting them is illustrated by the parable of the Banquet (*Mt.* 22.1–14). But Christ also reveals certain things about God's attitude towards us which, besides bearing on how we ought to behave, shed light on something which pertains to ethics in a way, divine justice. The revelation is partly cheering, partly disturbing.

On the disturbing side we are warned that God will come and judge us unexpectedly. A series of menacing images are collected at *Mt.* 24.37–25.13. 'If the householder had known at what hour the thief would come, he would have stayed awake.' Also disturbing is the parable of the man who did not do anything with the money his master entrusted to him:

> You wicked and lazy slave! You knew that I reap where I have not sown and gather where I have not scattered. You should have deposited my money with the bankers, and when I came I should have got it back with interest ... Throw out this useless slave into the outer darkness where there will be weeping and grinding of teeth. (*Mt.* 25.26–30.)

On the cheering side we have the parables of the Prodigal Son (*Lk.* 15.11–32) and the Workers in the Vineyard who worked for only one hour at the end of the day, but were paid as much as those who had worked all day long (*Mt.* 20.1–16). Both these stories, however, jar on our ideas of human justice. We sympathise with the non-prodigal son, and the workers who had worked through the heat of the day. The non-prodigal son in fact receives some consolation: 'All I have is yours.' But the owner of the vineyard is uncompromising: 'I am not being unjust to you. Did you not agree on one denarius? Take it and go. I wish to give this last-comer as much as you. Can I not do what I like with my own?'

No doubt Christ wishes to impress it upon us that we should not grudge good things to other people, even if they appear not to deserve them. I think, however, that he is also putting in his own way the view of the Book of Job (and of Aristotle) that there is no justice between God and men. God owes us nothing; all that we receive from him is gift. In *Lk.* 17.9–10 he says:

> Must a master be grateful to the slave for doing what he is told? So with you: when you have done all you have been told to do, say 'We are useless slaves; we have done no more than our duty.'

Such is Christ's teaching on the behaviour by which we are to achieve salvation. I mentioned the particular importance he attaches to forgiving injuries (abstaining from judging, *Mt.* 7.1, is probably to be treated as part of this). I think it could be held that it is here more than in ordinary beneficence that the unordained Christian shares in God's life-giving activity. As Christ says (*Mt.* 5.46–8) there is nothing particularly divine in loving and benefiting one's friends; that is part of what it is to be a rational being at all.

There is opportunity for forgiveness not only when people injure us but when, in our view, they injure themselves. We are distressed when we are betrayed by someone close to us, especially a spouse or a lover; but it is hardly less distressing if one of our children takes to crime or neglects his or her talents and consorts with people we think inferior. That forgiveness in these cases is divine we are told again and again in the scriptures. A constant theme of the Old Testament (see, for example, *Hosea* 1–3), is that God forgives his people as a husband forgives an unfaithful wife. In the New Testament we have the parable of the Prodigal Son. Not only is this sort of forgiveness like God's; it is a channel for his power, since it is creative, whereas witholding forgiveness and judging are blighting. Everyone has seen how children are paralysed by parental disapproval, and how married couples become desiccated and boring through jealousy and resentment. We see less often, but life is grim indeed if it is not the case, that reconciliation, forgiveness and obliteration of the past restore life to both parties.

On the other hand it is extremely difficult to behave like this. It is impossible without God's help. Christians seek that help through the Church and the sacraments. It may be that the Eucharist is the basic institutional means of receiving that help, but there are at least two others.

First, Christ said to his apostles: 'Whose sins you shall forgive, they are forgiven; whose sins you shall retain, they are retained.' (*Jn.* 20.23.) Most Christians recognise some kind of official penitential rite. The penitent may confess his sins to a priest and receive an official absolution. Many Christians reckon this a sacrament. If it is, it is one that makes it easier for the recipient to forgive. Hatred for past injuries is a sin; the sinner who makes use of the sacrament will normally be required to forgive, and will find it easier to do so. Now the penitential rite is enough to reconcile the penitent with the Christian community, but not with the person whose behaviour was resented. If the priest who gives absolution imparts life, why should not the penitent who forgives, and still more the injured person who forgives without ever having harboured resentment?

Second, the persons by whom we can most easily be hurt and whom it is hardest to forgive are our spouses; after them come our children and the rest of our immediate family. These are also the persons whom we are most able to benefit and harm, and on our dealings with whom in general our spiritual destiny chiefly turns. If Christ is present in living human beings, two people who live together meet him first of all in one another. I have followed the majority of Christians in holding that there is a sacrament of marriage. This is administered by two parties to one another, and is supposed to help them to do good to one another and forgive one another. From the point of view of the Church this sacrament is administered at the wedding ceremony. There is no need to suppose, however, that the infusion of divine help occurs only at that ceremony: as if it were the once-and-for-all handing over of a sum of money on which the recipients must live from then on. The divine life should be passing into each partner through the other throughout their lives. This transmission, however, cannot be supposed to take place independently of any physical action. If it occurs at all it occurs in the obvious actions, those by which the parties speak to each other and help each other. (No doubt sexual intercourse is one such act; not, however, the only one or one which is effective independently of others.) Exactly how these acts are related to the sacrament of marriage is a matter for theological debate, but it should be possible to see the persons performing them as imparting divine life in as genuine a fashion as ordained priests administering the sacraments reserved to them.

In marriage it seems that the institutional act of taking a

person in wedlock flows without a discontinuity into the most uninstitutional and informal acts of domestic life. There is not the same continuity between the institutional act of the absolving priest and the non-institutional act of the forgiving layman, but I have suggested that each could be an equally valid participation in Christ's giving of his life to the faithful. If that is right, we should not exaggerate the difference between the institutional and the non-institutional means of union with God. If we do, then since the institutional are administered by a small minority to the great majority, we give the impression that the mystical body of Christ is in a very moribund condition; like a man lying in a hospital bed receiving a blood-transfusion which he regulates with the tips of two fingers. But that is a body from which life has almost fled. If the vine is healthy, if Christ is living properly in the Church, each member should be receiving life from the rest and giving it to the rest.

6

We have now seen how Christians hope to share in the life of Christ. There remains some obvious questions. First, does this account of the mechanics of salvation allow individual Christians to retain their identity as distinct persons? Secondly, does it allow Christ to retain his identity as a person distinct from other human beings? Thirdly, is it an account which a reasonable person can believe to be true? The branches of the vine are not individuals distinct from one another, still less is the vine an individual additional to them. The members of a nation are distinct from one another and from their head of state, but a political society is not a single body animated by a single life. If we attend to these models it may seem impossible to believe we can share in the life of Christ in more than a metaphorical way. I hope, however, that the problem will appear less intractable now that the Christian conception of the Church has been examined in some detail.

What is needed for individuality is consciousness of one's reasons for action and free acceptance of them as reasons.

Nothing in the account of Christian belief which I have offered conflicts with this. Rather the reverse. For self-awareness and responsibility for oneself depend essentially on believing (truly or falsely) that there are other persons who care for one, and trying to benefit these persons. To that extent existence as a distinct individual depends on membership of a society.

An ordinary human society does not attain the same degree of unity as a living organism. But why not? The reason is not that the members are separated from one another by gaps and can move independently. A living organism turns out not to be a continuum when viewed through a sufficiently powerful microscope. A swarm of bees is not a single organism, but it has a greater degree of unity than a human society. A Portuguese man of war is a kind of colony of organisms which really is a single living thing. A human society fails to achieve the unity of a vine because it is not a genuine purposive agent. If it can be said to act at all, say in going to war or making laws, its acts are logical constructs of acts by the members, and they occur in order that acts by the members should occur – in order that the members should be able to carve wooden bowls, bring up their children and so forth. The acts of the society are means to these private acts, whereas the private acts are ends in themselves.

It will be noticed that some of these acts which are private relatively to the State are nevertheless essentially social. Sculpting and philosophising are not; making love and bringing up children are. Social acitivities which are an end in themselves constitute a kind of life of the society in which they occur, and give that society some of the unity of a living organism. Even a state has some of this unity, and a family has more of it. But the degree of unity is limited in two ways. It is limited if there are no essential external activities, activities of the society as a whole relative to something outside it; and it is limited if the social activities are comparatively unimportant in the lives of the members.

In the Church, I suggest, these limits are or can be removed. The immanent activity of the Church, we have seen, includes the social life of the family; it takes over such importance to us as that may have. But it goes further. It is part of the concept of religion that it governs what is most important. In proportion as something is important to a person it pertains to that person's religion. When religion takes over, say, the mutual activity of husband and wife or parent and child, in sanctifying this and making it like a sacrament it makes it more important in the individual's life. And the Christian believes that carrying out Christ's moral teaching is the most important thing possible.

The immanent life of the Church, then, can be the most important part of the life of the members. But the Church also has an activity directed to something outside it, its worship of God. This is essential to the Church (not accidental, like conducting vendettas to a family), and it is an activity of the Church as a whole, not something an individual can do at all satisfactorily on his own. Someone who has never heard of Judaeo-Christianity might wish to worship a supernatural person who is responsible for the universe; but he would have to guess at what sort of person this might be, and what worship, if any, would be acceptable. The God the individual Christian worships is the one revealed by Christ, and the Christian doctrine is that he can be approached only through Christ. The worship of the Father, then, is an activity of the Church. It is also an end in itself and important. Christians believe that benefits come to them in consequence of it but, particularly when they thank God and praise him for creation, they think this should be done for its own sake. And it is not a logical construct out of acts performed by the faithful, because central to it is Christ's offering of himself.

Christ's role as High Priest in the Church's worship of the Father provides an answer to the question how he remains a person distinct from other human beings. In the immanent life of the Church his existence as a distinct individual is less evident. The faithful try to put his teaching into practice, to make their aims conform as closely as possible to his, to act as if they were animated by him; but we can do as much with any dead teacher or legislator we admire. So far as the immanent life of the Church is concerned, either Christ has left the world, or he lives within the faithful. But in relation to the Father he has the distinct individual role of priest-king: priest who offers himself as a victim, and king who presents to his Father a unified people.

This, I suggest, preserves Christ's identity as one member of the human race distinct from the others; and the external and immanent activity of the Church give it the unity of a single living thing. But the degree of unity it has, of course, depends on the individual Christians. It depends on the extent to which they carry out the moral teaching of Christ and think it important. The Christian to whom it is the most important thing in life can hope to be incorporated in Christ in a more genuine way than someone whose commitment is limited, say, to a perfunctory weekly appearance in church.

Here, perhaps, we have an answer to the final question: is it believable that we can share in the life of Christ? There is not much point in asking that question from the armchair. If we do, the answer must be 'No'. If the account I have been proposing is true, believing it will already be sharing in the life of Christ. Believing it will be what is called 'faith'. Faith is a kind of practical knowledge – knowledge, that is, of what is advantageous and disadvantageous – which we apply in leading a superhuman existence. We cannot have it without giving religious activities, or activities which have been sanctified by religion, the first place in our lives.

> May they all be one; as you, Father, are in me and I in you, may they too be in us ... The glory which you gave me I have given them that they may be one as we are one; I in them and you in me, may they be completely one, that the world may come to know that it was you who sent me.

So, according to *Jn.* 17.21–3, prayed Jesus the night before he died. Is it an empty prayer, or can it be fulfilled? Philosophy cannot tell us. Only by trying the life Christ proposes can we find the answer.

Notes

CHAPTER ONE *Christianity and Philosophy*

1. See Kruger, G., *History of Early Christian Literature in the First Three Centuries*. E.T. New York 1897. For other schools: Harnack, H. D., *History of Dogma*. E.T. New York 1958, Vol. II, pp. 319ff.
2. Wiles, M., *The Making of Christian Doctrine*, Cambridge 1967, p. 117.
3. Stoic influence on Christian ethics: Troeltsch, E., *The Social Teaching of the Christian Churches*, E.T. London 1931, pp. 64–9. The will a Judaeo-Christian concept: Dihle, A., *The Theory of the Will in Classical Antiquity*, Berkeley, Ca., 1982.
4. Al-Ghazali, *Incoherence of the Philosophers* (*Tahafut al-Falasifah*), E.T. by Kamali, S. A., Pakistan Philosophical Congress 1963, pp. 6–7. Further on Arabian philosophy of religion see Craig, W. L., *The Cosmological Argument from Plato to Leibniz*, London 1980.
5. 'The criticisms we shall make derive from him [Hume]': Flew, A., *God and Philosophy*, London 1966, s. 3.25; Mackie, J. L., *The Miracle of Theism*, Oxford 1982 uses Hume in Chapters 1 and 8. Similarly Nielsen, K., *Contemporary Critiques of Religion*, London 1971: 'Hume's critique of religion is one of the most thorough and probing critiques ever made' (p.16).
6. For instance Smart, J. J. C., 'The existence of God', in Flew, A., and MacIntyre, A., ed., *New Essays in Philosophical Theology*, London 1963.
7. Paine, Thomas, *The Age of Reason*. Secaucus, N.J., 1974, p. 186.
8. Bell, Clive, *Art*, London 1914, p. 69.
9. This expression appears in Käsemann, E., *Essays on New Testament Themes*, E.T. London 1964, p. 48.
10. Strauss, D. F., *The Life of Jesus*. E.T. London 1975, pp. 87–8.
11. *Ibid.*, p. lii.
12. Bultmann, R., *The History of the Synoptic Tradition*, E.T. Oxford 1963, p. 371.

13. Wiles, M., *The Remaking of Christian Doctrine*, London 1974, pp. 118, 121–2; *cf.* also his *Working Papers on Doctrine*, London 1976, pp. 158–61.
14. Phillips, D. Z., *Death and Immortality*, London 1970, pp. 68, 71, 74. The two quotations which follow are from p. 55.
15. Also classed as Wittgensteinian fideism is Malcolm, N., 'Is it a religious belief that "God exists"?' in Hicks, J., ed., *Faith and the Philosophers*, New York 1964. The criticisms quoted are from Swinburne, R., *The Coherence of Theism*, Oxford 1977, p. 93, Nielsen, K., *op. cit.*, p. 110 and Mackie, J. L., *op. cit.*, p. 11.
16. Donald Davidson's 'On saying that' (*Synthese* 19, 1968–69, pp. 130–46) is one of the first attempts to come to grips with nonscientific discourse. Davidson is also an influential and articulate spokesman for the view that mental states are causes, effects or both of physical events: see his *Essays on Actions and Events*, Oxford 1980, Essays I and XI.

CHAPTER TWO *The Existence of God*

1. The notion of a cumulative argument is well explained in Mitchell, B., *The Justification of Religious Belief*, London 1973. Flew (*God and Philosophy*. s. 3.9) makes the objection: 'If one leaky bucket will not hold water, that is no reason to think that ten can'. The reply of Swinburne (*The Existence of God*, Oxford 1979, pp. 13–14) is accepted by Mackie (*The Miracle of Theism*, p. 7).
2. Al-Ghazali, *Incoherence*, tr. Kamali, p. 32. The same argument is used by deists: Paine, *Age of Reason*, p. 70.
3. Among theists who think the universe might have existed for an infinite length of time are, in the Middle Ages, Aquinas (*On the Eternity of the World*) and Maimonides (*Guide for the Perplexed* I. 71–4, E.T. Chicago 1963), and today Swinburne, 'Whole and part in cosmological arguments', *Philosophy* 44 (1969) pp. 339–40, and Geach, P. T., (*Three Philosophers*, Oxford 1963, p. 112. Finitism (the doctrine that there cannot be an infinite number of objects or events) is maintained by Philoponus (*De eternitate mundi*, ed. Rabe, Leipzig 1899, pp. 9–11); Ghazali (*Incoherence* q. 1); Bonaventure (E.T. in Vollert, C., *et al.*, ed., *St. Thomas Aquinas, Siger of Brabant, Bonaventure, On the Eternity of the World*, Milwaukee 1964); and most recently Pamela Huby, 'Kant or Cantor?', *Philosophy* 46 (1971), pp. 121–32, criticised in Sorabji, R., *Time, Creation and the Continuum*, London 1983, Ch. 14.
4. The example belongs, I think, to Macintosh, J. J.

5. So Mackie, J. L., in 'Evil and Omnipotence', *Mind* 64 (1955), pp. 200–12; for a powerful reply see Plantinga, A., *God and Other Minds*, Cornell 1967, Ch. 5 and 6.
6. The argument from uniformity appears in Plato, *Laws* X 886 a and Cicero, *Nature of the Gods*, II.95, and is Aquinas's argument 'ex gubernatione rerum' (*Summa Theologiae* I.2.3); the argument from adaptation to needs of living things goes back to Xenophon, *Memorabilia* I.iv.
7. See Davies, P., *The Accidental Universe*, Cambridge 1982, especially Ch. 5 ss. 2–3. John Hick in *Arguments for the Existence of God* (London 1970) protests against arguments based on scientific considerations (pp. 14–17) but considers only the argument that the odds are vastly against the chance formation out of atoms of a molecule of protein. Swinburne in *The Existence of God* has an elaborate argument based on the difference between the probability of a universe like ours given a benign creator and the probability of such a universe without a benign creator.
8. *An Enquiry concerning Human Understanding*, s. x. For criticism see Swinburne, *The Concept of Miracle*, London 1970.
9. The classic statement of the 'critical' view is Wellhausen's *History of Israel* (1878; E.T. Edinburgh 1885; summarised in his article 'Israel' in *The Encyclopedia Britannica*, Ninth Edition). Wellhausen argues that the narratives in *Genesis* and *Exodus* hardly date back beyond the sixth century and were intended to justify the endowment of a numerous clergy and the institutionalisation of what had been a simple nature-religion. For a contrasting view see Harrison, R. K., *An Introduction to the Old Testament*, London 1970.
10. Ghazali, *Incoherence*, tr. Kamali, pp. 98–9. Aquinas, *Summa Contra Gentiles* 42 (among other arguments). Spinoza, *Ethics* I. 4–5.

CHAPTER THREE   *A Non-material, Personal Creator*

1. Gregory of Nyssa, *Great Catechism* 25 (PG 45, 65). Augustine, *De Genesi ad litteram* (PL 34, 335).
2. The connection of time with change is asserted in Aristotle, *Physics* IV. 10–11; for a recent defence, see my 'Time', *Philosophy* 56 (1981) pp. 149–60 where I argue that time is the going on or taking place of change.
3. On the side of Schleiermacher see Williams, B. A. O., 'The Makropulos Case', in *Problems of the Self*, Cambridge 1973; against him: Sorabji, *Time, Creation and the Continuum*. Ch. 12.

4. Martha Kneale in 'Eternity and Sempiternity' (*Aristotelian Society Proceedings* 69 (1968/9) pp. 223-38) is doubtful about any kind of timeless truth. That existence for persons must always be temporal is maintained in Pike, N., *God and Timelessness*, London 1970, Ch. 6 and 7 (following Schleiermacher), Sorabji, *op. cit.*, Ch. 16, Swinburne, *The Coherence of Theism*, Ch. 12. For a contrary view see Davies, B., *An Introduction to the Philosophy of Religion*, Oxford 1982, Ch. 8.
5. The difficulty of dating thoughts is exploited by Geach in *God and the Soul*, London 1969, Ch. 3.
6. Intentional action is explained as movement caused by acts of will in Locke, *Essay* II. xxi and Mill, *System of Logic* I.iii.5; for criticism see Ryle, G., *The Concept of Mind*, Ch. 3. O'Shaughnessy, B., *The Will*, Cambridge 1980 is an elaborate effort to revive the notion of an act of will. For the idea that intentional actions are caused by desires see Davidson, *Essays on Actions and Events*, Essay 1. My *Weakness of Will* (Oxford 1988) Chs. 4 and 6 contains a survey of some recent work on volition and sketches an alternative to viewing desires as causes.
7. The Swinburne quotation is from *The Evolution of the Soul* (Oxford 1984) p. 17. On the concept of the body see (besides Chapter Five below) Harrison, J., 'What use is having a body?', *Aristotelian Society Proceedings*, 74 (1973/4) pp. 33-55, applied to God and the world by Swinburne, *The Coherence of Theism*, pp. 102-4. For something like my view see Athanasius, PG 25. 168-9.
8. See Dennett, D. C., *Brainstorms*, Montgomery, Vt., 1978; Wilkes, K. V., *Physicalism*, London 1978.
9. For a positive answer see Schlick, M., *Problems of Ethics*, E.T. New York 1962, Ch. VII; for a negative Campbell, C. A., *In Defence of Free Will*, London 1967. The disagreement is projected back in the interpretation of Aristotle: see my 'Aristotle and the Harmonia Theory' in Gotthelf, A., ed., *Aristotle on Nature and Living Things*, Bristol 1985. The idea that sentient reality can be divided up in infinitely many mutually exclusive ways may underlie Spinoza's doctrine that there are infinitely many 'attributes' (*Ethics* I. 9-10, Letters 9, 64).
10. Geach, P. T., *Providence and Evil*, Cambridge 1977, Ch. 4.
11. Translation by Speiser, E. A., in Pritchard, J. E., ed., *Ancient Near Eastern Texts*, Princeton 1955.
12. There is disagreement about whether *Genesis* attributes to God creation from nothing or operation on pre-existing matter and whether it alludes to the Divine Spirit or merely to a divinely excited wind; for contrasting views see Cassuto, U., *Commentary on Genesis*, E.T. Jerusalem, 1961, and the *New Jerusalem Bible*.

CHAPTER FOUR *The Divinity of Christ and Historical Truth*

1. Käsemann, 'The Problem of the Historical Jesus', in *Essays on New Testament Themes*, pp. 20, 24.
2. Heidegger, *An Introduction to Metaphysics* E.T. London 1959, p. 7.
3. *Ibid*., pp. 5–6.
4. Sanders, E. P., *Jesus and Judaism*, Philadelphia 1985, p. 1.
5. *Op. cit*., p. 19.
6. *Op. cit*., pp. 45–6.
7. Sandmel, S., *The Hebrew Scriptures*, New York 1978, pp. 337–8.
8. Bousset, W., quoted by Sanders, *op. cit*., p. 25. Sanders gives quotations from Bultmann, Bornkamm and Käsemann (pp. 31–4) showing the same view.
9. A classic statement of the 'critical' position is Bultmann, R., *History of the Synoptic Tradition* (1921), E.T. Oxford 1963. For the methods of 'form criticism' see Dibelius, M., *From Tradition to Gospel* (1919), E.T. London 1934. Among contemporary Roman Catholic scholars representative of the current orthodoxy are Raymond Brown and Joseph Fitzmyer. But other scholars are more conservative, e.g. Albright, W. F. and Mann, C. S., authors of the Anchor Bible *Gospel According to Matthew*, New York 1971.
10. Quoted by Bultmann, *op. cit*., p. 4, from *Theologische Rundschau* NF 1 (1929) p. 187.
11. Bultmann, *op. cit*., p. 5.
12. *Op. cit*., p. 12.
13. See Heidegger, *Being and Time*, E.T. London 1962, pp. 148–53; Ricoeur, P., 'The task of hermeneutics' in Murray, M., ed., *Heidegger and Modern Philosophy*, New Haven, Conn., 1978. The discipline of hermeneutics descends to Heidegger from Schleiermacher via the historian Dilthey, W. (1833–1911).
14. There are classic statements of the sense-datum theory in Russell, *Problems of Philosophy*, London 1912, Ch. 1 and Ayer, A. J., *Language, Truth and Logic*, London 1936, Ch. III.
15. The chief evidence from Papias, Origen, Clement and others, is collected by Eusebius in his *Ecclesiastical History* (finished c. 324), III. xxiv. 5–11, xxv, xxxix. 15–16, V. xx. 6, VI. xiv. 1–7, xxv. 3–13.
16. Strauss makes much of the Younger Pliny's quoting a surviving poem of Martial's in his *Letter* III. 21. He omits to say that this is the only early evidence we have about Martial apart from his own works.
17. They are less than, for example, the discrepancies between the excellent eye-witness reports by Cortes and Bernal Diaz of

memorable events in the conquest of Mexico, such as the burning of the boats, the ascent of Popocataptl and the first meeting with Montezuma. See Cortes, *Letters from Mexico*. E.T. New Haven 1968; Diaz, *The Discovery and Conquest of Mexico*, E.T. London 1928.
18. For references to recent discussions see Brown, *The Gospel According to John*, London 1971, pp. 555–6.
19. A word much used by Strauss here: *New Life*, Vol. I, pp. 402–4.
20. *Op. cit.*, p. 49
21. *Op. cit.*, p. 332. [Emphasis added.]
22. Strauss, *New Life*. Vol. I, pp. 101, 142.
23. Philostratus, *Life of Apollonius of Tyana*, Loeb ed., London 1912. Among scholars who have recently referred to this are Sanders, *op. cit.*, p. 320 and Frances Young in Hicks, J., ed., *The Myth of God Incarnate*, London 1977, p. 92. They say that in VIII 30ff., Apollonius 'appears after his death'. How carefully have they read the passage? 'Fails to appear' would be a more natural description.
24. Pannenberg, W., *Jesus, God and Man*, E.T. London 1968.
25. Brown, R., *The Birth of the Messiah*, London 1977, pp. 8, 28–9; *Gospel According to John*, p. 378.

CHAPTER FIVE   *Soul, Good and Evil*

1. A quasi-Platonic conception was favoured by Augustine (Holscher, L., *The Reality of the Mind*, London 1986), and has always survived in popular thinking (e.g. Shakespeare, *Sonnet* 146); but Aquinas caused a quasi-Aristotelian conception to become orthodox with Catholic theologians (*Summa Theologiae*, I.75,1–2 etc.) Swinburne in *The Evolution of the Soul* (Oxford 1984) advocates an extreme dualistic position: human beings are partly composed of 'soul-stuff'; 'soul-stuff comes in indivisible chunks which we may call souls' (p. 154), and my soul is non-identical with yours because 'they differ in soul-stuff' (p. 297). For a recent version of the Thomistic view see Geach, *God and the Soul*, London 1969, Chs. 1–3.
2. For a fuller statement see my *Weakness of Will*, Chs. 5 and 6.
3. Aquinas, *Summa Theologiae*, II–II.23.1; Marquesan 'ka'oha'.
4. Aristotle, *Nicomachean Ethics* X.4–5; for a good modern statement see Kenny, A., *Action, Emotion and Will*, London 1963, Ch. VI.
5. So Hume, *Treatise* II.iii.3 and III.i.1, *Enquiry Concerning Morals* Appendix I. The notion of a reason for action is defended in Anscombe, G. E. M., *Intention* (Oxford 1957) and Nagel, T., *The Possibility of Altruism* (Oxford 1970).

6. So Armstrong in Armstrong, D. M., and Malcolm, N., *Consciousness and Causality*, Oxford 1984. The alternative view I propose here is defended in my 'Knowing what we think' in Stevenson, L., et al., ed., *Mind, Causation and Action*, Oxford 1986.
7. The basis for all subsequent accounts of character is Aristotle, *Nicomachean Ethics* II.1–6.
8. For the difficulty in societies without police see Pestieau, J., *Guerre et paix sans état*, Montreal 1984.

CHAPTER SIX *The Soul and God*

1. That God can be benefited and harmed is insisted by the so-called process theologians; see, e.g., Hartshorne, C., 'The God of religion and the God of philosophy' in Vesey, G., ed., *Talk of God*, London 1969.
2. This idea is put forward by Malebranche in his *Search After Truth* VI.ii.3. Malebranche, however, gives God sole responsibility not only for the continued existence of our limbs but for what we (in his opinion wrongly) take to be our intentional movements of them.
3. The Fathers speculated on whether if Adam had not sinned he would still have died a natural death. *Genesis* is unclear on this point and so is the official teaching of the Church: compare Denzinger 222 and 1978.
4. See Midgley, M., *Beast and Man*, Hassocks 1978, Ch. 2.
5. I translate Christ's quotation of the passage at *Mt.* 19.5–6. Christ supports it, not with talk about ribs, but with the 'Male and female he made them' of *Gen.* 1.27: is it fundamentalism to suggest that he was not a fundamentalist?
6. The Easter Liturgy suggests a doubt: 'O truly necessary sin of Adam! O happy fault, that earned so good and great a Redeemer!'

CHAPTER SEVEN *Life after Death*

1. Alt, A., 'The God of the Fathers' in *Essays on Old Testament History and Religion*, Oxford 1966.
2. Aquinas, *Summa Theologiae* I.75 2 and 6. Aristotle's discussion is in *De Anima* III.4–5.
3. See Harris, C., *Duns Scotus*, Oxford 1927, Vol II, p. 301; *Opus Oxoniense* lib. IV, d. 43, q. 2, nn, 16, 26.
4. For an exposition see Penelhum, T., *Survival and Disembodied Existence*, London 1970, Chs. 5–6. Confusion of the notion of a physical body with that of a person's body seems to infect Bernard

Williams' 'Are persons bodies?' in *Problems of the Self*, Cambridge 1973. Spatio-temporal continuity is made constitutive of identity in Quinton, A., *The Nature of Things*, London 1973, Ch. 3.
5. *Op. cit.* pp. 71–2.
6. Hume 'On the immortality of the soul', *Essays*, Oxford 1963.
7. Geach in *God and the Soul*, Ch. 2, argues that we could not have an after-life without a bodily resurrection; for a contrasting view (which does not, however, make use of the theological ideas deployed above) see Wiles, *The Remaking of Christian Doctrine*, Appendix.

CHAPTER EIGHT *The Incarnation*

1. Wiles, *The Remaking of Christian Doctrine*, p. 45. For his views on historical relativism see ibid. and *Working Papers on Doctrine*, pp. 157–8.
2. The objections may be found in Fitzmyer, *Gospel According to Luke I–IX*, New York 1981, pp. 304–9; Brown, *Birth of the Messiah*, pp. 32–7, Brown et al., *Mary in the New Testament*, pp. 13–14.
3. The adoption theory was condemned by Pope Hadrian I: Denzinger 595. Pannenberg seems to find it in Luke in *Jesus, God and Man* p. 143. The compromise theory (neither incarnated nor adopted) is preferred by Catholic scholars like Brown (*Birth* pp. 311–16) and Fitzmyer (*Gospel According to Luke I–IX*, pp. 207, 351).
4. This idea is associated with Sabellius (fl. 220).
5. So Rahner, K., 'Remarks on the *De Trinitate*' in *Theological Investigations*, London 1974, Vol. IV.
6. Brown, R., in *Jesus, God and Man* (London 1968) after an extended discussion of Jesus' knowledge concludes (pp. 93–6) that he had only a kind of inarticulate knowledge of his divine nature and mission.

CHAPTER NINE *The Redemption*

1. Paine, *Age of Reason*, p. 67.
2. So, e.g., Hamlyn, D. W., *Aristotle's De Anima*, Oxford 1968, p. xiii.
3. Carroll, R., *Jeremiah, A Commentary*, London 1986, p. 612.

CHAPTER TEN *The Church*

1. The term was introduced by J. L. Austin (Austin, J. L., *Philosophical Papers*, Oxford 1961, paper 10); his fullest account is *How to Do Things with Words*, Oxford 1962.
2. I use the excellent translation of Roberts and Donaldson in *The Ante-Nicene Fathers*, Edinburgh 1867) Vol. I.
3. Aquinas' theory of transubstantiation seems to spring from a misinterpretation of Aristotle according to which in any natural change there must always be some material which remains throughout the change. For discussion of this supposed Aristotelian doctrine see my *Aristotle's Physics I and II*, Oxford 1970, Appendix. On 'Cambridge' change see Russell, *The Principles of Mathematics*, s. 442, and Geach, *God and the Soul*, Ch. 5.

Index

Abelard, 7
adoptionism, 167
Alexandria, 2, 5–7, 96
Alt, A., 143
Ambrose, 205, 211–12
Ammonius Saccas, 5
Anscombe, G. E. M., 236
Anselm, 7–8, 57, 80, 85, 189–90
Antioch, 2, 5
Apollonius of Tyana, 97
Aquinas, 55, 57, 144–5, 174–5, 182, 210, 232–3, 239
Aristotle, 7, 21, 56, 100, 110–11, 114, 144–5, 154, 223, 237, 239
Armstrong, D. M., 237
Athanasius, 190, 192, 234
Athens, 2, 6–7
Augustine, 3, 57, 173–5, 233, 236
Augustus, 163–5
Austin, J. L., 21, 239
Averroes, 6
Avicenna, 5

baptism, 203–4, 221
Basil, 3
belief and behaviour, 28, 60–1, 111–12, 154–5
Bell, C., 14
Boethius, 57
Bousset, W., 235
Bosanquet, B., 21

Bradley, F. H., 21
Brown, R., 98, 143, 235–6, 238
Bultmann, R., 18, 90, 92–3, 97, 235

Caiaphas, 195
Calcidius, 7
Calvin, 28
Campbell, C. A., 234
Carroll, R., 238
causality, 32, 64–5, 68–9, 112
Chalcedon, Council of, 3–4
character, 123–4, 140, 161
charity, 114
Church, the, 201–5, 214–17, 226–9
Cicero, 233
Clement of Alexandria, 2–3, 235
Constantinople, Third Council of, 183
Cortes, H., 235–6
cosmological arguments, 11
Covenant, the New, 190, 198–9, 208–9
Cranmer, 88
creation, 63–9, 75–9, 127–30
criticism, Biblical, 89–91, 95, 98–9, 143, 163–7
Croce, B., 14
cumulative proofs, 26, 29

Darwin, 137

INDEX

Davidson, D., 23, 234
Davies, B., 234
Davies, P., 233
demons, 85, 136–7
Dennett, D. C., 234
Descartes, 8–9, 23, 110, 117, 144, 154, 181
design, arguments concerning, 37–45
Diaz, B., 235–6
Dibelius, M., 90, 235
Dilthey, W., 235
Duns Scotus, 145
duty, 113–14

Eliot, George, 15–16
Enuma Ellis, the, 82–3
epiphenomenalism, 72
Eucharist, the, 191, 202, 207–13, 217–18, 221
Eusebius, 96, 106, 235
evil, 37–43; *see also* good, hatred

faith, 27–8, 229
Fall of Man, the, 137–9, 162
Feuerbach, 15–16
Fitzmyer, J., 198, 235, 238
Fleetwood, J., 88
Flew, A., 10, 43
forgiveness, 125, 195–7, 219, 224–6
free will, 42–3, 73–5
Frege, 23
fundamentalism, 91–2, 107, 237

Gadamer, H. G., 14
Geach, P. T., 79, 232, 234, 236, 238–9
Genesis 1.1–2.4, 80–3
Ghazali, 6, 30–1, 55

Gnostics, 5
good and evil, 112–15, 119–21
Gregory of Nazianzum, 3, 171–2
Gregory of Nyssa, 3, 176, 179, 182, 188–9, 233

Hamlyn, D. W., 238
Hanina ben Dosa, 97
Harrison, J., 234
Harrison, R. K., 233
Hartshorne, C., 237
hatred, 121–6, 135–6
Hegel, 14–16, 21
Heidegger, 14, 22, 87–8, 90
Hell, 85–6, 133–6
Herod the Great, 165
Herodotus, 94
Hick, J., 233
Horace, 200
Huby, P., 232
Hume, 9–10, 12, 16–17, 19, 32–3, 37–42, 44, 46–9, 53, 95–6, 128, 150–2, 189, 236

immortality of the soul, 5, 10, 13–14, 20, 131, 141–57
Incarnation, the, 3, 18, 23, 131, 139, 152, 156–7, 160–1, 180–7, 192, 196–7
infinity, 31–6, 58
inspiration, 81–2
Irenaeus, 134–5, 171

Jewel, J., 88
Jews, 46–7, 50–1, 193
John the Baptist, 103, 165, 205
John Chrysostom, 3
Josephus, 142, 165, 208
Jowett, B., 21
Judas Maccabaeus, 141

INDEX

justice, divine, 223
Justin Martyr, 2, 207–9, 211
Justinian, 6

Kant, 4, 10–12, 19, 21, 23
Käsemann, E., 92, 231, 235
Kenny, A., 236
Kneale, M., 234
Kripke, S., 176

Leibniz, 9, 23
Lessing, G. E., 14
Locke, 9, 41, 234
logos, 169–71
Lucian, 97–8
Luther, 87–9

Mackie, J. L., 10, 20–2, 31–2, 42–3, 232
Maimonides, 232
Malebranch, 9, 237
marriage, 80, 138–9, 205, 211–13, 225–6
Mary, 164
Marx, 16
Midgley, M., 237
Mill, 234
miracles, 10, 14, 16–17, 19, 39–40, 46–9, 92, 95–8
Mitchell, B., 232
Moore, G. E., 91
moral teaching of Christ, 218–23

Nagel, T., 236
Necker, J., 12
Neoplatonists, 5
Nielsen, K., 20–1, 231

omniscience, 61–3, 183–4
ontological arguments, 11

Orders, sacrament of, 216–17
Origen, 3, 5, 235
O'Shaughnessy, B., 234

pain, 41–2, 113, 122
Paine, T., 11–12, 190, 232
Paley, W., 11
Pannenberg, W., 98, 238
pantheism, 69–70
Papias, 235
Paris, 7–8
Pascal, 93–4
Paul, 1, 28, 84–5, 94, 105–6, 141, 143, 201, 205
Peake, M., 122
Penelhum, T., 237
performative utterances, 206
person, notion of, 63, 116, 118–20, 125, 177–80; identity of, 146–9
Pestieau, J., 237
Peter, 105–6, 195
Phillips, D. Z., 20–21
Philo, 2, 80
Philostratus, 97
physicalism, 70–2, 120, 151–2
Pike, N., 59, 234
Pilate, 166, 194
Plantinga, A., 233
Plato, 3–5, 7, 58, 99, 110, 144, 154, 160, 233
Plotinus, 5
prayer, 155–6, 213–14
Price, H. H., 91
process theology, 237
propositions, 18–19, 22–3, 100, 192

'Q', 18
Quinton, A. M., 238
Quirinius, 164–5

Rahner, K., 237
Redemption, the, 23, 78, 84–6, 88, 107, 161–2, 188–97
reasons, 111–12, 115–23, 127–30, 153–5
Regnier, M., 22
Reimarus, H. S., 14
responsibility, moral, 64–6, 130
resurrection, of bodies, 157–9; of Christ, 92–3, 98–9
Ricoeur, P., 235
Russell, 21, 23, 91, 210, 239
Ryle, G., 21, 234

Sabellius, 238
sacraments, 202, 205–7, 213–18
sacrifice, 190–1, 217, 228–9
salvation: *see* Redemption
Sanders, E. P., 88, 90, 93, 235
Sandmel, S., 88–9
Schleiermacher, 12–15, 20, 58, 235
Schlick, M., 234
sense data, 91
Sherwin-White, A. N., 92
sin, 85, 120, 127, 131–3, 137–40
Smart, J. C. C., 231
Socrates, 197
Solzhenitsyn, A., 122
Sorabji, R., 60, 232–3
soul, 69–70, 107–11, 154
Spinoza, 7, 13, 23, 55
spirit, 171–2
Stephen, 106

Stoics, 4
Strauss, D. F., 16–18, 92, 94, 99, 103, 235–6
Swinburne, R., 20, 60, 70, 232, 234, 236

Tacitus, 96
teleology, 72–3, 111–13
Tertullian, 1, 3, 175
Theodore of Canterbury, 7
Tiberius, 92, 163, 166
time, 58, 66
timelessness, 57–63
transubstantiation, 210
Trinity, the, 3, 5, 18, 98, 167–80, 184, 187, 193, 197

unity of human race, 54, 139–40, 155–6, 158, 162–3, 193, 227–9

Vermes, G., 89, 97, 105

Weinberg, S., 67–8
Wellhausen, J., 233
Wiles, M., 4, 18–19, 161, 238
Wilkes, K., 234
will, the, 4, 65–6, 183
William of Champeaux, 7
Williams, B. A. O., 149–50, 233, 237–8
Winch, P., 53–4
Wittgenstein, 20

Xenophon, 232